I0003874

Python on Symbian

Mobile app development made easy

Pankaj Nathani and Bogdan Galiceanu

With

Hamish Willee, Marcelo Barros de Almeida, Mike Jipping

Reviewed by
Christophe Berger, Marcel Caraciolo, Herb Jellinek, Jouni Miettunen, Aapo Rista, Rafael Szuminski

Managing Editor
Satu Dahl

Editors
Jo Stichbury, Tim Williams

Table of Contents

Foreword

Hamish and I are delighted to be able to introduce this book about Python on Symbian.

This book is a historic first for Symbian. Created by a team of expert volunteers from the Python development community, and coordinated by Pankaj and Bogdan (two of the hardest working software developers in the Symbian world!), the book was fully written and reviewed on a wiki. Once the authors had polished the text, our colleague Satu created a typeset layout so that it can be read as an eBook or printed book as well as on the wiki. This open approach has meant that the book was available to the developer community while it was written, allowing it to benefit from significant real-world testing and feedback. It also means that we can reasonably hope to keep the book fresh and up to date in future, as Python on Symbian evolves. Best of all, apart from the production costs for a printed book, it's all free.

We can't express our gratitude deeply enough to the authoring team who have shared their wisdom so generously, and, in doing so, have created a significant resource for current and future Symbian developers. Thanks Pankaj, Bogdan, Mike and Marcelo!

Whether you're holding this book in your hands as a printed book, reading it on your eBook reader or desktop, or using the Symbian wiki, you're going to find it very helpful in your Python journey. It is aimed at anyone interested in using

Python to create apps for Symbian devices quickly, easily and without having to take a deep dive into C++. If you don't yet know Python, the book gently introduces you to the language and guides you through to the more advanced topics. Once you're ready, or if you already know desktop Python, the later chapters of the book take you on a tour of Python on Symbian, and include how to write applications that use Symbian APIs for telephony, messaging, graphics and multimedia. Advanced chapters on network programming, location-based services and platform services are included, and the book also covers the basics of extending Python on Symbian, debugging techniques and how to create standalone apps.

With a number of working examples for Symbian devices, this book makes it easy to get up and running with Symbian app development. As former Symbian C++ developers, we both encourage you to give it a try and compare just how rapidly you can put together Python apps, which can be used equally well as prototypes or as bona fide products sold through a commercial app store. We're converted - and think you will be too!

Jo Stichbury, Hamish Willee, July 2010.

Author Biographies

Bogdan Galiceanu

Bogdan is a Computer Science student from Romania. He develops mobile applications and helps others through the maze that is software development. Having been selected as a Forum Nokia Champion numerous times, Bogdan does everything he can to ensure he is worthy of the title by aiding others in the areas in which he is skilled: Python on Symbian, Java ME and Qt.

Bogdan's current endeavours include learning Symbian C++, graduating from college with good results and continuing to be a very active member of the mobile developer community, while still spending quality time with family and friends.

Hamish Willee

Hamish lives in Melbourne (Australia) with his wife Jen, sons Oscar, Sam and Leo, and a cat 'Biscuit' (who drops in from time to time). They spend a lot of time on the trampoline (I guess you could say life has its 'ups and downs').

Hamish has worked with Symbian and the Symbian Foundation since 1998. In that time, he's primarily been involved in developer technical support, providing white papers, software validation, consultancy and training to the wider Symbian community. Currently, he is responsible for evolving both the content and infrastructure of the Symbian Foundation developer wiki, through direct effort and engagement with the global developer community.

Hamish holds a Bachelor of Engineering (Electronics & Communications) and Masters of Engineering (Micromachining). He's contributed to a number of Symbian books, including 'Common Design Patterns for Symbian OS'. This is his first wiki book!

Marcelo Barros de Almeida

Marcelo is 37 years old at the time of the writing, lives in Brazil and tries to divide his time between his family (wife Elaine and son Mateus) and friends, his mobile programming hobby, working nights as a professor in a local college and his daily work as a developer/engineer.

Marcelo is a graduate electrical engineer with MSc and PhD degrees in computational intelligence. In the last seven years, he has been working as an embedded software developer, creating controllers for the industry automation field. Strong computer network and TCP/IP programming skills complete his profile. Mobility and Python programming are his current hobbies and he combines their powers with PyS60 for Symbian smartphones.

Mike Jipping

Mike is a Professor of Computer Science at Hope College in Holland, Michigan, USA. He has worked with the Symbian Platform since its days as EPOC when it ran on Psions. He has written two books for Symbian Press.

Mike holds MSc and PhD degrees in Computer Science. His current interests lie in mesh networking of handheld devices and in using handheld devices as assistive technology for those with low vision and hearing impairment. He spends time with Python and C++ on Symbian and Maemo platforms. He also enjoys his family: a wife, three children, a son-in-law, and a new grandson.

Pankaj Nathani

Pankaj, a Forum Nokia Champion from India, has been working on the mobile platform and developing mobile applications for more than three years. He has been most interested in developing applications for location-based services, information services, utilities and automation. His current research focuses on developing innovative solutions for mobile security, healthcare and location tracking. He has been helping and guiding students and developers of mobile applications across the globe.

He holds a Bachelor of Engineering degree (Electronics & Communications) and is currently studying Management. He primarily develops applications and research solutions with Python on Symbian, Symbian C++ and Qt.

Author Acknowledgements

This book has been possible by the joint and supportive efforts of many people working together over the last few months. We are deeply grateful to Symbian Foundation and Nokia for their kind and gracious support.

The idea of the book germinated while during a discussion with Mark Wilcox 18 months ago in Budapest. With Mark's support we came into contact with the right people at the Symbian Foundation who guided and helped us throughout this book project. We would like to extend our sincere thanks to Mark for pitching us through!

We'd like to acknowledge our deep sense of gratitude to Jo Stichbury, Satu Dahl and Tim Williams from the Technical Communications Team for being patient with us while we wrote the book. They played a significant role in structuring it, finalizing the chapters and typsetting them for the book. Moreover, they introduced us to the numerous people and experts while we needed any help; some of them also authored several chapters of the book and helped us bring it to you! We are thankful to Jo for dedicating her time to the book out of her tenure at Symbian Foundation during the final stages of the book.

We are grateful to the co-authors for their key contributions, and for investing their personal time to make this book a reality. Hamish Willee, Marcelo Barros de Almeida and Mike Jipping have spent time on authoring and editing significant sections of the book. We are grateful for their extraordinary support. We would like to thank all the contributors and technical reviewers - Aapo Rista, Christophe Berger, Herb Jellinek, Jouni Miettunen, Marcel Caraciolo and Rafael Szuminski - for their invaluable comments and help to improve the text significantly for the readers.

Special thanks to Hamish and Jo from Symbian Foundation, who successfully kept us constantly motivated and supported us in every way they could. Jo has made huge difference in terms of readability during copyediting chapters. Hamish has also authored, reviewed and edited several chapters of this book. His efforts towards the book have been extremely significant and this book wouldn't have been possible without his support. Thanks to Jo again, for allowing Hamish time to spend on this book!

We would thank T.S.Vijayan and his team from Nokia, for their essential support and help on the book. We would also like to acknowledge the support of Jürgen Scheible during the project.

Last but not the least, we would like to thank the Almighty and our families who supported and motivated us at all times.

Pankaj Nathani and Bogdan Galiceanu, June 2010

Preface

Python on Symbian is a great way to start your adventure in mobile programming! Python applications (apps) look like native C++ apps, can access the same important platform services, and can be distributed through the same channels.

The main difference between Python apps and native C++ apps is that, because of Python's simple human readable syntax, you can write quite remarkable apps after only a few hours of study. Although some computationally intensive applications cannot be written in Python it is, for almost every other purpose, a fun, fast and completely free alternative to native C++ development.

Some example Python apps include:

- Birthdays for S60, more information at ***bit.ly/3LQSAb***.
- Nixie Watch, more information at ***bit.ly/bej9lU.***
- TouchComic, more information at ***bit.ly/2Y2jQ3.***
- GoogleVoiceForS60, more information at ***bit.ly/4vwDPL.***
- GTranslate, more information at ***bit.ly/AmLI8***.
- Niime, more information at ***www.niime.com***.
- Unity, more information at ***bit.ly/a0ihPx.***

Here are few screenshots of Python applications.

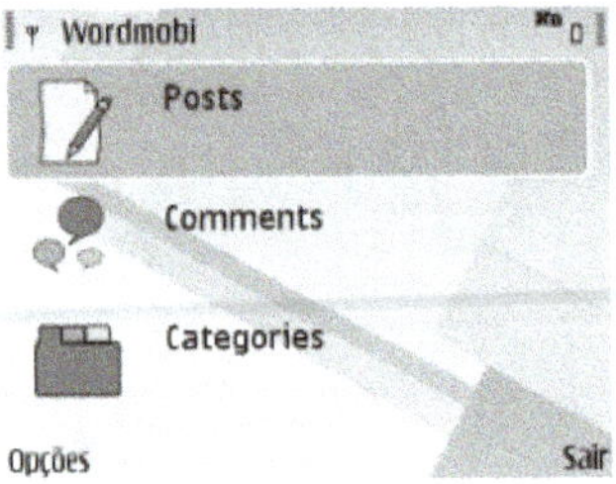

Figure 1 Wordmobi: A client for Wordpress which helps you to manage your blog while saving time and bandwidth.

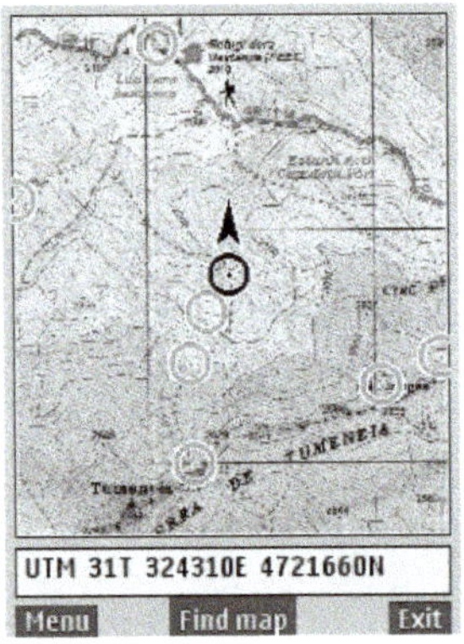

Figure 2 Tracker: A GPS mapping application for hikers who want to track their position on a digitized map.

Figure 3 A Paint-like application which demonstrates the use of touch support.

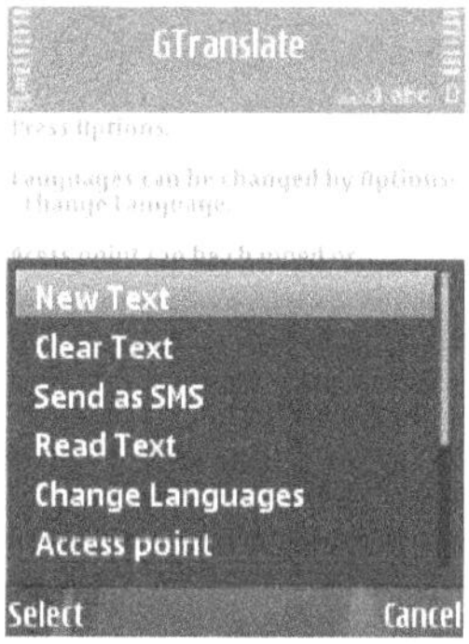

Figure 4 GTranslate: Translates text from English into 37 different languages.

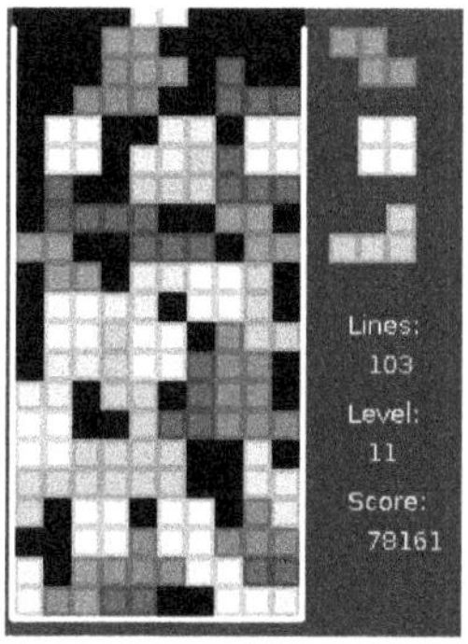

Figure 5 Jomtris: A Tetris-like game.

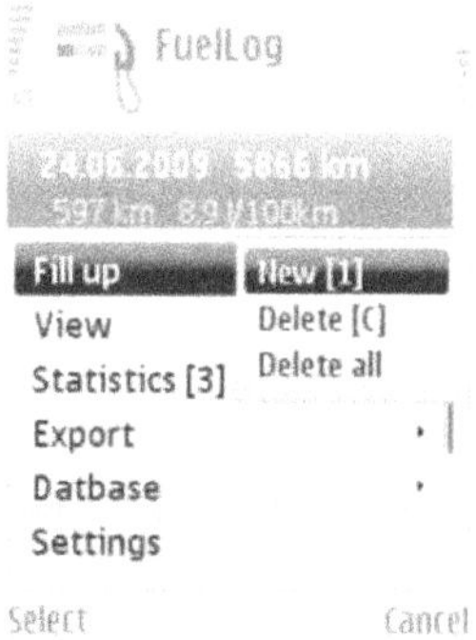

Figure 6 Fuelog: A fuel consumption and fuel expense monitor for recording, storing, calculating and exporting fueling data and fuel consumption for your vehicles.

Who is this book for and what does it contain?

If you want to develop powerful mobile apps with the minimum effort and learning curve, this is the book for you!

It's intended for readers of all levels of experience, from beginners to advanced users of Python on Symbian. We don't assume any knowledge of Python and we cover (almost) everything from basic Python concepts, such as variables, functions and classes, to advanced concepts like platform services and advanced network programming.

We've divided the book into a series of self-contained chapters, each of which discusses a specific and important feature of Python on Symbian:

- The first couple of chapters of the book introduce you to generic Python and to Python on Symbian. They cover the language, coding conventions, basic programming elements and how to get started.
- The following chapters explore the user interface and show you how to write applications using telephony, messaging, graphics and multimedia.
- Later in the book we look at advanced features: network programming, location-based services and platform services.
- Two chapters briefly describe extending Python on Symbian and debugging techniques.
- The book also describes how to package and sign your apps so that they can be published to the Symbian Horizon directory, Nokia's Ovi store and other app stores.

Throughout the book you'll find illustrations, screenshots and example code. It's a book to boost your knowledge of mobile phone programming and make it fun!

If you're already familiar with the popular book about using Python on Symbian published in 2007 (***eu.wiley.com/WileyCDA/WileyTitle/productCd-0470515058.html***), you'll find this book to be its natural successor. This book has a focus on developing fully fledged Python applications, so even if you're already a Python expert from reading Jurgen's book we hope that you will still get something out of this one. Python for Symbian has been updated since that book was released and has new ways of deploying and installing apps.

Python version used in the book

This book is based on Python on Symbian v2.0.0, the most recent version available at time of writing, which is in turn based on the Python 2.5.4 release.

Even though the book targets Python on Symbian v2.0.0, much of the information is applicable to earlier versions and most is likely to remain relevant in future versions. Since we are publishing the book on wiki, we will update sections as they become out of date (and encourage readers to do likewise). If you are reading this book in print version, you may wish to check the main wiki page (***croozeus.com/Python_on_Symbian***) to see if there have been major updates to the text since your book was printed.

Python on Symbian is hosted by the Symbian Foundation. See ***croozeus.com/Python_Package*** for the package landing page.

Where do I find supporting example codes and the online edition of this book?

This book is part of the Symbian Foundation wiki books project. So besides the printed version of the book, which can be purchased from ***www.amazon.com***, an online book is available at ***croozeus.com/Python_on_Symbian***. The eBook is licensed under Creative Commons Attribution-Share Alike v2.0 England & Wales license. For more information, see our copyrights page: ***croozeus.com/Symbian_copyrights.***

The book is also available directly from the Symbian Foundation developer wiki, at ***croozeus.com/Python_on_Symbian***.

The example code quoted in this book is made available wherever possible and can be downloaded from ***croozeus.com/Python_on_Symbian/Example_code***. The code is available under Public Domain license and may be reused freely.

1
Introduction

1.1 A brief introduction to Python

The Python programming language was created by Guido van Rossum in the early 1990's. It is a high-level scripting language that benefits from a simple and human readable syntax, a comprehensive core library, and the ability to be extended using native code. Python is a multi-paradigm language, supporting object-oriented and functional programming styles, among others, giving you the freedom to approach a problem in a variety of ways.

Python on Symbian (also known as 'Python for S60' or 'PyS60') is Nokia's port of the Python language for the Symbian platform, and is the subject of this book. Python on Symbian was first released by Nokia at the end of 2004, and was contributed to the Symbian Foundation in early 2010. In the following chapters, we describe the latest version of Python on Symbian, v2.0.

1.2 Why should I use Python on Symbian?

The main reason to use Python on Symbian is that it is easy to learn, and you can do a lot with very little code. Most people can read Python code with only a few hours of study, and can start developing mobile applications not long afterwards!

Applications created in Python are indistinguishable from native C++ applications and, for most purposes offer much the same performance. Most of the important functionality that is available to native applications (for example, access to the camera, device position, sensors etc) is exposed to Python applications through simple APIs.

If you are a developer proficient in another programming language (such as Symbian C++, Java ME or others) you can also benefit by using Python for rapid application development. So little code is needed when compared to other languages, that fully functional applications can be prototyped, demonstrated and tested very quickly!

1.3 Getting started

Python applications ("scripts") are simply text files containing code written in the Python programming language and named with the file extension ".py". The scripts can be written using any text editor and can be run either from within the *Python Interactive Shell* application on a device or device emulator, or as stand-alone applications that can be installed onto a Symbian device.

This section explains how to download and install Python onto your Symbian device or emulator.

1.3.1 Downloading the installation files

The Python on Symbian installation files can be downloaded from the Symbian developer wiki: ***croozeus.com/Python_Downloads***. The installation package contains Python reference documentation, the "Application packager" for making your scripts into stand-alone applications and the SIS files to be installed to a device.

Developers using Windows need to download the following files:

- `PythonForS60 2.0.0 Setup.zip`: a zip file containing Python on Symbian Windows Installer. Extract to obtain `PythonForS60_2.0.0_Setup.exe`
- `Python_2.0.0_SDK_3rdEdFP2.zip`: a patch for the SDK to support Python development.

Developers using Linux/Mac need to download the following:

- `PythonForS60_2.0.0.tar.gz`: An all-in-one archive includes all the contents provided by the Windows installer except the GUI for the packaging tool.
- The above files can be downloaded from ***croozeus.com/Python_Downloads***.

1.3.2 Setting up your computer

Run the following setup file to install on windows, or unzip the archive to install on Mac/Linux:

- (Windows): `PythonForS60_2.0.0_Setup.exe`
- (Mac/Linux): `PythonForS60_2.0.0.tar.gz`

On Windows, the tools and documentation are accessible from an option on the Start menu (Start | Programs | PythonForS60 2.0.0). Mac and Linux users will need to execute files directly (that is, you need to run the Application Packager by executing `ensymble_gui.py`).

Python 2.5.4 for PC is needed in order to use the PyS60 Application Packager, which can be downloaded from ***www.python.org/download/releases/2.5.4***. While it is possible to use simple editors like Windows Notepad to write Python scripts, we recommend using a more powerful and flexible text editor to take advantage of built-in Python syntax highlighting and code folding. A couple of good editors are Notepad++ and Textpad.

> ***Note***
> While you can write code in the classic Python IDLE IDE (***python.org/idle***), it is not possible to run code that depends on PyS60-specific libraries in this or any other Python IDE. Python scripts for Symbian must be run inside the Symbian platform emulator or on the target device.

1.3.3 Installing Python onto your Symbian device

The easiest way to test your Python application is simply to run it on a Symbian device. PyS60 v2.0.0 is compatible with any Symbian device (including Nokia S60 5th Edition phones and the earlier S60 3rd Edition devices). But, if you don't have a compatible phone, don't worry, the next section explains how you can run your scripts on the Windows-hosted Symbian emulator.

The SIS files you need are available in the `\PythonForS60\PyS60Dependencies\` directory of your Python installation. Windows users can open the directory from the start menu.

Following the instructions on ***nokia.com/pcsuite***, install the following files to your Symbian device (based on Symbian^1 or S60 3rd Edition):

- `Python_2.0.0.sis`: the PyS60 runtime
- `PythonScriptShell_2.0.0_3_2.sis`: a Python Interactive Shell application for Symbian^1 and S60 3rd Edition FP2 (and later)

(`PythonScriptShell_2.0.0_3_0.sis` should be used for earlier S60 3rd Edition devices). PC Suite software is currently available for Windows operating system only. However, Linux users can install the above sis files by copying them to the SD card and launching them by the File Manager application of the phone. To verify the installation, you should be able to launch the code using the Python icon, usually found in Installations folder.

> ***Note***
> If you wish to use Python on a non-Nokia Symbian device, you need to obtain manufacturer signed SIS file of the Python runtime. This could be available at the respective manufacturer developer websites. For example, a Samsung signed version of Python runtime (1.4.5) is available at ***bit.ly/bxc7Fl***.

1.3.4 Installing Python on your Symbian Emulator (Windows only)

If you don't have a Symbian device, you can still test your PyS60 scripts by running them within the Symbian platform emulator on Windows.
You'll need to install the following files (in order):

1. Symbian^1 SDK
2. `Python_2.0.0_SDK_3rdEdFP2.zip` (Python_Downloads from

Symbian Foundation Wiki)

Note that you'll first need to unzip the SDK to a temporary directory, and then run setup.exe. The installation will warn that you need to install Perl, but this is only necessary for C++ development, so you may ignore the warning. The patch will then need to be unzipped over the SDK so that it writes into the SDK's \epoc32\ directory. Accept all prompts to replace files during unzipping to allow this to happen.

On first use, the Symbian^1 SDK may prompt you to register it, which is a straightforward process, although you will need to sign up with Forum Nokia at ***www.forum.nokia.com*** if you haven't already done so.

You can launch the emulator by clicking on epoc.exe which is stored at <SDK installation directory>/epoc32/release/winscw/udeb/epoc.exe. Navigate to the Python icon in the Installations folder in the same way as you would on a device and click on the Python icon to launch the Python Interactive Script shell.

If Python shows an error message stating that the Python Runtime or PIPS Library are not installed, you will need to download and install the Open C/C++ Plugin for your SDK, which is available from Forum Nokia.

1.4 Testing sample scripts

Python's Interactive Script Shell makes it very easy to test your scripts during development. The shell is simply an application that allows you to type in and run arbitrary Python commands, or to load and run whole script files. Let's create a simple Python application. Write the following line in your text editor:

```
print "Hello Python on Symbian"
```

Save the file as `firstscript.py`. Note that the extension of the file is .py and not `.txt`.

That's it, you're a programmer!

1.4.1 Testing on a Symbian device

To test the script on the phone, we first need to transfer the script using the Nokia PC Suite (Linux users can transfer the script by copying it to the SD card). Connect to the phone and copy the script to either `C:\Data\Python` or `E:\Data\Python`.

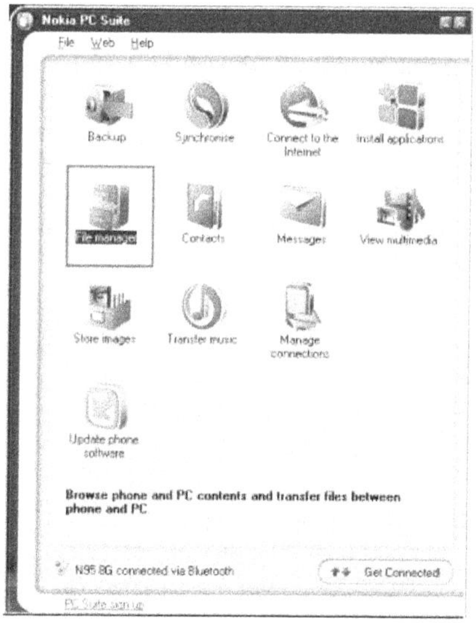

Figure 1.1 Transferring the script

Once the file has been successfully transferred to the Python folder, it is ready to be tested. You can start the Python shell on your device by clicking on the Python icon in the Installations folder. Select Options | Run Script, and you'll see your script listed among other pre-installed scripts. Choose your script from the list by pressing OK. Your script should now start up and you should see the text "Hello Python on Symbian".

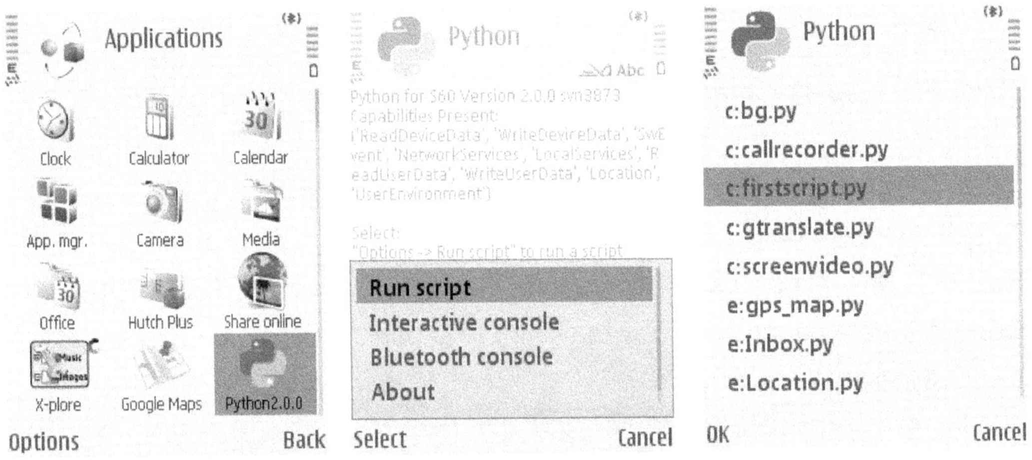

Figure 1.2: Testing scripts on a Symbian device

Hurray! You have just successfully deployed and tested your first Python script on the phone. You can also run and test the other pre-installed scripts like ball.py and snake.py, which demonstrate the power of Python on Symbian. Have fun!

1.4.2 Testing on Symbian Emulator

Testing scripts on the emulator is quicker than testing scripts on the device. The advantage of testing on the emulator is that you can make quick fixes to the script and test them instantly. However, it is strongly recommended to thoroughly test scripts for usability on the target devices before releasing them as 'finished'. This is because the script may behave differently on the hardware in some rare cases.

To test firstscript.py we need to place it in <SDK installation directory>\epoc32\winscw\c\data\python. Launch the Symbian emulator, navigate to the Python icon in the Installation folder and launch the script shell. You can test the script by selecting Options | Run Script and choosing firstscript.py from the list.

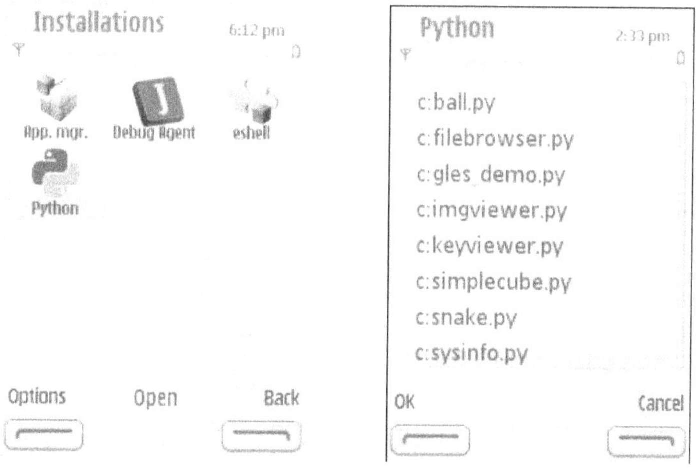

Figure 1.3: Testing scripts on Symbian Emulator

1.5 Summary

This chapter provides a brief overview of Python on Symbian and explains the main reasons why you should consider using it instead of Symbian C++ or Java ME. In addition, the chapter explains how to set up your Python development environment on the PC, Mac or Linux, and explains how to get scripts running on a Symbian device and on the Windows emulator. You also get to write and test your first small program!

While you're unlikely to have run into any problems following the instructions in this chapter, there are lots of excellent resources you use if you get stuck. The Python frequently asked questions have answers to lots of common questions, and the Symbian Python discussion boards are a good place to ask new questions (we and many other fellow Python developers are happy to you).

This is just a taster of how simple things can be when developing with Python on Symbian. IF you have any cool ideas, note them down, because you should be ready to implement them as you proceed through this book.

In the next chapter we start to understand the basics elements of the Python language.

2

Basic Python Elements

This chapter introduces the basics of the Python language. When this wiki book is complete, the first chapter will describe how to set up the Python environment for your PC and your Symbian device. In this chapter, we begin to write code that runs in both environments.

This chapter is not meant to be a definitive guide to Python. Instead, we provide an overview of the basic elements of the language and some simple examples to help you start programming. Where useful, we include comparative examples to explain how Python behavior differs from that of C++ and Java.

This chapter is applicable to all versions of Python. We cover the basics of the Python language; specifics of the Symbian implementation of Python are covered in later chapters.

2.1 Introduction

Python was designed as a reaction to, and an improvement on, compiled languages such as C++ and Java, and scripting languages such as Perl. It has a mixture of features from several languages — even functional languages — and was designed to put the best features of each into a language that could support the type of rapid development that scripting languages are able to support. Its design philosophy focused on code readability.

This means that Python supports multiple programming styles and paradigms. It is primarily an imperative language and programs can be written entirely from an imperative perspective. Python supports object-orientation at its core and supports structured programming. However, there is also support for functional programming (Lisp programmers will be comfortable with its use of lambda calculus) and you can even find aspect programming in Python's design (for example, meta-programming).

Python combines the best parts of programming languages into a highly readable language that executes in a scripting environment. By 'scripting', we mean that Python programs are executed directly by an execution engine without being translated into some native machine code. This execution engine is often referred to as an 'interpreter'; it interprets Python statements by reading and parsing them, and executes that interpretation by running machine code on the host computer's hardware. When compared to languages like C++ that compile to machine language the Python interpreter represents an extra layer of execution, which can be a program performance issue. Interpreted Python programs tend to run slower than similar programs written in compiled languages. However, much work has been done on Python interpreters to minimize this performance issue.

The scripting nature of Python has many benefits. Interpreters can take many forms, which means Python can be used in many places. It can become part of other software systems, such as Web browsers or system controllers, and can be ported to different architectural platforms with ease. Python supports experimentation with language features because its environment can be extended with new plugin programs.

All of Python's many design aspects will become more apparent as we introduce Python programming.

2.2 Variables

A strength of Python is the ability to abstract that concept of computer memory into something that is easy to use: the idea of variables. In Python, variables hold objects and objects represent data. Variables have identifiers, or names.

Names must begin with a letter, but can have any combination of letters, numbers, and the "_" character. Python uses assignment to give a variable a value and, references the value of the variable when the variable is used by name.

Python does not require variables to be declared and provides no mechanism to do so — simply assigning a value to a variable makes it exist (this is a significant difference between Python and more structured, compiled languages like C++ or Java). Thus, we can assign values like this:

```
>>> hours = 42.5
>>> hourly_wage = 12
>>> payment = hours * hourly_wage
>>> payment
510.0
```

Using a variable without first assigning it a value, however, is an error. Consider the attempt below to use overtime without assigning a value:

```
>>> payment = hours * hourly_wage + overtime * hourly_wage * 1.5
Traceback (most recent call last):
File "<stdin>", line 1, in <module>
NameError: name 'overtime' is not defined
```

2.3 Basic Types

Another strength of Python is its ability to view data in many different ways — as numbers, strings of characters, or pixels in an image. As with other programming languages, variables in Python are typed, that is, they are classified by the values they can take and the operations that can be performed on them. Types that are so fundamental to Python programming that they are built into the language are referred to as core types. Python has 11 built-in types. These are summarized in Table 2-1.

Table 2.1: Python built-in types

Object Type	Description
int	A whole number with fixed precision of unlimited magnitude
float	A floating point number with a fractional part of system-defined precision
complex	A number with real and imaginary parts
boolean	A truth value
string	A sequence of Unicode characters
byte	A sequence of 8-bit bytes
list	A sequence of objects, which can be of mixed types
tuple	A sequence of objects, which can be of mixed types
dictionary	A group of key/value pairs, which can be of mixed types
set	An unordered sequence of objects, which can be of mixed types, with no duplicates
file	The representation of data kept in storage

Several of these types will look familiar: *int, float, boolean, string*, and even *complex* are represented in many programming languages. Note that boolean True and False values are capitalized. There are a few types, however, that require more explanation:

The byte type is a representation of 8-bit quantities. Characters fit into 8-bit chunks (ASCII characters do; UNICODE characters do not) and Python represents bytes as the character 'b' followed by a string. In Table 2-1, b'one' is a sequence of three bytes: `01101111`, `01101110`, and `01100101`.

The list and tuple types can be viewed as collections, like arrays or vectors in other languages. Actually, they are like a combination of structs and arrays from C and C++, and may have any type of data in them. In Table 2-1, we can see an integer, a string and a boolean in each collection. Lists are represented using square brackets; tuples are represented using parentheses.

The difference between lists and tuples is their immutability. Immutable objects in Python cannot be changed. Tuples (and strings) in Python are immutable. This means you cannot change a tuple once it is set. Lists, on the other hand, can be changed.

For example, we can assign a list of values to a variable, change the list, then print it back out:

```
>>> thelist = ['trees', 'birds', 'flowers']
>>> thelist
['trees', 'birds', 'flowers']
>>> thelist[1] = 'cows'
>>> thelist
['trees', 'cows', 'flowers']
```

Here, we were able to change items in the list using array-like notation. If we tried this with a tuple, however, we would get an error:

```
>>> thetuple = ('trees', 'birds', 'flowers')
>>> thetuple
('trees', 'birds', 'flowers')
>>> thetuple[1] = 'cow'
Traceback (most recent call last):
File "<stdin>", line 1, in <module>
TypeError: 'tuple' object does not support item assignment
```

The concept of immutability can be used to guarantee that objects remain constant throughout a program. Immutability forces programmers to assign new values to new variables, rather than changing values in place.

A dictionary in Python is a mapping — like the hash table type in Java. Items in a dictionary are stored in key/value pairs. Variables that hold dictionary objects can be referenced with the key and return the value. Consider these examples:

```
>>> thedictionary = {"item": "coffee", "onshelf": True, "quantity":
10}
>>> thedictionary["item"]
'coffee'
>>> thedictionary["quantity"] += 1
>>> thedictionary["quantity"]
11
```

Note how the keys are used to reference each item, but that the value is returned; and that, unlike arrays, dictionaries can be referenced with any type. Sets are collections of objects that support standard mathematical set manipulation operations: union, intersection and difference. Consider the examples below:

```
>>> theset = set(['t', 'r', 'e', 'e'])
>>> theset
set(['r', 'e', 't'])
>>> anotherset = set('flower')
>>> theset & anotherset
set(['r', 'e'])
>>> theset | anotherset
set(['e', 'f', 'l', 'o', 'r', 't', 'w'])
>>> theset - anotherset
set(['t'])
>>> 't' in theset
```

```
True
```

Intersection is represented by the '&' operator, union is represented by the '|' operator, and difference is represented by the '-' operator. The operator 'in' is used to test set membership. Note how sets do not contain duplicate items.

One final word about data types in Python. Python is 'dynamically typed', this means that the type of a variable can change if the value assigned to it changes. Many other languages are 'statically typed', that is, the type of each variable is set when the variable is declared. You might think that dynamic typing can get a little confusing, but each type in Python has a unique notation. For example, lists are specified with square brackets, tuples with parentheses, and sets with the 'set' function.

2.4 Operators

Each data type in Python has two properties: the values used for the type and the operators that may be used with values of that type. Below is a brief overview of the operators that can be used with number types, strings and sequences.

Integers and floating point numbers use the standard arithmetic operators. Python includes a '**' operator for exponentiation.

Strings and other sequences support concatenation (the '+' operator) and repetition (the '*' operator). Consider these examples:

```
>>> listing = [1, 2, 3, 4, "DONE"]
>>> listing + listing
[1, 2, 3, 4, 'DONE', 1, 2, 3, 4, 'DONE']
>>> listing * 3
[1, 2, 3, 4, 'DONE', 1, 2, 3, 4, 'DONE', 1, 2, 3, 4, 'DONE']
```

The types in Python that involve sequences are characterized by sequential ordering. Sequences are referenced using square brackets to examine individual items in each sequence. Sequences are organized from left to right, as you might expect. Reference notations are offsets from the leftmost item. Python allows some special notation that are shortcuts, as demonstrated below:

```
>>> drsuess = 'The Cat in the Hat'
>>> animal = drsuess[4:7]           # take out the cat
>>> animal
'Cat'
>>> onmyhead = drsuess[15:]         # get the Hat
>>> onmyhead
'Hat'
>>> lastone = drsuess[-1]           # last character
>>> lastone
't'
```

Extracts of a sequence are called slices (for strings, you might know these as substrings). Negative index references refer to the end of the sequence.

Sequences can also hold other sequences, as shown below.

```
>>> drsuess = ["Horton Hears a Who", "Green Eggs and Ham"]
>>> drsuess[1][0:5]
'Green'
>>> drsuess[1][0:5][2]
'e'
```

It is important to remember that strings are just sequences. In this example the variable `drsuess` holds a sequence of two items, each of which is a sequence. The double reference `drsuess[1][0:5]` extracts the second item in the `drsuess` sequence and then extracts characters 0 through 4 from that sequence, giving the value `Green`.

Finally, it is important to remember that though Python is dynamically typed, it is also 'strongly typed'. This means that Python enforces the rule that only the operators that are defined for a data type may be used on that data type. Python does not try to figure out how to apply invalid operators; it simply throws an error.

2.5 Statements

In Python, as in other languages, a 'statement' is an executable element in the language. It is the element of the language that drives a program's actions.

The syntax of statements in Python is a bit different from other languages. Consider the following Java statement:

```
while (x < y) {
   x += 2;
   y = y - 2;
}
```

This `while` loop statement has a block of statements, the loop body, surrounded by "{" and "}". The statements within the loop are terminated by a semicolon. The entire statement set is flexible. It could be on one line or many because whitespace characters are ignored by the Java compiler.

In Python, the syntax is cleaner, but more restrictive. Consider the Python equivalent `while` loop below:

```
while x < y:
   x += 2
   y = y - 2
```

The code is cleaner: the semicolons and brackets of Java are not needed in Python. However, the code is also more restrictive. The block of statements formed by Java's of brackets is formed by indentation. Python relies on indentation to form statement blocks. In addition, individual statement must appear on individual lines - unless semicolons are used. Finally, note the colon that serves as a terminator to the while statement; colons are used when blocks of code are expected.

You can use semicolons to separate statements from each other. The code below is identical to the code above, though it does not look as clean:

```
while x < y: x += 2; y = y - 2
```

Consider the simplest statement in Python. It is the 'pass' statement. It does nothing, but is used often as filler for an empty statement block. In a language like Java, an empty block is simply an empty set of brackets: {}. However, in Python an empty block is an indented empty line, which is invisible, so 'pass' is used instead. For example, an empty while loop might look like:

```
while x<y:
   pass
```

In summary, it is best to say that Python syntax is 'different' but not necessarily better. Python enthusiasts get very eloquent on how the language supports all the same constructs as other languages, but with cleaner code. It is probably truer to say that Python's syntax serves its purpose well ...and leave language comparisons to linguists.

2.6 Expressions and Assignments

An expression is a combination of object references and operators. Expressions create and manipulate objects. Consider the expression here:

```
x + 15 * L[2]
```

The variable x is referenced and that reference creates an object whose value and data type match the data contained in x. Using the number 15 in the expression causes Python to creates an integer object whose value is 15. The list reference L[2] retrieves the third item in the collection named L and creates another object. All three newly created objects are nameless.

In Python, the above expression is a valid statement: you can use expressions as statements. All expressions return values. Unless the expression causes a side effect the value is thrown away. In the above expression produces no side effects (because no functions are called) so a value is computed and discarded. As long as they contain operators valid for the data types they are working with, expressions can comprise any combination of objects and operators. Table 2.2 illustrates some common expressions and their interpretation:

Table 2.2: Common expressions and their interpretation

Expression	Interpretation
x + 15 * L[2]	arithmetic expression
a < b	boolean expression
x + 15 * L[2] < 100 and a < b	compound boolean expression
`a < b < c`	combination of boolean expressions
`f(x,y)`	function call

These should look familiar if you are familiar with how other languages deal with expressions. Precedence rules apply in Python just as they do in other languages. In the first expression, for example, the * operator is executed before the + operator. Boolean combinational operators are spelled out (`and` , `or`, and `not`) rather than specified by symbols as in Java or C++.

Assignment is the operation of changing the object value of a variable. The syntax look just like it does in other languages:

```
variable = expression
```

The expression is computed first and the resulting object is assigned to the variable specified.

Here, a common mistake in Python which involves function calls, which are valid statements. Consider the following code:

```
>>> aList = [10,20,30]
>>> aList.append(40)
>>> print aList
[10, 20, 30, 40]
```

This works as you might expect. The statement aList.append(40) is an expression, but a valid statement nonetheless. It simply returns the value None which is discarded.

The common mistake is to think this expression can be assigned to a new list, like this:

```
>>> aList = [10,20,30]
>>> aNewList = aList.append(40)
>>> print aNewList
None
```

Instead, the new list gets the value None, which is the return value from the function call in the expression.

Finally, note that we have used a useful statement in the examples above. The print statement can be used to generate output based on the expression given to it. Python computes the expression and prints the result. If you are familiar with C or C++, this is the same as using stdout. However, we will also use the print statement to work with files later.

2.7 Conditional Statements

All programming languages feature the conditional execution of statements; Python is no exception. Python's `if` statement features multiway branching.

The general format of the `if` statement is below:

```
if <condition1>:
   <statementset1>
elif <condition2>:
   <statementset2>
else:
   <statementset3>
```

Even with no knowledge of Python syntax it looks very similar to an `if` statement for many other languages. Here, `<condition1>` is an expression that produces a boolean result. If the resulting value is `True` the statements in the block called <statementset1> are executed. If the resulting value is `False` the next condition is evaluated, and so on. If all the conditions evaluate to `False`, the default block <statementset3> after the else keyword is executed. Note the use of the colon after each condition and the indentation of the statement sets. These are Python standards.

Here is an example:

```
theString = "The Mad Hatter"
length = len(theString)
if length < 10:
   category = "short"
```

```
elif length < 20:
   category = "medium"
elif length < 30:
   category = "kind of long"
else:
   category = "long"
```

In the example the first condition is `False`, because `theString` has a length of 14, but the second condition is `True`. Therefore, the variable category takes the value medium. The remaining conditions are not evaluated.

Boolean expressions in Python resemble those in other languages. They use the standard relational operators (for example, "<" and ">=") and the boolean operators `and` , `or` and `not`. Boolean variables may also feature in boolean expressions. For example, the code below is valid:

```
theString = "The Mad Hatter"
length = len(theString)
toolong = length > 40
printable = not toolong and length > 10
if printable:
   print "The string is OK"
```

Values other than booleans are also valid as boolean expressions. As in other languages (pioneering in C, continued in C++ and Java), you may use numeric quantities as boolean expressions. When a number is used alone, Python translates it into the expression 'number != 0'. So, the code below is valid:

```
theString = "The Mad Hatter"
length = len(theString)
if length:
   print "The string has characters"
```

The numeric value may be an integer or a floating point number. In fact, this idea of non-booleans being considered True is extended to other cases:

- Nonempty objects are considered `True.`
- Zero numeric quantities and empty objects are considered `False`
- The special value None is considered `False.`

Things get a little complicated when combining non-boolean values using boolean operators. Python uses 'short-circuiting' to evaluate boolean expressions. In other words, when the result can be predicted, Python stops evaluating. For example, the boolean expression `False and x == 2` can stop immediately after `False` because `False and 'anything'` is `False.` Python stops evaluating and returns the first object it sees that can predict the result of the expression.

Consider this code as an example:

```
theString = "The Mad Hatter"
length = len(theString)
value1 = length or theString == "The Mad Hatter"
value2 = theString == "The Mad Hatter" or length
value3 = 0.0 or theString == "Mad Hatter"
```

In this code, value1 takes the value 14. This happens because `length` is nonzero and thus true, making the boolean expression true. Python stops evaluting and returns that first object that made the expression true. `value2` takes the value `True`, because the comparison is the first true object in the expression and it makes the whole expression have the value true. The variable `value3` takes the value `False.`

Finally, as in C++ and Java, inline if statements are possible in Python. Their form is a little different. Let's take this simple if statement:

```
if x < 10:
    x = 1
else:
    x = -1
```

The inline version of this would be:

```
x = 1 if x < 10 else -1
```

This functions like a normal if statement: all the rules apply to the boolean expression and the value assigned depends on the boolean value. Note that the entire right-hand side of the "=" operator is an expression; the entire string x = 1 if x < 10 else -1 returns a single value.

Can You Do This?
Using inline if statements, can you write a statement that increments or decrements a variable (say "a") based on another value? If "b == 10" then increment by 2 else decrement by 2. Do this in a single statement.

2.7.1 Loops

Iterative algorithms are handled by two main looping constructs in Python: `while` loops and `for` loops. We examine these in this section. Python extends looping by using an iteration protocol specifically designed for lists and sequences. We look at this as well.

Where is the goto?
It has been shown that all programs can be written with sequential execution, if statements and a goto statements. goto is available in many languages (even C++ has a goto statement) and usually takes the form of goto label, where the label is located somewhere in a program. Execution of the program jumps to the statement at the specified label.

Note: Python does not have a goto statement. Goto statements can result in very poor, very unstructured programming. Though some argue that goto statements are very handy — or even essential — most programmers agree that structured programming is better, and that goto statements are not needed when a rich set of looping constructs is available. Python provides such a rich set of looping constructs.

For more on goto statements, see the original work on the subject (***userweb.cs.utexas.edu/users/EWD/ewd02xx/EWD215.PDF***) and a retrospective on the original (***david.tribble.com/text/goto.html***) which is a great review of the subject.

2.7.2 While Loops

The `while` loop in Python mimics the `while` loop in other languages and adds Python's special spin on boolean conditions. The general format of the syntax looks like this:

```
while <condition>:
   <statementset1>
else:
   <statementset2>
```

The basic `while` loop behavior is to execute <statementset1> while <condition> is true. Using this basic construct, however, many different looping forms are possible. Infinite loops are easy:

```
while True:
   print "Help! I'm running away..."
```

Most loops depend on relational operators:

```
while x < y + 2:
   x += 1
```

```
    y -= 1

while a**2 < b**2 and c+d == e:
    a = c - d
    b += 1
    c -= 2
```

You might be familiar with the break and continue statements in other languages. Python has them too. `break` causes the current iteration to stop at the break statement and terminates the loop execution entirely. `continue` stops the current iteration only and allows the loop to continue execution. Consider the following examples:

```
a = 20
while a:
    a -= 1
    if a % 2 == 0: continue
    print a
```

This code prints all the odd numbers from 20 down to 0. The continue statement stops the iteration so that the print statement does not execute for even numbers.

```
while a**2 < b**2:
    if c+d != e: break
    a = c - d
    b += 1
    c -= 2
```

This code works just like the simple example above. When c+d != e the loop shuts down.

Spot the difference:

Note the effect of the subtle difference between the two coding styles. Because Python uses short-circuiting to evaluate boolean expressions, the while loop that starts with:

```
while a**2 < b**2 and c+d == e:
...
```

might never execute the right-hand side of the "and" operator because it will be short-circuited if the the left-hand side evaluates to False. However, if the form:

```
while a**2 < b**2:
    if c+d != e: break
    ...
```

is used, "c+d != e" is guaranteed to be evaluated.

This behavior has a significant impact when we use functions and class methods with side effects. The distinction becomes very important.

The else part of a while loop is rare in Python and a feature that few other languages have. It is optional. If included, it executes when the loop condition evaluates to False and the loop is about to terminate. It only executes when a while loop is terminated in the normal fashion. When a loop terminates with a break statement the else part does not execute. Consider this example:

```
number = int(raw_input("Enter number: "))
count = 0
while number:
    count += 1
    total = total + number
    number = int(raw_input("Enter number: "))
```

```
else:
    print "The average is ", total/count
```

This code reads numbers until a 0 is entered, then prints the average and exits.

2.7.3 For Loops

`for` loops are useful when you wish to iterate over a specific set of objects – for example, a range of integers or a list. The syntax for a for loop generally looks like this:

```
for <index> in <objectsequence>:
    <statementset1>
else:
    <statementset2>
```

As in other languages, a for loop executes by assigning to <index> an object from <objectsequence> for each iteration of the loop. For example:

```
thesum = 0
for x in [1, 2, 3, 4, 5, 6]:
    thesum += x
print "Average is ",thesum/6
```

The output is "Average is 3" as you might expect.

We could write the above using a tuple instead of a list:

```
thesum = 0
for x in (1, 2, 3, 4, 5, 6):
    thesum += x
print "Average is ",thesum/6
```

Any sequence works in a `for` loop. The example below shows a for loop

list, the next one is the sixth (i.e., 'list[5]'). Python uses these ideas for all iterable data types and specifies a syntax for iteration.

Consider this example:

```
 countries = ["France", "Germany", "United States", "Austria",
"Norway"]
iterator = iter(countries)
print iterator.next()
```

This code creates an iterator for the countries list and begins to step through the values in the list using that iterator. The result of the print statement is 'France'. Another call to `iter(countries)` will produce 'Germany'.

Some data types have iterators built in. For example, file types have iterators:

```
fd = open("data.txt")
print fd.next()
print fd.next()
print fd.next()
```

This snippet prints the first three lines in the file "data.txt" (the function `fd.readline()` does the same, but we are not discussing files here).

The `enumerate()` function is a variation on range generation and is useful for iteration in for loops. The `enumerate()` function takes a list and generates an iterator over list as tuples: the first item in each tuple is an integer representing the place of the second item in the original list. Consider the example below:

```
countries = ["France", "Germany", "United States", "Austria",
"Norway"]
for (offset, country) in enumerate(countries):
```

```
  print country, 'is the', offset, 'item in the list'
```

Again, the use of the `enumerate()` function produces an iterator, not a list. We could have simply used "`iter(countries)`", but we would not have the offset included in a tuple. This fragment produces the result:

```
France is the 0 item in the list
Germany is the 1 item in the list
United States is the 2 item in the list
Austria is the 3 item in the list
Norway is the 4 item in the list
```

Here, we should make a note: '`for` loops work with iterators as well as with sequences'. Working with sequences may seem to be their primary duty, but the fact that they work with iterators means they are very flexible.

There are some variations on for loops and iteration that might look a little strange at first. For example, if you want to generate a list of the powers of 2 between 1 and 5, you might try:

```
powers = [2**1, 2**2, 2**3, 2**4, 2**5]
```

This is fine for short lists. However, if you wanted to generate a list of the powers of 2 between 1 and 32, you might do this:

```
powers = [2 ** x for x in range(32)]
```

This type of inline for loop is much easier to use and more convenient.

2.7.5 Functions

A function is a collection of statements, treated as a special unit, that can be used many times in a program. Using the group of statements in a function is known as calling the function. When one part of a program calls a function, it can pass data to the function for the function to use; these data are known as parameters. As part of their execution, functions can return values back to the calling statement (but are not required to do so).

We have already seen functions at work. In previous examples, we called the `range()` function, passed it an integer parameter, and used the list of integers that it returned. We also used the `next()` function for iterators and the `enumerate()` function. If you have used other programming languages, calling functions should be very familiar.

In this section, we focus on writing user-defined functions and explaining how the various semantics of functions affect this type of function.

Writing User-Defined Functions

User-defined functions are written using the `def` statement. The general form of this statement is here:

```
def <function name>(<parameter list>):
   <statementset>
```

The '<function name>' should take the form of all other names in Python: it must start with a letter and can be made up of letters and numbers after that. The '<parameter list>' is optional and is a list of names that will be used to reference the parameters that are sent during a function call. The '<statementset>' is the block of statements, appropriately indented, that executes when the function is called.

Consider this simple example:

```
def listaverage(aList):
   thesum = 0
   for x in aList:
      thesum += x
```

```
    print "Average is ",thesum/len(aList)
```

This is a repackaging of an earlier example. We can call this function by executing the statement:

```
listaverage([1,2,3,4,5])
```

and we get the output:

```
Average is  2
```

In the definition, the list '[1,2,3,4,5]' is assigned to the parameter aList and that parameter is used as a variable in the defining code.

Coding Habits and Discipline

It is natural for programmers to develop habits when writing programs. Some like to use a certain style of naming for functions and parameters. Language designers might even use a certain style in designing a language to help programmers write better code. For example, the 'declaration before use' rules of C++ and Java are designed to force programmers to be intentional about using variables in those languages.

It is important in a language like Python to develop and maintain good coding habits. The language design is loose and rarely enforces a specific kind of coding practice. Therefore, it is up to you to use good practices.

For example, because you may use any names as parameters and variables, it is easy to get them mixed up in a function definition. However, good coding discipline should ensure that you can identify them. Notice that the name of the parameter in the example above begins with the letter 'a' followed by a capital letter. This is to distinguish it as an 'argument' to the function.

Function definitions are 'executable' and are created at program runtime. This happens because of the interpreted nature of Python. This means that the def statement can occur anywhere any other statement can occur. You can also treat the function name just like a variable and assign it to other names. Consider this example:

```
if x < y:
   def announcement():
      print "x is indeed less than y!"
else:
   def announcement():
      print "Sorry, x is not less than y!"

shout = announcement
shout()
```

The result of this code fragment, when x is "1" and y is "2" is:

```
x is indeed less than y!
```

This might be obvious, but the way the definitions work is unique to Python. Definitions can be nested inside an `if` statement because they are executable and function objects can be assigned to other names because executing a function definition produces a function object. This may be a little contrived for this simple an example, but these mechanisms are useful for more complex programs.

Function parameters

Python function parameters are specified as a comma separated list of zero or more named parameters (or "arguments"). When the function is called the parameters can be passed either unnamed in the order of the function definition, or in any order using their names. In the example below a function which takes three parameters and adds them is called using both named and unnamed parameters:

```
def adder(a,b,c):
    return a+b+c

x=1
y=2
z=3

#specify parameters in original order of function definition (un-
named)
print adder(x,y,z)

#specify values of named parameters
print adder(b=x,c=y,z=a)
```

We can declare default values for parameters in the function definition using the assignment operator. The combination of default values and named parameters gives us a lot of flexibility. In the example below we set the non-default parameter explicitly, without having to define the other parameters.

```
def adder(b,a=3,c=0):

x=1
print adder(b=x)
```

> ***Tip***
> Care should be taken when assigning mutable default parameters. A default parameter, like every other named object in Python, is a reference to an object. If the object is mutable its value can be changed in your executing program.

The examples above are great if we only want to add zero, one, two or three numbers, but what if we want to add an arbitrary number of numbers? One way would be to use a list or tuple as an argument. Another is to use Python's special syntax to specify a *variable number of arguments:*

- a single asterisk (*) in front of a parameter is a tuple of all remaining unnamed values.
- a double asterisk (**) in front of a parameter is a dictionary of all remaining named parameters.

If both single and double asterisk arguments are specified, the double asterisk must be specified last.

The example below shows an add function that uses the single asterisk syntax to add any number of unnamed parameters.

```
def add(firstValue=0,*myArgumentList):
    sum=firstValue
    for number in myArgumentList:
        sum+=number
        return sum

print add(1,2,3,4,5)
```

Python passes parameters into a function body as object references. This means that if an object passed as a parameter is of a mutable type (like a list, set or dictionary) changes to it within the function affect the referenced global object. If the object is immutable (like a tuple, string or integer) it cannot be modified by the function. If the function attempts to modify an immutable object type Python creates a local scope copy of the object for use within the function.

Care must be taken to ensure that you don't accidentally modify mutable variables within your function. If the intention of passing a mutable object is simply to assign values to it within the function, a safer and more "Python" approach is to assign the result of your object to the return value of the function (as discussed in the following section).

Returning values

Python functions can return a value (or values) back to the caller by executing the 'return' statement, as shown below. This mechanism for returning values is preferred over modifying the values of mutable function arguments.

```
return <expressions>
```

The <expressions> are computed, the function execution is terminated, and the value is returned to the caller. That value can then be used as any other value or variable reference. Note that if no value is explicitly returned, a function will return `None`.

Consider the code here, a proper rewriting of the `listaverage()` function:

```
def listaverage(aList):
    thesum = 0
    for x in aList:
        thesum += x
    return thesum/len(aList)
```

Now a call to `listaverage()` prints nothing, but returns the average and can be used in an expression or other statement.

Functions in Python can return multiple values. For example:

```
def listaverage2(aList):
    thesum = 0
    for x in aList:
```

```
        thesum += x
    return len(aList),thesum/len(aList)
```

This function returns both the length of the list and the average of the numbers. We can use it like this:

```
l,a = listaverage2(range(32))
print "l is ", l, " and a is ", a
```

The result is:

```
l is  32  and a is  15
```

Scope Rules

As we have seen, Python has the notion of 'statement blocks' — sets of statements, grouped by indentation. Identifier names for variables and other objects can be used in these blocks without declaration. Blocks can be nested inside each other and then the names in use can become confusing.

What is the value of a that gets printed in the example below?

```
a = 100
def f():
   a = 99
f()
print a
```

Python has scope rules which define the visibility of identifiers.

To understand the scope rules of Python, we need to understand some definitions. We first need to make the distinction between 'global scope' and 'local scope'. Global scope is the space of identifiers for an entire Python module or program. All blocks at all levels in a Python program can see and use global names. Local scope is the space for identifiers in the innermost function definition. Between global and local there is 'enclosing scope'; this is the space of identifiers defined outside of a statement block. And there is one more scope: all built-in Python identifiers are available to all parts of a Python program.

Figure 2.1 shows the relationships between these scope areas. This set of rules is often called the 'LEGB scope rule'.

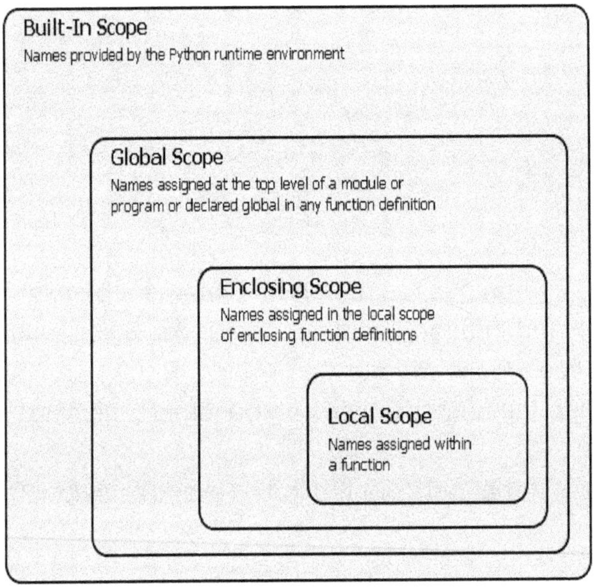

Figure 2.1: Python Scope Areas

Let's make a couple of observations on this LEGB rule before we get into an example.

Since we do not declare variables in Python, the operation that establishes the block where a name is defined is 'assignment'.

When a name is used, the LEGB rule defines the lookup sequence that Python uses. Python starts looking for an assignment in the local block, then in the enclosing blocks, then in the global block, and then finally in the set of built-in

Python definitions.

A name may be declared global, which places it into the global scope area. Here are some examples.

```
a = 100
def f():
    a = 99
f()
print a
```

This is the example that opened this section. What is the value of `a` that gets printed? To figure this out, we need to know which a the print statement refers to. There are two a definitions, one in the `f()` function block and one in the global program block. The lookup rule starts in the current block and looks "outward" to outer blocks, so the `a` is from the global block, which has the value `100`. Note that the function changes its own value of `a`, so it does not affect the global definition of `a`.

```
a = 100
def f():
    print a
f()
print a
```

In this example, two values are printed, both refer to global name `a`. The first print statement needs to find an `a` to print. The search begins in the local scope, but no assignment defines an `a` in that scope. So, the search moves to the enclosing scope (which happens to be the global scope as well) and there is an `a` defined there with the value `100`. Both print statements reference this definition of `a`.

```
a = 100
def f():
    print a
    a = a+100
    print a
f()
print a
```

This code actually produces an error. The inner scope of the function needs a definition of `a` to print. The Python interpreter looks for the definition in the function's scope area and finds it in the assignment statement after the print statement. This results in an error because the variable is referenced before it has a value. The interpreter ***might*** have used the name from the enclosing scope, but the rule is to use the local scope first.

```
a = 100
def f():
    global a
    print a
    a = a+100
    print a
f()
print a
```

This code is identical to the previous code but with the addition of a `global` declaration. Now it works. Because of the `global` declaration, the assignment statement in the function uses the global definition of a instead of attempting to create a new one.

Here is a final note about parameters to functions. Parameters are passed to functions as if they were assigned to the local function names of the parameters. This means that parameters are in the local scope area of a function. This means that changing the values of parameters has no effect on definitions in the enclosing scope.

Ramifications of Scope Rules: Redefinition of Names

There are many ramifications of scope rules; some are more obvious than others. One ramification is that you can redefine names from an outer scope in an inner scope.

You should avoid such redefinitions. The biggest reason is that you will hide the outer definition by the inner definition, making the outer definition inaccessible. For example:

```
def min(a,b):
   return a if a>b else b
min(2,3)
```

This is the wrong definition of a min() function; it is actually a max() function. However, once this is defined, it will be used in place of the built-in min() function and always return the wrong result.

Another reason why redefinition is not useful is that it can get confusing. Constantly redefining the variable mileage, for example, might result in some very complex code, especially if you need to track down a bug that sets the variable incorrectly.

lambda functions

There is a way to define a function in Python without giving that function a name through the `def` statement. This type of anonymous function is defined using a lambda expression.

A lambda expression allows you to express parameters and an expression that defines its return value. The general form looks like this:

```
lambda <parameterlist>: <expression>
```

For example, we could use a lambda function like this:

```
func = lambda a, b, c: (a + b + c) / 3
x = func(1,2,3)
```

In the code above, we define an anonymous function that returns the average of three numbers. That definition is assigned to a variable and that variable is used to invoke the function. At no time did that function get a name, so if the variable `func` were to be reassigned, the definition of that function would be lost.

We should note some properties of lambda functions. First, the use of the lambda function is an expression, not a statement. This means that the definition of the lambda function returns a value — a function value — that can be assigned to a variable as we did above. Second, the body of a lambda definition is an expression, not a set of statements. This means that is not as flexible as a `def` definition.

However, lambda functions can be used conveniently in several situations. They are simpler code constructs than using a def statement. We will see them in use in later chapters as callback functions. One common use of lambda functions is as a 'jump table'. A jump table is typically a dictionary construct with lambda functions as values.

Consider this example:

```
table = {'green': (lambda: x * y),
      'orange': (lambda: x + y),
      'blue': (lambda: x - y + 2),
      'yellow': (lambda: x / y -1)
      }
```

functions, so you know about methods!

Each method in the above definition has at least one parameter. This parameter refers to the instance of the class that has been created. We use this instance above in references to data. When we use `self.amount`, for example, we are referring to the amount variable that exists in a specific instance of this class, referred to by `self`. Programmers in C++ and Java will recognize the `self` variable as the this object.

We can use this class as follows:

```
bankaccount = Account(1000)
bankaccount.balance()
bankaccount.deposit(250)
bankaccount.withdraw(100)
bankaccount.balance()
```

The first line of the code creates an 'instance object' called `bankaccount` of the 'class object' called `Account`. We initialize the `amount` of the `bankaccount` object to `1000` by including it in the instance creation statement. This calls the constructor and passes it the value 1000.

The remainder of the example above uses methods from the class. The results of running the above code is below:

```
1000
1150
```

Inheritance

Inheritance occurs when classes are defined in terms of other classes and take their data components and methods. This establishes a relationship between classes that can be exploited for software reuse. Inheritance is one of the most useful and important concepts of object-orientation and Python supports it fully.

Let's say that we want to define two more banking classes: `CheckingAccount` and `SavingsAccount`. We could go through the same definitions as we did with the `Account` class and each of three classes would have their own definitions. However, it would be advantageous if these classes had a relationship: if we could use one of these new classes in the same places as `Account`. In fact, a `CheckingAccount` is exactly the same as an `Account`, and a `SavingsAccount` is an `Account` with a special definition for `withdraw` that does not allow `amount` to go below $100.

We can define these subclasses like this:

```
class CheckingAccount(Account):
   pass

class SavingsAccount(Account):

   def withdraw(self, aWithdrawalAmount):
      if (self.amount-aWithdrawalAmount > 100):
         self.amount -= aWithdrawalAmount
      return self.amount
```

In this definition, `CheckingAccount` has the same definition as`Account` and therefore only includes the 'pass' statement (class definitions need a block of statements). `SavingsAccount` is defined in terms of `Account`, but redefines the `withdraw()` method.

Here, anytime an `Account` is required, we can use `CheckingAccount` or `SavingsAccount`, because they inherit the `Account` type. For example, let's write a function that transfers money between two accounts:

```
def transfer(aAmount, aAcct1, aAcct2):
```

```
aAcct2.deposit(aAcct1.withdraw(aAmount))
```

This code would work equally well with `Account`, `CheckingAccount`, or `SavingsAccount`.

Often the hierarchical nature of the inheritance relationship is exploited to provide a programming interface of “expected” method implementations. This way of providing an interface assumes that a method exists or provides a method but leaves its implementation empty.

Let’s redefine the `Account` class as below:

```
class Account():
   def __init__(self, aStartingAmount):
      self.amount = aStartingAmount

   def deposit(self, aDepositAmount):
      self.amount += aDepositAmount
      return self.amount

   def withdraw(self, aWithdrawalAmount):
      if (self.amount-aWithdrawalAmount > self.limit):
         self.amount -= aWithdrawalAmount
      return self.amount

   def balance(self):
      print self.amount
```

This code now has the `withdraw()` method based on a variable called `self.limit`, which is not defined by the `Account` class. This makes the `Account` class unusable for regular programming and turns it into an ‘abstract class’, one that is used as a base class to define other classes and to force those classes to have a specific definition. Now, to be usable, both `CheckingAccount` and

SavingsAccount must define self.limit. Here is the new definition of these classes:

```
class CheckingAccount(Account):
    def __init__(self, aStartingAmount):
        self.amount = aStartingAmount
        self.limit = 0

class SavingsAccount(Account):
    def __init__(self, aStartingAmount):
        Account.__init__(self,aStartingAmount)
        self.limit = 100
```

Both definitions define a self.limit variable that is assumed by the Account definition.

Notice how the above definitions have different ways of using the parent class. The CheckingAccount definition rewrites the __init__() method completely; the SavingsAccount definition calls the parent class' __init__() method before making refinements. The second approach is better because it does not assume a definition in the parent class. If the __init__() method changes in the parent class the SavingsAccount definition will still be correct, whereas the CheckingAccount definition will not.

Multiple Inheritance

We should make a note here about Python's ability to use multiple inheritance. We discussed inheritance and showed how a subclass can inherit the properties of a parent class. In Python, this inheritance relationship can extend to multiple parent classes.

Multiple inheritance is useful when a class needs access to the data objects and methods of more than one class. Let's say that a Python program has a set of definitions that define, among other objects, an Employee class and a

`Student` class. There might be a class that defines student employees, which would have to inherit both `Employee` and `Student` class properties. Again, let's say that a user interface has a class that depicts items on a menu and buttons on a page. There would also be classes that inherited aspects from both of these classes to put buttons on items on menus.

Muliple inheritance is specified in Python by putting multiple classes in the `class` statement. For example, we could define:

```
class MenuItemWithButton(MenuItem, Button):
    ...
```

The `MenuItemWithButton` class has two parents and must implement the proper abstract properties from both.

It can happen that some of the classes that are inherited have properties with the same name. In the above, both `MenuItem` and `Button` classes could have a method named `isPressed` or `setVisible`. The rule for which one is referenced is the "left to right" rule: the classes specified in the class statement are searched in specification order left to right. So the `setVisible` method from the `MenuItem` would be used for that method unless it is redefined for the new class.

Multiple Inheritance considered controversial

Like some other language features (e.g., the goto statement), multiple inheritance is a controversial feature. Some languages (C++, Python) include it while others (Java,C#) specifically exclude it. Proponents find it useful and actually necessary to properly depict certain object-oriented relationships; detractors find it confusing and not needed for most programs. Some languages (Java) implement multiple inheritance, but cloak it behind language features designed to encourage better programming (in Java, the interface concept is an attempt to incorporate single inheritance with a cleaner multiple inheritance implementation).

Operator Overloading

One specialized way of working with class methods is through operator overloading. It is possible to 'overload' — or redefine — operators in Python classes. This applies to the basic common operators used in the built-in data types as well.

For example, consider the following definitions:

```
class MyNumber:
   def __init__(self, aInitialValue):
      self.value = aInitialValue
   def __add__(self, aValue):
      return MyNumber(self.value + aValue)
```

Now, the operator "+" can be used with instances of the `MyNumber` class. We can now execute the following:

```
x = MyNumber(100)
y = x + 100
```

`y.value` now has the value "200". Whilst that might not be surprising, the beauty of the code is the we used the "+" operator. This is a nice way to provide intuitive operators when classes demand it. If a class denotes a collection of objects, for instance, redefining the "[]" operator would be an intuitive thing to do.

Almost all operators in Python can be overloaded in this manner. See the Python Documentation for a list, ***docs.python.org/reference/datamodel.html#special-method-names***.

Overloading Accounts

It would make a lot of sense to use "+" as `deposit()` and "-" as the `withdrawl()` definition in the Account definitions above. Can you show how these definitions would incorporate these operators?

2.9 Exception Handling

2.9.1 Exception Basics

Exceptions are events which define a condition that has arisen that needs to be dealt with. These events are typically errors that occur during the execution of a program, but exceptions can also be used in other situations to modify the execution of a program. The key feature of an exception is the need for it to be handled. Unhandled exceptions halt the execution of a program.

Python has a rich set of language constructs that implement exceptions. The most basic of these features is the `try/except` sequence of statements. This is the general format:

```
try:
   <statementset1>
except <name1>:
   <statementset2>
except <name2>,<data>
   <statementset3>
except (name3, name4):
   <statementset4>
except:
   <statementset5>
else:
   <statementset6>
finally:
   <statementset7>
```

Using exceptions is very flexible. Python starts by attempting (trying) to execute <statementset1>. If these statements execute without raising an exception the statements in the optional else part — <statementset6>— and `finally` part — <statementset6>— are executed. If an exception is raised, however, the `except` parts are searched for the <name> of the exception. When the matching exception is found the statements under that `except` part are executed. If the name of the exception is not found, the statements under the generic `except` part — <statementset5> — are executed. The `except` statement can be used with the "<data>" element to get more information about the exception. The `finally` part is always executed.

Consider an example. A very common programming error is division by zero. This has an exception associated with it:

```
a = 10
b = 0
try:
   c = a/b
except:
   print "Oops...something bad happened"
```

This code produces the message 'Oops...something bad happened' and it should be obvious why this exception was raised. In Python, this exception has a name: 'ZeroDivisionError'. We can look for this exception specifically with the following code:

```
a = 10
b = 0
try:
   c = a/b
except ZeroDivisionError:
   print "Oops...something bad happened"
```

This code produces the same result. Extra information can be obtained by adding a variable to the `except` part. In our simple case, this extra information is an error message that explains the error:

```
a = 10
b = 0
try:
   c = a/b
except ZeroDivisionError, message:
   print "Oops...something bad happened"
   print message
```

This code produces the output:

```
Oops...something bad happened
integer division or modulo by zero
```

Let's conclude this simple example with an `else` statement.

```
a = 10
b = 10
try:
   c = a/b
except ZeroDivisionError, message:
   print "Oops...something bad happened"
   print message
else:
   print "Hey!  Something good happened"
```

This code prints the message in the `else` statement, because the division completes successfully.

Because of the way that the `try` statement is structured multiple exceptions can be handled and common ways to complete the statement can be implemented. Multiple exceptions can be handled in the same way by naming them all in the `except` part.

There are many built-in exceptions in Python, too many to list here. They all have names and depict a specific kind of error condition. Python always prints the name of the exception when giving an error message. So, if you were use a division by zero in a Python program, you might get an error message like this:

```
Traceback (most recent call last):
File "<stdin>", line 1, in <module>
ZeroDivisionError: integer division or modulo by zero
```

Note the name of the exception in the last line.

Raising Exceptions

There are lots of built-in exceptions, but you can also raise your own exceptions. This is a useful feature when you want to force certain conditions (like errors) to be handled by programmers using a programming interface. You raise exceptions with the `raise` statement. It can be used in several ways:

```
raise <exceptionname1>
raise <exceptionname2>,<value>
```

These should make some sense given the way that we use the try statement to catch exceptions. The first form is the the more obvious; it raises the named exception. The name can be a built-in exception, a string that you make yourself, a class name or an an instance.

The second form adds a string value that serves as additional data. The string is usually an error message that augments the exception.

Let's take a couple of examples. Consider an addition to the `Account` class definitions above:

```
BalanceError = 'BalanceError'

class Account():
   def __init__(self, aStartingAmount):
      self.amount = aStartingAmount

   def deposit(self, aDepositAmount):
      self.amount += aDepositAmount
      return self.amount

   def withdraw(self, aWithdrawalAmount):
      if (self.amount-aWithdrawalAmount > self.limit):
         self.amount -= aWithdrawalAmount
      else:
         msg = "Account is overdrawn by "+str(-(self.amount-aWith-
drawalAmount))
         raise BalanceError,msg
      return self.amount

def balance(self):
   print self.amount

class CheckingAccount(Account):
   def __init__(self, aStartingAmount):
      self.amount = aStartingAmount
      self.limit = 0

class SavingsAccount(Account):
   def __init__(self, aStartingAmount):
      Account.__init__(self,aStartingAmount)
      self.limit = 100
```

We have added several things. We now have a global string that identifies 'BalanceError'. We will use this as our exception. We also added an 'else' part to the `withdraw()` method that creates an error message in the variable msg and raises the `BalanceError` exception. Now we can use the following code to catch this new exception:

```
newacct = CheckingAccount(100)
try:
   newacct.withdraw(200)
except BalanceError,errormsg:
   print errormsg
```

Exceptions and propagation

Exceptions must be handled somewhere or the program will terminate. Python 'propagates' exceptions: It passes them through the calling sequence and any of the functions in the sequence can handle them.

For example, if a function 'funcA' calls 'funcB', which calls 'funcC', we have a calling sequence like that in Figure 2.2:

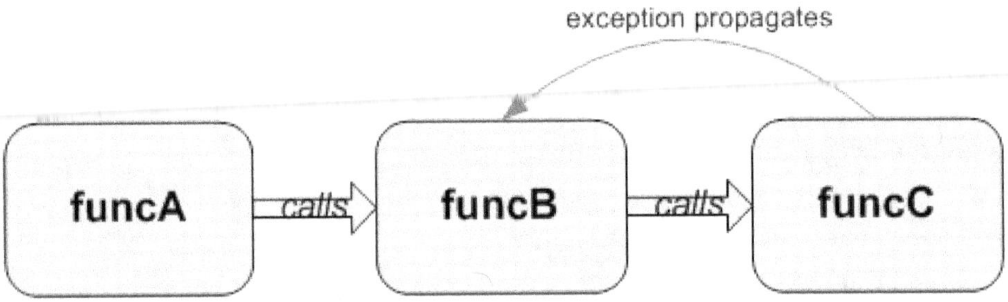

Figure 2.2: Calling Sequence Implies Exception Propagation

Let's say that an exception is raised in 'funcC'. If there is an exception handler in "funcC" Python uses that. If not, it looks for one in "funcB" and so on up the calling chain.

2.9.2 Importing Modules

It would be awkward if every Python program were a single file. Python programs depend on many built-in definitions and on code written by others. So it makes sense to split code definitions up into multiple files. This is where importing modules comes in.

Python program file names end in a '.py' suffix and are referred to as 'modules'. A program can reference items from other modules by 'importing' them. The contents of modules are known as 'attributes' and can be imported as a large unit or individually.

Here is an example. Let's assume that the Account class definitions above, the child classes `CheckingAccount` and `SavingsAccount`, and the `BalanceError` exception, are stored in a file called 'Account.py'. If we create a new file with an instance of the `SavingsAccount` class we must import the definition from 'Account.py' like this:

```
import Account
myaccount = Account.SavingsAccount(1000)
myaccount.balance()
```

The `import` statement made the attributes defined in the 'Account.py' file available to the current program. We reference the module's attributes — in this case, the `SavingsAccount` class — using the same dot notation we use to reference class attributes.

We can avoid this dotted notation and be a little more specific in our importing by using the `from` keyword with the import statement, as below:

```
from Account import SavingsAccount
```

```
myacct = SavingsAccount(1000)
myacct.withdraw(2000)
```

Executing the last line, however, raises an exception:

```
Traceback (most recent call last):
File "<stdin>", line 1, in <module>
File "Account.py", line 17, in withdraw
raise BalanceError,msg
BalanceError: Account is overdrawn by 1000
```

Importing module attributes can get a little tricky. Let's say that we want to trap the `BalanceError` exception in `try` statement, like this:

```
from Account import SavingsAccount
try:
   myacct = SavingsAccount(1000)
   myacct.withdraw(2000)
except BalanceError, errormsg:
   print errormsg
```

We get an error here too:

```
Traceback (most recent call last):
   File "accttest.py", line 6, in <module>
      except BalanceError, errormsg:
NameError: name 'BalanceError' is not defined
```

This is because we imported the `SavingsAccount` attribute, but no others. We referenced the `BalanceError` name without importing it. We can get around importing every attribute individually by using the following syntax for the `import` statement:

```
from Account import *
try:
    myacct = SavingsAccount(1000)
    myacct.withdraw(2000)
except BalanceError, errormsg:
    print errormsg
```

By using 'import *', we import every attribute and do not have to use the dot notation to reference them. This is the most commonly used form of the `import` statement.

We can also import an entire directory of files and definitions. This called a 'package' import. It is a somewhat advanced feature of Python, however, so we do not describe it here.

Miscellaneous Python Elements

As we conclude our brief overview of Python, there are a couple of miscellaneous items we should mention.

The first is docstrings. Docstrings are a special form of string that can be used in program files and function definitions. They are treated like comments at execution time and ignored. However, they are used and displayed by tools that work with Python, including the Python runtime environment. Docstrings are surrounded by three quote marks, as you can see below:

```
def sum(a,b,c):
    '''
    This is a contrived example to show
    off docstrings
    '''
    return(a+b+c)
```

When the Python runtime system parses a docstring, it stores it as the __doc__ attribute for the item being defined. We can print documentation by using the following code:

```
>>> print sum.__doc__

   This is a contrived example to show
   off docstrings
```

We can print documentation like this for built-in definitions too. For example, the function `max()` is built into the Python runtime system and we can read its documentation as follows:

```
>>> print max.__doc__
max(iterable[, key=func]) -> value
max(a, b, c, ...[, key=func]) -> value

With a single iterable argument, return its largest item.
With two or more arguments, return the largest argument.
```

The `help()` function is built into the Python runtime system and is defined to print docstrings if they exist.

This brings us to our second miscellaneous item. The `dir()` built-in function allows us to explore the runtime environment and determine the definitions that currently exist. The function has two forms: without parameters, it prints the names of all definitions; with one parameter, it prints the attributes of the name given by that parameter.

For example, if you want to see all the definitions built into the `sum()` function we described above, you could call `dir(sum)`. You would get something like this:

```
>>> dir(sum)
```

```
['__call__', '__class__', '__delattr__', '__dict__', '__doc__',
'__get__', '__getattribute__', '__hash__', '__init__', '__mod-
ule__', '__name__', '__new__', '__reduce__', '__reduce_ex__',
'__repr__', '__setattr__', '__str__', 'func_closure', 'func_code',
'func_defaults', 'func_dict', 'func_doc', 'func_globals', 'func_
name']
```

Usually, definitions that begin and end with the "__" character sequence are system-defined. All of these definitions can be used in Python code.

Explore!
We cannot go over all of these attributes in this chapter. So, go ahead and explore these yourself. Try using the help() function on these, like help(sum.__init__). You will get several screens of documentation.

Finally, a note about program formats and lines. As you now know, Python is designed to have one statement per line and to use indentation to group statements together. This means that if you write a statement that takes multiple lines, Python might mistake the extra lines as a new block and find the code to be in error. To write statements that span multiple lines put a "\" character at the end of lines that are continued. For example, this code is in error:

```
if (x < y and
   y > z and
   a > y):
   ...
```

but this code is fine:

```
if (x < y and \
   y > z and \
   a > y):
   ...
```

2.10 Summary

This chapter has provided a brief overview of Python's basic elements, covering many of the most import aspects of the language:

- Variables, along with data typing and operations on data
- Expressions and assignment operations
- Statements, including conditional statements and iterative looping constructs, with an introduction to Python iterators
- Functions, including parameter passing, scope rules, and lambda functions
- Object oriented features, including classes, inheritance, and operator overloading
- Exceptions.

While many of these concepts can be found in other programming languages, Python provide has a unique and developer-friendly perspective on them.

3

System Information and Operations

Having covered the basic Python conventions and coding syntax in Chapter 2, it's time to move on to discuss how to use Python on Symbian. This chapter describes how to access device and application information, how to perform system operations and how to work with files and time values.

This chapter introduces sysinfo and e32, the modules that provide information about the device and the current application respectively. The e32 module also contains utilities to perform system operations, such as running and pausing scripts and setting the device time.

Finally, the chapter discusses core functionality inherited from standard Python, such as how to perform operations related to time and how to manipulate files. It covers Symbian's file naming and handling conventions and shows how Python handles files in ways similar to other programming languages.

The methods described in this chapter are frequently used in Python applications for Symbian devices, including many of the examples in this book.

3.1 The System Information Module

The sysinfo module can be used to access the following device information:

- IMEI
- signal strength
- battery strength
- firmware version
- OS version
- screen display resolution
- current profile
- current ringing type
- RAM and ROM drive size
- the amount of free RAM, ROM and disk drive space.

The module is easy to use. For example, the following two lines in the interactive PyS60 console return the IMEI of the device:

```
>>> import sysinfo
>>> sysinfo.imei()
u'217402720272029 2'
```

> ***Note***
> Every mobile device on a GSM network is identified by a unique number called its IMEI (International Mobile Equipment Identity), about which you can find out more from ***en.wikipedia.org/wiki/International_Mobile_Equipment_Identity***.

The IMEI of the device can be retrieved manually by dialing *#06#.

The following code snippets show the methods used to obtain the information and their return types.

```
# Retrieve battery strength as an integer. The value is in the
range 0 (empty) to 100 (full).
>>> sysinfo.battery()
42

# Retrieve signal strength as an integer. The value is in the
range 0 (no signal) to 7 (strong signal).
>>> sysinfo.signal_bars()
7

#  Retrieve network signal strength in dBm (integer)
>>> sysinfo.signal_dbm()
81

# Retrieve the IMEI code of the device as a Unicode string
>>> sysinfo.imei()
 u'354829024755443'

# Retrieve the software version as a Unicode string. This is the
version number that a device displays when *#0000# is dialled.
>>> sysinfo.sw_version()
u'V 20.0.016 28-2-08 RM-320 N95(c)NMP'
```

```
# Retrieve the width and height of the display (in the current
orientation) in pixels
>>> sysinfo.display_pixels()
(240, 320)

# Get the current profile name as a string ('general', 'silent',
'meeting', 'outdoor', 'pager', 'offline', etc). If a custom profile
is selected - it returns 'user <profile value>'
>>> sysinfo.active_profile()
'general'

# Retrieve the ringing type as a string - 'normal', 'ascending',
'ring_once', 'beep' or 'silent'
>>> sysinfo.ring_type()
'normal'

# Get the OS version as a tuple
>>> sysinfo.os_version()
(2, 0, 1540)
```

Note

When running on the emulator some of the functions return dummy values:

- `battery()` and `signal_bars()` return 0.
- `sw_version()` returns u'emulator'
- `imei()` returns `u'000000000000000'`

Symbian devices usually have an internal disk (C:) and a memory card (E:). If there is a random access memory (RAM) drive it is mapped to D: and Z: is the read only memory (ROM) drive. There are exceptions: some devices use E drive for 'internal' mass memory and some have additional drives. The amount of ROM, RAM and disk space varies across devices.

`sysinfo` can also return information about the device memory, shown as follows:

```
# Get free RAM in bytes
>>> sysinfo.free_ram()
81838080

# Get total RAM in bytes
>>> sysinfo.total_ram()
125501440

# Get total ROM in bytes
>>> sysinfo.total_rom()
8716288

# Get free disk space in bytes. Drive can be C: or E:
>>> sysinfo.free_drivespace()['C:']
16207872
```

Note that the e32 module provides `drive_list()` to get the list of drives, as discussed in the following section.

3.2 The e32 Module

The e32 module contains a useful and varied collection of utilities. The utilities range from methods that retrieve information about the device and current application, to methods that pause the current script or reset the device inactivity timer. There are also methods available for filesystem operations, such as copying files and folders.

The e32 module provides the following 'system' information in addition to that provided by sysinfo:

- The Python runtime version
- The Symbian device runtime version
- The list of available drives
- The platform security capabilities of the current application
- The length of time since the last user activity
- Whether or not the current thread is a UI thread
- Whether or not the current application or script is running on an emulator

The code snippet below shows the methods used to obtain the above information.

```
# Get the Python runtime version - tuple of version number: major,
minor, micro and release tag,
>>> e32.pys60_version()
(1, 9, 7, 'svn2793')
```

```
# Get the Python runtime version - tuple of major, minor, micro,
release tag, and serial.
>>> e32.pys60_version_info()
(1, 9, 7, 'svn2793', 0)

# Get the Symbian platform device version - tuple of major and mi-
nor version
>>> e32.s60_version_info()
(3, 0)

# Retrieve a list of available memory drives. For example:
[u'C:',u'D:',u'E:',u'Z:']
>>>e32.drive_list()
[u'C:',u'D:',u'E:',u'F:',u'Z:']

# Get the time in seconds since the last user activity
>>> e32.inactivity()
3

# Get the platform security capabilities granted to the applica-
tion, returned as a tuple
>>> e32.get_capabilities()
('ReadUserData','WriteUserData')

# Test if application has been granted the specified platform secu-
rity capabilities. Returns True or False.
# querying single capability
>>> e32.has_capabilities('WriteUserData')
```

```
True

# Query whether the application has two capabilities
>>> e32.has_capabilities('WriteUserData','ReadUserData')
True

# Test if the calling script is running in the context of a UI
thread. Returns True or False
>>> e32.is_ui_thread()
True

# Test whether or not the application or script is running in an
emulator. Returns 1 if yes, 0 if no.
>>>e32.in_emulator()
1
```

The e32 module can perform the following system operations on the device.

Set the device's system time

The `set_home_time()` function sets the device system time to given time (for e.g. `user_time` in the example below). The device system time can be retrieved through the time module as explained in next section.

```
import e32
import time

# current time
user_time = time.time()
```

```
# modify the user_time
user_time -= 10.0

e32.set_home_time(user_time)
```

> **Note**
>
> The `WriteDeviceData` capability is required to use this function. For more information, refer to Chapter 16.

3.2.1 Copy files

The `file_copy()` function can be used to copy files from one folder to another.

```
>>> source_path=u"C:\\Python\\myimage.jpg"
>>> destination_path=u"C:\\Data\\Images\\myimage.jpg"
>>> e32.file_copy(destination_path,source_path)
```

To copy all of the files in the source folder append '`*.*`' to the source path.

```
>>> source_path=u"C:\\Python\\*.*"
>>> destination_path=u"C:\\Data"
>>> e32.file_copy(destination_path,source_path)
```

This copies all the files in the C:\Python directory to the C:\Data directory.

> **Note**
>
> Double backslashes '\\' must be used to specify directory paths
>
> The destination directory must already exist - the function fails if it doesn't.
>
> If the copy operation fails, it throws an exception.

3.2.2 Launch an application

The `start_exe()` method can be used to launch a specified executable (`.exe`) file, as follows.

```
>>> e32.start_exe(exe_filename, command,wait_time)
```

The parameter command passes command line arguments to the executable. If no arguments are required, it may be set to `NULL` or an empty string. The parameter `wait_time` is an optional parameter as described below.

The following statement is used to launch the Web browser with the default URL, and the `command` parameter is passed an empty string.

```
>>> application_exe='BrowserNG.exe'
>>> a=e32.start_exe(application_exe, "")
```

In order to open the web browser application with a particular URL, we pass it as a command as follows.

```
>>> url="http://developer.symbian.org"
>>> application_exe='BrowserNG.exe'
>>> e32.start_exe(application_exe, ' "%s"' %url
```

In both the previous examples the browser is launched asynchronously. We can use the optional `wait_time` integer parameter to launch an application synchronously.

If a non-zero value is specified for `wait_time` then `start_exe()` launches the application and waits for it to exit. It then returns 0 if the application exits normally or 2 if the application terminates abnormally.

```
>>> wait_time=1
>>> url="4 http://developer.symbian.org"
>>> exit_type=e32.start_exe(application_exe,' "%s"' %url , wait_
time)
>>> print exit_type
```

The '4' prefix in the url parameter indicates that the browser should launch the url specified. Other predefined prefixes for the parameter are shown below:

Table 3.1 Parameter prefixes

Prefix	Parameter	Description
None	<Any text>	Start (or continue) the browser with no specified content
1	"<Space>"+"<Uid of a bookmark>"	Start or continue the browser with specified bookmark
2	"<Space>"+"<Uid of a saved deck>"	Start or continue the browser with specified saved deck
4	"<Space>"+"<URL>"	Start or continue browser with specified URL
4	"<Space>"+"<Url>"+"<Space>"+"<Uid of AP>"	Start or continue the browser with specified bookmark and Access Point (AP)

5	`<Any text>`	Start or continue the browser with the start page. (Used when starting the browser with a long press of "0" in the Idle state of the phone)
6	`" <Space>"+"<Uid of bookmark folder>"`	Start or continue the browser with specified bookmark folder

The `start_exe()` function can also be used to launch other native and third party applications.

Launch a python script as a server

A Python script can be launched in the background (as a server script) with the `start_server()` function.

```
>>> server_script.py=u"C:\\Data\\Python\\myscript.py"
>>> e32.start_server(server_script)
```

> ***Note***
> The appuifw module cannot be used in a Python server script.

3.2.3 Reset inactivity timer

The `reset_inactivity()` method can be used to reset the inactivity timer programmatically .

```
>>> e32.reset_inactivity()
```

Resetting the inactivity timer at regular intervals prevents the device from entering a low power mode during periods of user inactivity. This can be useful if an application needs to remain visible when the user is not "doing anything" - for example, when using an in-car hands-free navigation system. See also `inactivity()`, which returns the current value of the inactivity timer.

3.2.4 Wait/Sleep

> ***Note***
> Active objects are used extensively in Symbian C++ to provide co-operative multitasking to applications and other code. The concept is used to implement much of Python's underlying behaviour on Symbian and, for this reason, many function names in Python on Symbian have an ao_ prefix. Active objects are discussed in detail elsewhere on the ***wiki.forum.nokia.com*** wiki.

`ao_sleep()`

The `ao_sleep()` method can be used to introduce a delay between the execution of statements, or to call a specified method after a given interval. The use of `ao_sleep()` is encouraged over the standard `time.sleep()` method (documented here: ***docs.python.org/library/time.html#time.sleep***, because `ao_sleep()` doesn't block the active scheduler, which means that the UI can remain responsive.

For example, the following code causes the script to wait for two seconds.

```
print "Waiting for 2 seconds"
e32.ao_sleep(2) #sleeps for 2 seconds
print "Wait over"
```

A call back function can be specified when calling `ao_sleep()`. In the example below, the function `foo()` is called after 3 seconds.

```
def foo():
    print "In function"

e32.ao_sleep(3,foo)
```

ao_yield() and ao_callgate()

Calling `ao_yield()` gives control back to the active scheduler (see the wiki page ***croozeus.com/Python_Downloads***) thereby allowing any active object-based code with priority above normal to run. In practice this keeps an application responsive to menu and softkey input, even while performing other long running events. For example, the following code fragment displays notes within a continuous while loop. The use of `e32.ao_yield()` ensures that we can exit the loop (and application) by pressing the right soft key. Without `e32.ao_yield()` in the loop, the active scheduler would never get to run the event handling code.

```
def quit():
    global running
    running=0
```

```
    appuifw.app.set_exit()

appuifw.app.exit_key_handler=quit

running=1

while running:
    appuifw.note(u"hello")
    e32.ao_yield()
```

The `ao_callgate()` method creates an active object wrapper around a callable Python function and returns another function object that can be used to start the active object. The original Python function will be called at some point after the wrapper function is called when its associated active object is run by the active scheduler. The wrapper object can be used to call the function from any Python thread; the function is run 'in the context of the thread where the `ao_callgate()` was created'.

The following example shows how the function `fun()` is registered with the callgate to return the wrapper object `foo()`. Method `fun()` is run by the active scheduler at some point after `foo()` is called.

```
import e32

def fun():
    print "Hello"
```

```
foo = e32.ao_callgate(fun)
foo()
```

Ao_lock and Ao_timer

Two important classes defined in the e32 module are `Ao_lock` and `Ao_timer`. They are classes, unlike the operational functions above, so they can only be used after they have been instantiated.

`Ao_lock` is an active object-based synchronization service that is at the heart of the Python application UI structure as Chapter 4 describes. An `Ao_lock` object is used by creating an instance of `Ao_lock`, adding a number of active objects, and then calling `wait()` on the thread, shown as follows:

```
#Create instance of Ao_lock
app_lock = e32.Ao_lock()

# Add active objects here - e.g. menu callbacks
...

#Wait for application lock to be signaled
app_lock.wait()
```

Python halts execution of the script at the wait, but any active objects that are already running will be serviced. Python implements menus as active objects, so they are still called and the UI remains responsive. When you're ready to continue execution of the script you call `signal()`. However, as the script execution is halted at the `wait()` you must signal it to restart through a menu callback. It is a convention to release the waiting script in the `quit()` function:

```
#Signals the lock and releases the "waiter"
def quit():
    app_lock.signal()
```

Remember that `wait()` can only be called in the thread that created the lock object and only one 'waiter' is allowed, so take care when using it in a loop. `Ao_timer` is a Symbian active object-based timer service. Like `Ao_lock`, it can be used in the main thread without blocking the handling of UI events. The following code snippet creates an instance of `Ao_timer` and illustrates use of its `after()` and `cancel()` methods.

```
#Create instance of Ao_timer
timer = e32.Ao_timer()

#Sleep for the 1 second without blocking the active scheduler and
call the callback_function() (user defined callback)
timer.after(1, callback_function)

#Cancels the 'after' call.
timer.cancel()
```

The callback function parameter of the `after()` method is optional; if it is not specified the thread simply sleeps for the specified time.

The `cancel()` method can be used to cancel a pending `after()` request. It is important to cancel pending timer calls before exiting the application. If you forget, the application will panic on exit.

> ***Tip***
>
> Use `Ao_timer` instead of `ao_sleep()` where possible, because a pending `ao_sleep()` cannot be canceled, which means that a user cannot exit the application while the application is sleeping.

3.3 Time Operations

Python's concept of time comes from the Unix operating system. Unix measures time as the number of seconds since the epoch, which started on January 1, 1970 at 00:00:00 UTC (also known as Greenwich Mean Time). For example, midnight on 1 January 2010 was 1,262,304,000 seconds since the Unix epoch.

> ***Tip***
>
> Generally speaking you don't need to think about the number of seconds! Python provides methods to allow you to convert to more friendly units. If you do need to do a manual conversion, there are several sites on the Internet that will convert them for you:
>
> - ***www.epochconverter.com***
> - ***www.onlineconversion.com/unix_time.htm***

There are several system functions that display and manipulate system time. Before we look at them, however, we should review the possible values accepted for time values. There are two sets of values:

- float values represent seconds since the epoch as described above (the float data type must be used because this number of seconds is large).
- time structure values are nine integers that correspond to specific time components, as shown in the table below.

Table 3.2 Time component integers

Python Name	Description
`tm_year`	four digit value depicting the year
`tm_mon`	integer in the range 1 to 12 depicting the month
`tm_mday`	integer in the range 1 to 31 depicting the day of the month
`tm_hour`	integer in the range 0 to 23 depicting the hour
`tm_min`	integer in the range 0 to 59 depicting the minute
`tm_msec`	integer in the range 0 to 61 depicting the second (the 60th and 61st values account for leap and double leap seconds)
`tm_wday`	integer in the range 0 to 6 depicting the day of the week (Monday has the value 0)
`tm_yday`	integer in the range 0 to 365 depicting the day of the year (accommodating for leap year)
`tm_isdst`	integer in the range 0 to 1 depicting a boolean value to determine Daylight Savings Time (can be -1, see `mktime()` below

For example, consider the code below, where `time.localtime()` returns the `time` structure values as a tuple:

```
import time
(a,b,c,d,e,f,g,h,i) = time.localtime()
```

If this code were executed on 8 September 2009, at 9:15:38 am, then the variables would have the following values:

```
a = 2009
b = 9
c = 8
d = 9
e = 15
f = 38
g = 1
h = 251
i = 1
```

Let's briefly overview the functions in the time module:

- `time.asctime([t])` converts the time - either the current time, if the parameter is absent, or the time represented by the optional tuple representing a time structure value - to a string that depicts the time described.
- `time.clock()` returns the current processor time as a float in seconds. You cannot really depend on this value for anything other than comparative uses.

- `time.ctime([secs])` converts a time value in seconds since the epoch to a time structure value UTC. For this conversion, the `dst` flag is always zero, which means adjustment for Daylight Savings Time is not done. If `secs` is not provided or is `None`, the current time as returned by `time()` is used.
- `time.gmtime([secs])` converts a time expressed in seconds since the epoch to a time structure value in UTC in which the `dst` flag is always zero. If `secs` is not provided or is `None`, the current time is used.
- `time.localtime([secs])` converts to local time, returning a time structure value. If `secs` is not provided or is `None`, the current time is used.
- `time.mktime(t)` can be viewed as the inverse function of `localtime()`. Its argument is a tuple depicting a time structure value, which expresses the time in local time, not UTC. It returns a floating point number of seconds since the epoch. If the input value cannot be represented as a valid time, either `OverflowError` or `ValueError` is raised.
- `time.sleep(secs)` suspends execution of the current program for the given number of seconds. This number may be a floating point number to indicate a precise sleep time.
- `time.strftime(format[, t])` converts a tuple representing a time structure value to a string as specified by the format argument. If t is not provided, the current time is used. `format` must be a string. A `ValueError` exception is raised if any field in `t` is outside of the allowed range. More on this function below.
- `time.strptime(string[, format])` parses a string representing a time according to a format. The return value is a `time` structure value. The format follows the same directives as `strftime()`, which are de-

scribed below.

- `time.time()` returns the time as a floating point number expressed in seconds since the epoch, in UTC.
- `time.tzset()` resets the time conversion rules used by the library routines. The environment variable `TZ` specifies how this is done.

The `strftime()` and `strptime()` functions use special directives embedded in a format string. These directives are shown here:

Table 3.3 Directives for the `strftime()` and `strptime()` functions

Directive	Description
`%a`	abbreviated weekday name
`%A`	full weekday name
`%b`	abbreviated month name
`%B`	full month name
`%c`	date and time representation appropriate for region
`%d`	day of the month as an integer
`%H`	hour as an integer on the 24-hour clock
`%I`	hour as an integer on the 12-hour clock
`%j`	day of the year as an integer
`%m`	month as an integer
`%M`	minute as an integer
`%p`	AM or PM as a string
`%S`	seconds as an integer

%U	week number of the year as an integer (with Sunday considered the first day of the week)
%w	weekday as an integer (Sunday is day numbered 0)
%W	week number of the year as an integer (with Monday considered the first day of the week)
%x	date representation as a string
%X	time representation as a string
%y	year as an integer without century
%Y	year as in integer with century
%Z	time zone name (no characters if no time zone exists)

Here are some examples. Consider the following code:

```
time.strftime("Now is %a, %d %b %Y at %H:%M:%S", time.gmtime())
```

This format string combines regular text with time specifiers. It also gets the time value from `time.gmtime()`. This code produces the output:

```
Now is Wed, 09 Sep 2009 at 13:58:37
```

Now consider this code:

```
thedate = "31 Dec 08"
t = time.strptime(thedate, "%d %b %y")
```

```
if t[7] == 366:
    print thedate, "was in a leap year"
else:
    print thedate, "was not in a leap year"
```

In the above example, the results showed that 2008 was a leap year, because '31 Dec 08' was day number 366 in the year. Notice that the format string for `time.strptime()` describes the way that the first string depicting the date is formatted.

There are also some variables represented in the time module. These are:

- `time.accept2dyear` is a boolean value indicating whether two-digit year values will be accepted.
- `time.altzone` represents the offset of the local DST timezone, in seconds west of UTC, if one is defined.
- `time.daylight` is nonzero if a DST timezone is defined.
- `time.timezone` is the offset of the local timezone, in seconds west of UTC.
- `time.tzname` is a tuple of two strings. The first is the name of the local timezone; the second is the name of the local DST timezone.

Does this look familiar?

These calls and variables may look familiar. Python is based heavily on C and C++, so you might have recognized these methods as Unix system calls. The time structure values are also taken from Unix system calls. In fact, there is one more method - `struct_time()` - that works with the time values in the C struct time structure (see the struct values in the table above). Though you do not need to use it, most time methods accept a structure in the C form, much like this:

```
:time.struct_time(tm_year=2010, tm_mon=0, tm_mday=0, tm_hour=0,
tm_min=0,tm_sec=0, tm_wday=6, tm_yday=0, tm_isdst=-1)
```

The description here is of the system time module. There are other modules that provide a less primitive, more object-oriented approach to dates and times:

- The datetime module generally handles dates and times.
- The locale module implements internationalization services; its settings can alter the return values for some of the functions above.
- The calendar module implements calendar related functions.

Finally, there is one more system function we should look at: `e32.set_home_time()`. This call comes from the e32 module and is used to set the current time for the device. The parameter required is the time, to be set in Unix 'seconds past the epoch' format. For example:

```
import e32

e32.set_home_time(1262304000)
```

This code sets the global device time to midnight on 1 January 2010.
To execute the code, an application requires the `WriteDeviceData` platform security capability. Capabilities are discussed in Chapter 16.

3.4 File Operations

As we discuss in Chapter 2, a file is a built-in data type for Python. Python handles files in ways similar to other programming languages. There are also some extended file operations in the modules unique to Python on the Symbian platform.

We'll start with the file naming conventions for the Symbian platform. Symbian uses conventions similar to those used in Microsoft Windows. Drive letters are used to indicate storage units such as memory or SD cards, there is a hierarchy of directories, and pathname components are separated by backslashes.

The following table outlines some of the common file operations provided by Python.

Table 3.4 Common file operations

Operation	Description
`log=open("C:\logfile2.txt", "w")`	Create a new file (the 'w' flag is for writing)
`inlog = open("C:\images\logfile.txt")`	Open the file for reading (the 'r' flag, for reading, is the default flag)

`contents = inlog.read()`	Read the entire contents of a file into a single string variable
`bytes = inlog.read(count)`	Read "count" bytes into a string
`line = inlog.readline()`	Read a single line into a string (includes end-of-line marker)
`linelist = inlog.readlines()`	Read the entire contents of a file into a list of strings, each holding a line
`log.write(someContent)`	Write a string into a file
`log.writeLines(stringList)`	Write a sequence of strings to the file (does not add end-of-line markers)
`log.flush()`	Flush the buffer holding data for a file into that file
`log.truncate()`	Cut off the file at the current position, discarding all data after that position
`log.seek(position)`	Move the current position in a file to 'position'
`log.close()`	Close a file

Most of these operations are similar to those used in other languages and platforms. Because of the way Python organizes data objects, some are more streamlined, such as the `readlines()` and `writelines()` functions, which make reading or writing a large amount of content quite easy.
Consider the following code:

```
html = ["<HEAD>"]
## ... generate HTML and append it to the list using "html.ap-
pend(...)"
htmlfile = open("E:\Images\announce.html", "w")
htmlfile.writelines(html)
htmlfile.close()
```

Languages like Java would require each line of HTML to be written separately to a file, probably using a `for` loop. Here, however, one statement writes all lines to the file.

Note that data is always retrieved from files as a string - even non-readable data. This means that if you need data in another form, say numbers, you have to convert the data from strings to the form you need. Likewise, writing data to a file is always done using strings. Even if you want to write integers or floats, you must format the data into a string first, then write that string to a file. For example:

```
line = str(10) + "," + str(data) + "," + str(value) + "\n"
out.write(line)
```

This code builds three data items into a single string for writing. Likewise, we might read this data like:

```
line = input.readline()
pieces = line.split(',')
data1 = int(pieces[0])
data2 = int(pieces[1])
converter = float(pieces[2])
```

Here we read a comma separated line, split it into pieces and convert the individual strings into the type of data we need.

We can also use some string formatting to construct the line we need for a file. Consider the following example, which rewrites the previous code:

```
line = "%d,%d,%f\n" % (10, data, value)
out.write(line)
```

The code works for simple data types, but native Python objects might be harder to convert to strings and back. This is where the `pickle` module comes in. The pickle module contains methods that allow almost any Python object to be written to a file, with no conversion to and from strings. Consider the example below:

```
import pickle
dict = {'one': 1, 'two': 2, 'three': 3, 'four': 4}
dictFile = open('dictfile', 'w')
pickle.dump(dict, dictFile)
```

```
dictFile.close()
```

The code allows the data store in the dictionary `dict` to be stored in the file 'dictfile' as a native Python dictionary. We can get the dictionary back using the code below:

```
infile = open('dictfile')
newdict = pickle.load(infile)
infile.close()
```

Now the variables dict and newdict have the same value.

In addition to these basic file operations, the os module has many file descriptor and directory operations. The file descriptor operations reveal the Unix operating system method of dealing with files. Unix uses integers to keep track of files at the system level (really indexes into a file table) and there are several primitive operations that work with these descriptors. There are useful operations to retrieve status information for files from the operating system. You can get more information at ***pys60.garage.maemo.org/doc/lib/os-fd-ops.html*** about file descriptors.

Many directory operations in the os module also deal with system-level manipulation of the file system, but some can prove useful in general use, including the following:

- `chdir(path)` changes the current working directory of the application. This is useful, for example, when many files are manipulated and long pathnames are undesirable.

- `getcwd()` retrieves the current working directory.
- `chmod(path, mode)` changes the mode of the path given. The mode of a file is a set of permission flags kept by the operating system. Please refer to the list of permissions on ***pys60.garage.maemo.org/doc/lib/os-file-dir.html*** to understand everything you can change for a file.
- `listdir(path)` returns a list of names for the files and directories in the directory specified as a parameter.
- `mkdir(path[, mode])` creates a directory with the pathname given and the (optional) permissions given by mode. Without the permissions given, the directory is created with all permissions for all users.
- `remove(path)` deletes the file specified by path. If you specify a directory, Python raises an exception.
- `rename(src, dst)` renames `src` to `dst`.
- `rmdir(path)` removes the directory given by `path`.
- `stat(path)` returns (a lot of) information about the `path` specified. See ***pys60.garage.maemo.org/doc/lib/os-file-dir.html*** for a complete list.
- `tempnam([dir[, prefix]])` returns a unique path name that can be used for creating a temporary file.

There are several additional file system-related calls available in the `e32` and `sysinfo` modules that can be useful, as seen in the following table.

Table 3.5 File system-related calls

System Call	Module	Description
`drive_list()`	`e32`	Returns a list of visible, accessible drives
`file_copy(target_name, source_name)`	`e32`	Copies a file from target_name to source_name
`free_drivespace()`	`sys-info`	Returns the amount of free space left on drives as a dictionary object using drive/space pairs

More information can be found at ***pys60.garage.maemo.org/doc/s60/node10.html*** and ***pys60.garage.maemo.org/doc/s60/module-sysinfo.html***.

3.5 Summary

This chapter describes the system operations and information provided by two basic PyS60 modules: e32 and sysinfo, such as how to perform operations related to time, and how to work with files and directories. To cover a lot of ground quickly, we've used some rather simplistic examples, however we believe these are still very illustrative!

These features are combined with other ingredients of PyS60 in many of the examples in forthcoming chapters. We suggest you to use this chapter as a reference and come back to it whenever you need to apply these concepts in practice.

4

Basic User Interface

This chapter explains how to create a Python application with native look and feel, and how you can generate notifications and queries from non-GUI applications.

4.1 Introduction

Python provides access to most of the UI elements available on the Symbian platform, allowing rapid development of applications that are indistinguishable from those written in native code. With a few lines of code you can write menu-driven applications that include text editors, listboxes, dialogs and forms, and that display notifications and queries.

The functions and classes that create an application's native-looking UI are part of the `appuifw` (**app**lication **u**ser **i**nterface **f**rame**w**ork) module. This module also provides the functionality for creating the application's menu and handling the application's exit process. Another module, globalui, provides visual elements (notifications and queries) for applications that do not have a UI environment or are running the background.

4.2 The UI structure of a Python application

Python applications have the same visual structure as Symbian applications written in other programming languages. The large number of UI elements available to Python means that the UI can be customized to meet the needs of most developers.

The following figure represents the skeleton of a Python application. It shows which UI element corresponds to each area. Except for dialogs, every element is part of the Application instance (an instance that is always present when the `appuifw` module is used and which is referred to as app).

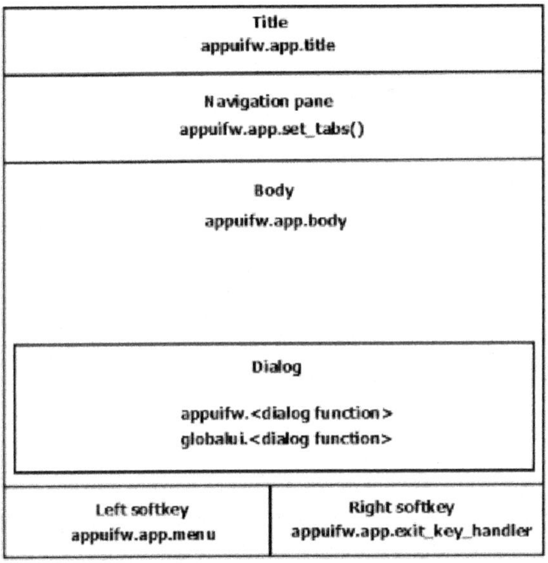

Figure 4.1 The structure of a Python application

A basic Python application does not *require* you to specify anything about its visual construction - there are default implementations for the menu and title so a script still runs if these are not defined. The application also has default softkey labels which cannot be changed: the left softkey is always called 'Options' and the right one is always called 'Exit'.

> ***Note***
>
> Though Python does not provide a way to modify the softkey labels, you can modify them using a native extension (see Chapter 13).

Most serious applications define the main elements of the user interface - a UI control for the application's body (the 'body' is the main part of an application - see Figure 4.1 above), a menu and a right softkey. Note that the right softkey should, unless the nature of the application dictates otherwise, call a function that closes the application.

The code fragment below shows a basic application with title, a text control for its body, and a menu. The application displays the current time in the text editor whenever the Show time menu option is selected. The user can exit the application with the Exit menu option or by selecting the right softkey.

```
import appuifw, e32, time

#Set the application title
appuifw.app.title = u"MyApplication"

#Create an instance of a Text control and set it as the applica-
tion's body
appuifw.app.body = t = appuifw.Text()

def show_time(): t.add(unicode(time.ctime()))
```

```
def quit():
      app_lock.signal()
      appuifw.app.set_exit()

#Create a menu, defining callback functions show_time and quit re-
spectively
appuifw.app.menu = [(u"Show time", show_time), (u"Exit", quit)]

#Set the function to be called when the right softkey is pressed
(quit)
appuifw.app.exit_key_handler = quit

#Create an instance of Ao_lock - an active object based synchroni-
zation service
app_lock = e32.Ao_lock()

#Wait for application lock to be signalled
app_lock.wait()
```

A normal Python script runs from start to end and then exits - the behavior of the application is a little different.

First, the application imports the application framework and e32 modules, and defines the individual UI elements (these are largely self-explanatory, as you would expect in a Python code). It then creates an instance of `Ao_lock` and waits on it. `Ao_lock` is an active scheduler based synchronization service. Even though the execution of the script stops at this point the application is still running and responding to menu and softkey events.

The application continues to run until the user selects Exit from the menu or the right softkey (both of which have been set up to call the `quit()` method). The `quit()` method signals the application lock and the active scheduler terminates.

A standalone application remains open until the application framework object's `set_exit()` method is called - this contrasts with a script run in the shell, which terminates once it reaches completion. In order to exit gracefully, an application must call `appuifw.app.set_exit()` in the exit callback (the `quit()` function in our examples).

The following sections of this chapter describe the elements that can make up an application's graphical user interface (GUI). We recommend that you consult the PyS60 documentation in addition to these tutorials for further information.

4.3 Title, orientation and screen size

The application title can be changed by assigning a Unicode string to the `title` attribute of the `Application` instance. For example, the line:

```
appuifw.app.title = u"MyApplication"
```

sets the title to "MyApplication".

Figure 4.2 Changing the application title

Python applications automatically respond to orientation change events. If an application needs to maintain a certain orientation then you can do this using the orientation attribute of the `Application` instance, which can be given one of the following values: 'automatic' (the default value), 'portrait' or 'landscape'.

```
import appuifw, e32

#Set the orientation to 'landscape'
appuifw.app.orientation = 'landscape'
#Wait 3 seconds
e32.ao_sleep(3)
#Set the orientation to 'portrait'
appuifw.app.orientation = 'portrait'
```

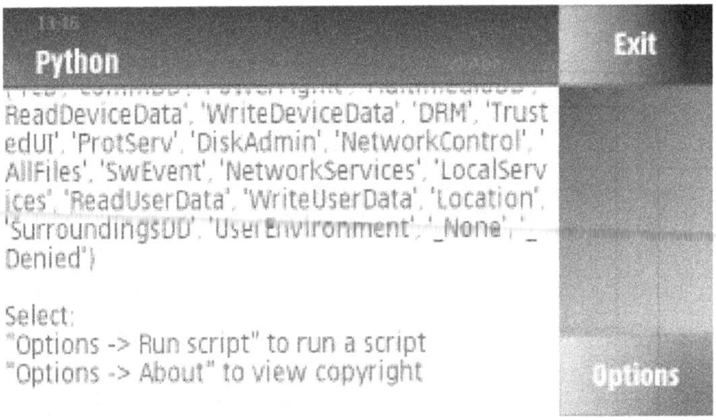

Figure 4.3 The application in landscape orientation

The size of the application body can be modified using the `screen` attribute, which takes one of three possible values:

- 'normal' - the default. The title and navigation panes and the softkey labels are visible
- 'large' - the application uses the entire upper area of the screen. The soft-key labels are visible
- 'full' - the application uses the whole screen.

The following snippet and screenshots demonstrate the three screen sizes:

```
import appuifw, e32

#Set the screen to 'full'
appuifw.app.screen = 'full'
#Wait 3 seconds
e32.ao_sleep(3)
#Set the screen to 'large'
appuifw.app.screen = 'large'
#Wait 3 seconds
e32.ao_sleep(3)
#Set the screen to 'normal'
appuifw.app.screen = 'normal'
```

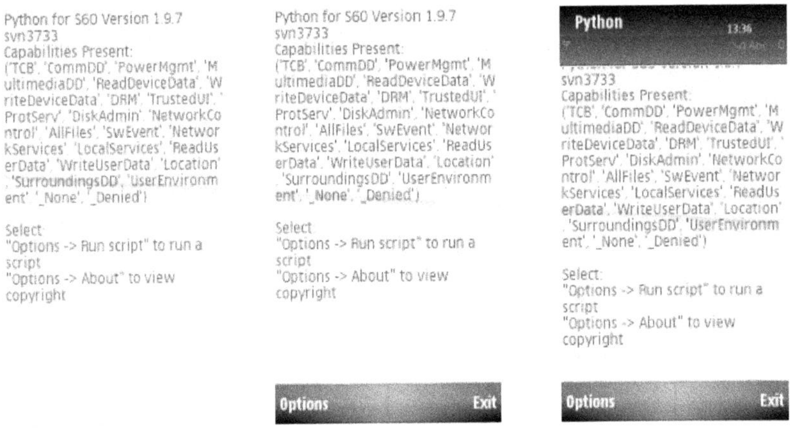

Figure 4.4 The three screen sizes

4.4 Notifications

Notes are native-looking popup messages that an application can display to inform the user about various things. Three types of notes are provided: 'conf' (confirmation), 'info' (information) and 'error' (error). Each type has a different icon and plays an appropriate sound.

Example code:

```
import appuifw

appuifw.note(u"Process complete", 'conf')
appuifw.note(u"Low memory", 'info')
appuifw.note(u"Operation aborted!", 'error')
```

The following screenshots show the result:

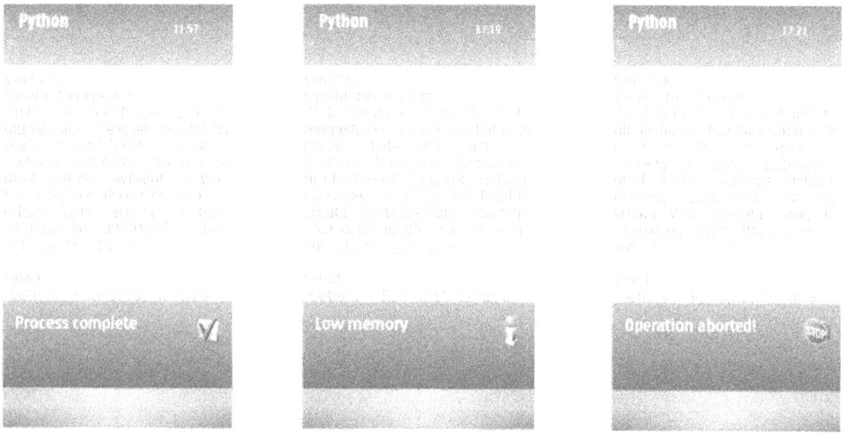

Figure 4.5 appuifw notes

The notifications in the `globalui` module are slightly more varied, as you can be seen in this code snippet and the screenshots that follow:

```
import globalui

globalui.global_note(u"Item available", 'info')
globalui.global_note(u"An error has occured!", 'error')
globalui.global_note(u"Message", 'text')
globalui.global_note(u"Warning!", 'warn')
globalui.global_note(u"Operation in progress", 'wait')
globalui.global_note(u"Permanent note", 'perm')
globalui.global_note(u"Operation complete", 'confirm')
globalui.global_note(u"", 'charging')
globalui.global_note(u"", 'not_charging')
```

```
globalui.global_note(u””, ‘battery_full’)
globalui.global_note(u””, ‘battery_low’)
globalui.global_note(u””, ‘recharge_battery’)
```

Figure 4.6 globalui notes

4.5 Queries

Queries enable applications to request user input - such as a password or the answer to a question. The input can be in various formats depending on the type of the query ('text', 'time', 'date', 'number', 'float', 'code' or 'query').

Example code:

```
import appuifw

word = appuifw.query(u"Enter a word", 'text')
time = appuifw.query(u"Enter desired time", 'time')
date = appuifw.query(u"Enter a date", 'date')
number = appuifw.query(u"Enter a number", 'number')
decimal_number = appuifw.query(u"Enter a decimal number", 'float')
password = appuifw.query(u"Type in a password", 'code')
answer = appuifw.query(u"Are you sure?", 'query')
first_name, last_name = appuifw.multi_query(u"Enter first name",
u"Enter last name")
```

The following screenshots illustrate what each query looks like.

Figure 4.7 appuifw queries

Now, we take a look at the `globalui` queries. There are only two kinds available: `global_query` and `global_msg_query`. The first one is a simple confirmation style query while the second one allows you to specify a title in addition to the text. Both kinds can have a timeout (given as the last argument to their functions), which means that if the user doesn't answer after a number of seconds, the query disappears.

```
import globalui
```

```
globalui.global_query(u"Are you sure?")
globalui.global_msg_query(u"File transfer will begin in 5 sec-
onds", u"Confirm operation", 5)
```

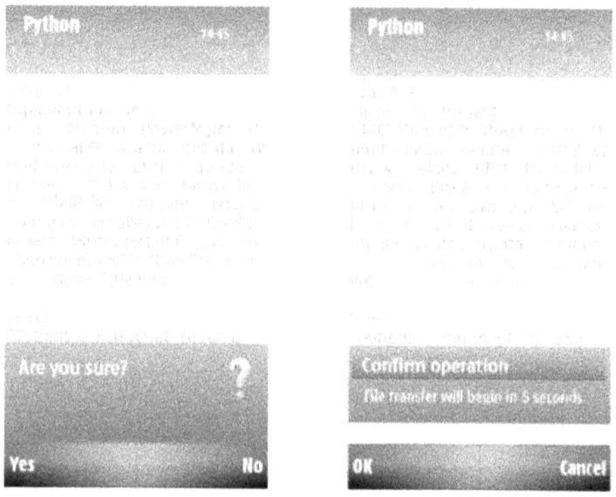

Figure 4.8 Queries of globalui

4.6 Menu

The application's menu consists of a list of tuples containing labels (Unicode strings) and callbacks (functions that are executed when the corresponding menu item is selected). There are two kinds of tuples that can be used:

- `(label, callback)` - a simple menu
- `(label, ((label, callback)))` - a menu with a submenu

The menu can be set simply by assigning the list of tuples to the `menu` attribute of the `Application` instance (`app`).

A simple menu:

```
import appuifw, e32, time

#Create an instance of Ao_lock - an active object based synchroni-
zation service
app_lock = e32.Ao_lock()

#Define a function that stops the script execution; it will be
called when "Exit" is selected from the menu
def quit(): app_lock.signal()

def show_time(): print time.ctime()

appuifw.app.menu = [(u"Show time", show_time), (u"Exit", quit)]

#Do not stop the script execution until "Exit" is selected
app_lock.wait()
```

A menu with a submenu:

```
import appuifw, e32

app_lock = e32.Ao_lock()

def quit(): app_lock.signal()
```

```
def hello(): print "Hello"

def goodbye(): print "Goodbye"

appuifw.app.menu = [(u"Message", ((u'Say "Hello"', hello), (u'Say
"Goodbye"', goodbye))), (u"Exit", quit)]

app_lock.wait()
```

The following screenshots illustrate the two kinds of menus:

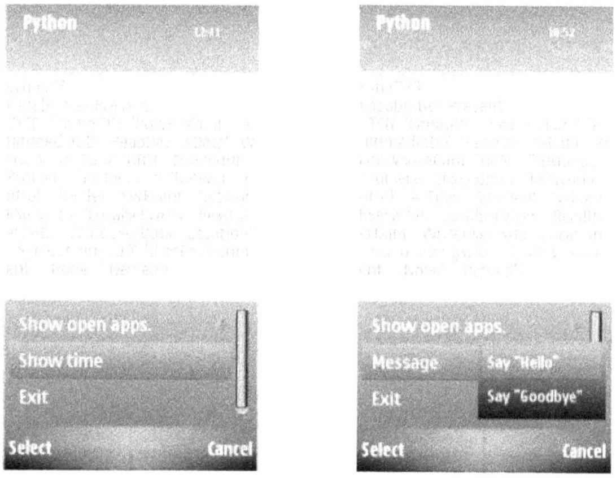

Figure 4.9 Menus

Another type of menu is the popup menu. Like the name suggests, it is displayed automatically when invoked. The function used to create one is `popup_menu(list[, label])`. list is a list of Unicode strings that represent the menu's entries. `label` is an optional title the menu can be given.

```
import appuifw

colours = [u"Red", u"Green", u"Blue"]

colour = appuifw.popup_menu(colours, u"Pick a colour")
```

Figure 4.10 Popup menu

The `globalui` module provides a global popup menu that can have a header and a timeout. It is almost identical in appearance to the popup menu from `appuifw`, but unlike that one, it can be shown outside the Python application.

```
import globalui

#Make a list of Unicode strings - the menu's entries
options = [u"Omlette", u"Bacon and eggs", u"Cereal", u"Sandwich"]
```

```
#Show the menu for 5 seconds and display what was selected
choice = globalui.global_popup_menu(options, u"Breakfast op-
tions:", 5)
print options[choice] + " was selected."
```

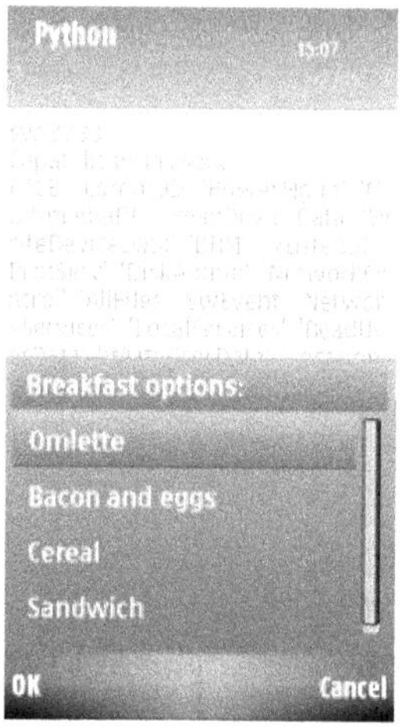

Figure 4.11 Global popup menu

4.7 Selection lists

A selection list is a dialog that displays a list from which the user can select an entry. It can have a search field that can be used to find entries (the search field only becomes visible when the user starts typing letters to search for). The multi selection list allows several entries to be selected.

To create a selection list, we use either the `selection_list` or the `multi_selection_list` function with a list of Unicode strings as its argument.

```
import appuifw

entries = [u"Carrots", u"Potatoes", u"Onions", u"Tomatoes"]

selected = appuifw.multi_selection_list(entries, style="checkbox",
search_field=1)

for i in selected:
      print entries[i] + " was selected"
```

Figure 4.12 A multi selection list

4.8 Listbox

A `Listbox` is similar to a selection list. While it doesn't allow multiple selections and doesn't have the search field option, it allows you to specify what keys perform actions on the listbox (key binding) and to control which item is highlighted, as well as using icons with the entries. It can even have two rows for every line.

The constructor for the `Listbox` class takes a list of tuples and a callback function as its arguments. The callback is executed when a selection occurs, and the list can have one of the following structures:

- `[Unicode_string1, Unicode_string2]` - one row on every line; without icons
- `[(Unicode_string1, Unicode_description1), (Unicode_string2, Unicode_description2)]` - two rows on every line; without icons
- `[(Unicode_string1, icon1), (Unicode_string2, icon2)]` - one row on every line; with icons
- `[(Unicode_string1, Unicode_description1, icon1), (Unicode_string2, Unicode_description2, icon2)]` - two rows on every line; with icons

The `bind(event_code, callback]` method binds the specified key code to the specified callback function. Basically, it detects when a certain key is pressed and executes the function.

Using the `current` method, one can retrieve the index of the currently highlighted entry. This can also be set by using the `set_list(list[, current]` method, where `list` is a list of tuples as described above, and `current` is the index of the item that we want to highlight.

As a first example, we will create a simple `Listbox` and bind the left and right arrow keys. When the right arrow key is pressed, the next item in the list becomes highlighted; the opposite happens for the left arrow key:

```
import appuifw, e32
from key_codes import *

app_lock = e32.Ao_lock()
#Define the exit function
def quit():
        app_lock.signal()
appuifw.app.exit_key_handler = quit

#The list of entries
items = [u"1", u"2", u"3", u"4"]

#Define the function for the arrow keys
def move(direction):
        if direction == 'right':
                if lb.current() == len(items) - 1:
                        lb.set_list(items, 0)
                else:
                        lb.set_list(items, lb.current() + 1)
        elif direction == 'left':
                if lb.current() == 0:
                        lb.set_list(items, len(items) - 1)
                else:
```

```
                    lb.set_list(items, lb.current() - 1)

#Create an instance of Listbox and set it as the application's
body
lb = appuifw.Listbox(items, lambda:None)
appuifw.app.body = lb

#Bind the keys
lb.bind(EKeyRightArrow, lambda:move('right'))
lb.bind(EKeyLeftArrow, lambda:move('left'))

app_lock.wait()
```

Now we can see what a more complex `Listbox` looks like - one with two rows for every entry and icons (details about the `Icon` class can be found in the PyS60 documentation).

```
import appuifw, e32


app_lock = e32.Ao_lock()
#Define the exit function
def quit():
      app_lock.signal()
appuifw.app.exit_key_handler = quit
#Define the icons to be used
file_icon = appuifw.Icon(u"Z:\\resource\\apps\\avkon2.mif", 17504,
17505)
folder_icon = appuifw.Icon(u"Z:\\resource\\apps\\avkon2.mif",
```

```
17506, 17507)

#Create a list of items to be displayed
#An item consists of two fields (Unicode strings) and an icon
items = [(u"File", u"Unknown type", file_icon), (u"Folder",
u"Empty", folder_icon)]

#Define a function that is called when an item is selected
def handle_selection():
      appuifw.note(items[lb.current()][0] + u" has been select-
ed.", 'info')

#Create an instance of Listbox and set it as the application's
body
lb = appuifw.Listbox(items, handle_selection)
appuifw.app.body = lb
app_lock.wait()
```

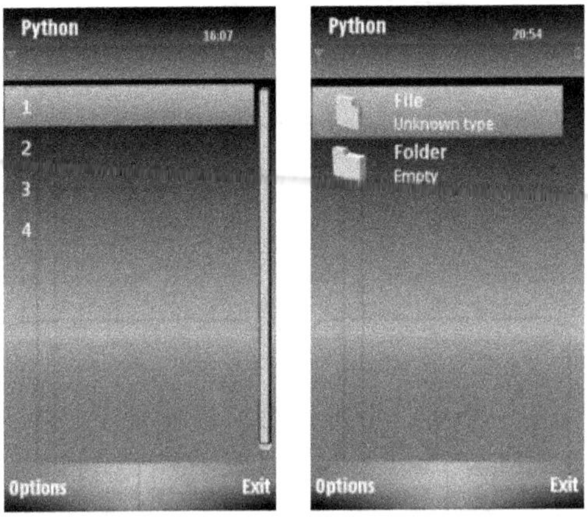

Figure 4.13 Listbox

4.9 Forms

The `Form` class allows us to create a customizable multi-field dialog. This means that it supports several fields at the same time, which can be of various types, editable or read-only.

The following example demonstrates how to create and use a `Form`:

```
import appuifw, time

#A list of objects, such as books
titles = [u"Quick Recipes on Symbian OS", u"Java ME on Symbian
OS", u"S60 Programming - A Tutorial Guide"]

#Create the fields to be displayed in the form
fields = [(u"Domain", 'text', u"Progamming"),
          (u"Title", 'combo', (titles, 0)),
          (u"Amount",'number', 1),
          (u"Date", 'date', time.time()),
          (u"Time", 'time')]

#Initialize a boolean variable to know whether the form is saved
saved = False

#Define a function to be called when the form is saved
def save(arg):
```

```
    global saved
    saved = True
    return True

#Create a Form object
myForm = appuifw.Form(fields, flags=appuifw.FFormEditModeOnly)

#Assign the save function
myForm.save_hook = save

#Execute the form
myForm.execute()

#After the form is saved and closed, display the information
if saved == True:
    print myForm[0][2]
    print titles[myForm[1][2][1]]
    print myForm[2][2]
    print time.strftime("%d/%m/%Y", time.localtime(myForm[3]
[2]))
    print time.strftime(time.ctime(myForm[4][2])[11:20])
```

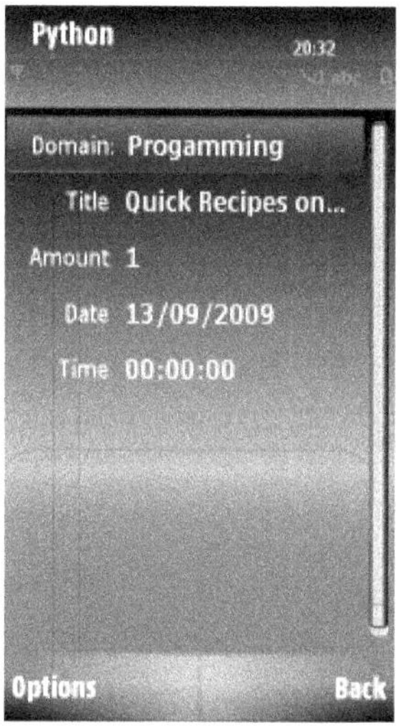

Figure 4.14 Form

Let's take a closer look at what each part of the code above does. First, we create the fields that will be used in the form as a list of tuples containing the label, type and, optionally, the default value for each field.

After that, we define a function that handles the saving. This function will be called every time when the contents of an executing Form dialog are saved. It takes a list representing the current contents of the form as an argument and returns a Boolean value. If it returns True, the list is set as the new contents of the form. If it returns False, the form's fields are reset to their previous values. We tell the form to use this save function by assigning it to the `save_hook` attribute. After creating a form and launching it (using the `execute()` method), we demonstrate how to check the information the user has entered. After it's saved, we simply print the new contents.

One noticeable fact is that the second argument passed to the form's constructor, `flags`, is set to `appuifw.FFormEditModeOnly`. This specifies that the form is to remain in edit mode while it is being executed. Other possible types of forms are:

- `FFormViewModeOnly` - the form cannot be edited
- `FFormAutoLabelEdit` - allows the user to edit the labels of the fields
- `FFormAutoFormEdit` - allows the user to add or remove fields from the form
- `FFormDoubleSpaced` - puts the label and value on different lines (practically makes each fields take up two lines)

4.10 Text Editor

The `Text` class provided by the `appuifw` module is a customizable way of displaying text and receiving input. It provides methods for modifying the text it contains (either the content itself or the font and color of the text) and retrieving it.

An instance of `Text` can be customized by giving different values to its attributes. A complete list of attributes along with their descriptions and possible values is available in the PyS60 documentation. There you can also find all the methods you can use to manipulate the editor's functionality.

```
import appuifw, e32
```

```
app_lock = e32.Ao_lock()

def quit():
      app_lock.signal()
appuifw.app.exit_key_handler = quit

#Create an instance of Text and set it as the application's body
appuifw.app.body = t = appuifw.Text()

#Set the color of the text
t.color = 0xEE00DD

#Set the color for the highlight of the text
t.highlight_color = 0xFFFF00

#Set the font by name, size and flags
t.font = (u"Nokia Hindi S60", 25, None)

#Highlight the text and set the style of the text to bold and
strikethrough
t.style = (appuifw.HIGHLIGHT_STANDARD | appuifw.STYLE_BOLD | ap-
puifw.STYLE_STRIKETHROUGH)

#Write text to see the effect
t.add(u"Your text here")

app_lock.wait()
```

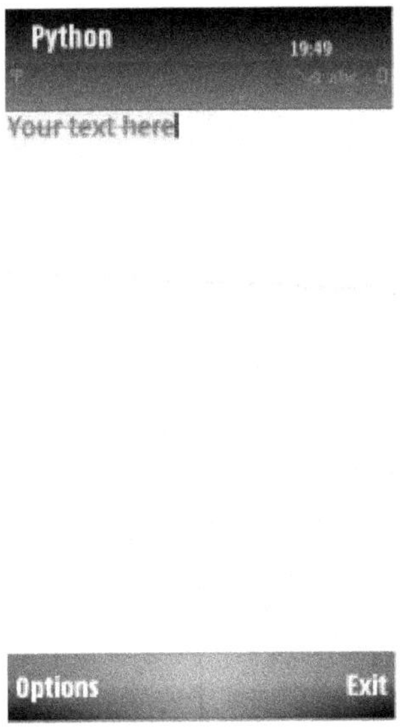

Figure 4.15 Text editor example

4.11 Tabs

A Python application can make use of tabs in order to allow the user to easily switch between interfaces. All you need to do is create the interfaces using the available UI controls and define a function that handles switching from one to another. When closing the application, the tabs have to be removed manually (i.e., giving an empty list of tab titles and setting the function to None). It should be noted that the tab handler function is called automatically by the framework and thus no explicit key mapping is needed.

Example code:

```
import appuifw, e32
```

```
app_lock = e32.Ao_lock()

def quit():
      appuifw.app.set_tabs([], None)
      app_lock.signal()
appuifw.app.exit_key_handler = quit

#Define the tabs
tab1 = appuifw.Text(u"This is tab #1")
tab2 = appuifw.Text(u"This is tab #2")

#Create a function that handles switching between tabs
def tab_handler(index):
      #Switch to the tab according to index
      if(index==0):
            appuifw.app.body = tab1
      if(index==1):
            appuifw.app.body = tab2

#Set the tabs
appuifw.app.set_tabs([u"One", u"Two"], tab_handler)

#Open the first tab
appuifw.app.body = tab1

#Wait for the user to request the exit
```

```
app_lock.wait()
```

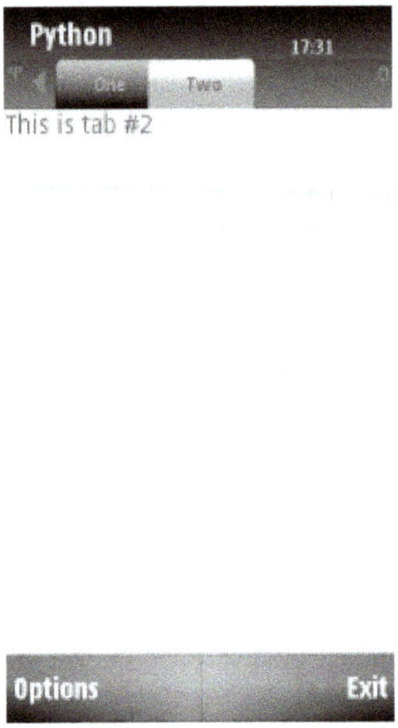

Figure 4.16 Tabs interface

What we've done is create two `Text` instances (`tab1` and `tab2`), one for each tab, and define the function that will be used for switching between them. The index argument is passed to the function by the framework and is used to decide which tab should become active.

4.12 InfoPopup

`InfoPopup` is a class that allows you to display a message in a certain place on the screen that is inaccessible to a standard note, and for a certain number of seconds. It is especially useful when you want to display tips or instructions.

The `show` method takes as its arguments the text as a Unicode string. Optionally, other arguments can be specified, such as the coordinates of the top left corner of the message box, the amount of time the message is shown, the amount of time to wait before showing the message (in milliseconds), and the alignment. A complete list of alignment constants and their descriptions is available in the PyS60 documentation.

Example code:

```
import appuifw

#Create an instance of InfoPopup
popup = appuifw.InfoPopup()

#Show the popup for 7 seconds at coordinates (150, 160)
popup.show(u"Message", (150, 160), 7000)
```

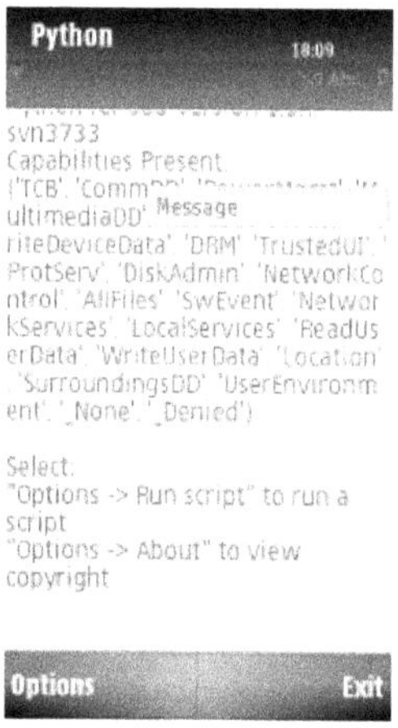

Figure 4.17 InfoPopup

4.13 TopWindow

The `TopWindow` class (defined in the topwindow module) allows you to create customizable popups containing an image or text.

A `TopWindow` is simply a rectangular area that obscures other screen elements and that displays an image. Its aspect can be customized to an extent, allowing you to specify whether or not it has a shadow, if the corners are round, and other things. It can be used dynamically, meaning it can be shown and hidden at any time and its position can be changed easily.

Example code:

```
import appuifw, e32, graphics, topwindow

app_lock = e32.Ao_lock()
#Define the exit function
def quit():
        app_lock.signal()
appuifw.app.exit_key_handler = quit

#Instantiate a TopWindow
window = topwindow.TopWindow()

#Define its size and the coordinates of its top left corner
window.size = (210, 160)
```

```
window.position = (10, 40)

#Create a new, blank image and colour it, then write a message on
it
img = graphics.Image.new((195, 110))
img.clear(0xFF0000)
img.text((25, 25), u"This is a topwindow example", font = 'title')

#Place the image on the TopWindow object and define some of the ob-
ject's visual characteristics
window.add_image(img, (10, 10))
window.background_color = 0x00FF00
window.shadow = 4
window.corner_type = 'corner5'

#Display the TopWindow
window.show()

app_lock.wait()
```

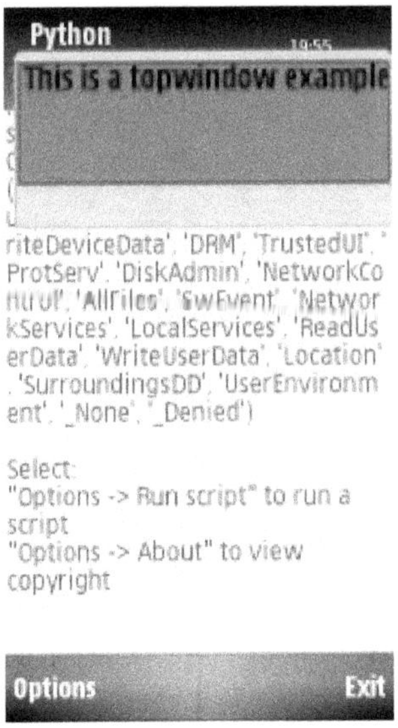

Figure 4.18 TopWindow

4.14 Summary

This chapter introduced to you the structure of standard Python applications and the UI elements that are available. With very little coding involved, these elements allow you to customize an application's look and feel to meet your requirements. In many examples, throughout the book, you will find these UI elements used again and understand how these can be a part of full-fledged applications.

5

Contacts and Calendar

Mobile devices are, for many people, the most important and personal tool that they own; they hold all their important contacts, and are used to organize their busy social and work lives.

Access to APIs that interact with a user's contacts and calendar enables compelling and personal applications to be developed. Python on Symbian provides access to contacts and calendar data through the `contacts` and `e32calendar` modules.

5.1 Contacts overview

The contacts module provides an API that allows you to open the default phone book on the device to perform operations such as searching, reading, adding, modifying and deleting entries.

The contacts database is represented by a `ContactDb`, which contains a number of Contact objects, which in turn contain `ContactField` objects. The `ContactDb` is a dictionary-like object that is indexed by the unique IDs of any `Contacts` that are contained. Contacts are list-like objects that are indexed using the field indices of the contained `ContactField` objects.

`ContactDb` represents a live view of the database. Changes committed to the database are visible to outside applications immediately and vice versa.

Contacts are locked for editing before modification, and released immediately afterwards.

The following sections explain how to search for, add, delete and modify contacts and how to work with contact groups. Additional information is available at ***pys60.garage.maemo.org/doc/s60/module-contacts.html.***

5.1.1 Opening the database

A database must be opened before any contacts operations can be performed. In order to open the device's default database, the contacts module `open()` method is called as shown below:

```
import contacts

#Open the default contacts database
db = contacts.open()
```

In theory, you can also create your own application-specific database by passing the name of the database and a mode to the `open()` method. However, this functionality is considered unreliable according to the official documentation found at ***pys60.garage.maemo.org/doc/s60/module-contacts.html*** and is, in any case, of limited use.

There is no need to explicitly close the contact database; it will automatically be closed when the contacts object goes out of scope.

5.1.2 Adding a contact

To create a new contact, first open the database, create a `Contact` object, add the desired fields and values and save it by calling `commit()`.

The following code fragment creates a new contact, specifying a first name and mobile number.

```
import contacts

#Open the default contact database
db = contacts.open()

#Add new contact's details
c = db.add_contact()
c.add_field('first_name', 'Samantha')
c.add_field('mobile_number', '0123456789')

#And save the changes
c.commit()
```

The following table lists the most common field types available from Nokia S60 (3rd Edition) onwards. Fields with these types are added using `add_field()`, which uses the same syntax as the previous code fragment.

Table 5.1: Contact fields

city	company_name	country	date
dtmf_string	email_address	extended_address	fax_number
first_name	job_title	last_name	mobile_number
note	pager_number	phone_number	po_box
postal_address	postal_code	state	street_address
url	video_number	picture	second_name
voip	sip_id	personal_ringtone	share_view
prefix	suffix	push_to_talk	locationid_indication

The official documentation at ***pys60.garage.maemo.org/doc/s60/node83.html*** explains what data type they can be assigned, and also lists a few fields that are recognized but that cannot be created.

5.1.3 Deleting a contact

The next section shows how to find the ID of a specific contact and, once the ID is known, a contact may be deleted from the database by using the `del` operator with its ID. The following code fragment shows how to delete the first `Contact` object that has 'Samantha' in its name:

```
import contacts

#Open the default contact database
db = contacts.open()
```

```
#Search for a contact whose name is Samantha
l = db.find('Samantha')

#l is a list of contacts matching the criterion
#We only need the first one, if it exists
if len(l) > 0:
	c = l[0]
	#Get its ID
	id = c.id

	#Delete it
	del db[id]
else:
	print "No such contact found"
```

5.1.4 Finding contacts

The contacts database can be queried for contacts that have a certain string in any of their fields using the `find()` method, passing the search string as its argument. The search can then be refined to see if a certain field matches the search criteria.

For example, the following code fragment first retrieves all contacts that have the text 'James' in any field, and then displays information for those contacts that have 'James' in the `first_name` field (only).

```
import contacts

#Open the database
db = contacts.open()

#Retrieve every contact that contains the name "James"
#and display only those that have it in the first_name field
for c in db.find('James'):
        if c.find('first_name')[0].value == u"James":
                print c.find('first_name')[0].value + " " +
c.find('last_name')[0].value + " " c.find('mobile_number')[0].value
```

5.1.5 Modifying existing contacts

Modifying a contact can be done in two ways: A simple way is to just make the changes and then call the contact object's `commit()` method, which saves them.

Alternatively:

1. Call the contact object's `begin()` method, which locks the contact for editing (thus making it inaccessible to other applications)
2. Make the changes
3. Call the contact object's `commit()` method, which releases the lock and saves the changes.

Should you wish to undo the changes, you can simply call the object's `roll-back()` method instead of `commit()`, which releases the lock and restores the contact to the way it was before `begin()` was called.

New fields can be added, as shown in the section *Adding a Contact*, and existing fields, labels and values can also be customized, as demonstrated in the following example.

```
#The changes are undone at the end
import contacts

db = contacts.open()
c = db.find('Jim')[0]

c.begin()

#Retrieve the "last_name" field if it exists, change its value to
#some other name and its label to "Surname"
if c.find("last_name"):
      c.find("last_name")[0].value = u"Cohen"
      c.find("last_name")[0].label = u"Surname"

#Undo the changes
c.rollback()
```

```
#The changes are saved and the contact remains modified
import contacts
```

```
db = contacts.open()
c = db.find('Jim')[0]

#Retrieve the "last_name" field if it exists, change its value to
#some other name and its label to "Surname"
if c.find("last_name"):
        c.find("last_name")[0].value = u"Cohen"
        c.find("last_name")[0].label = u"Surname"

#Save the changes
c.commit()
```

Finally, individual fields can be removed from the contact using the `del` operator.

5.1.6 Working with `groups`

Python on Symbian allows you to create and access related contacts using `Group` objects, and gives access to a set of `Group` objects through a `Groups` object.

In simple terms, a `Group` is a list-like object containing the IDs of Contact objects belonging to that group. A `Groups` object is a dictionary-like collection of all the `Group` objects from the database, which can each be accessed using a `Group`'s unique ID.

As with any contact operation, the database must be opened before any of the group operations may be performed.

Creating a new group

After creating a Groups object, its `add_group(name)` method is used to create a new group (a new `Group` object).

The following code fragment adds the group 'My new group' to the `Groups` object (and hence to the database):

```
import contacts

#Open the database
db = contacts.open()

#Instantiate a Groups object
groups = db.Groups(db)

#Add a new group
group = groups.add_group(u"My new group")
```

Retrieving existing groups

Groups are identified by their unique ID. A list of the unique group IDs can be obtained by calling Python's built-in `list()` function on the iterator object, which is returned by calling Python's built-in `iter()` function on the `Groups` object.

The following code fragment uses the list iterator to print out the names of all the groups, based on their id.

```
import contacts

#Open the database
db = contacts.open()

#Get a list of IDs of the available groups
ids = list(iter(db.groups))

#Show the names of the groups
for id in ids:
      print db.groups[id].name
```

Deleting a group

A group is deleted from a Groups object and, simultaneously, from the database by using Python's `del()` operator. The following code fragment gets the list of available groups by ID, then calls `del()` to remove a specific `Group` object:

```
import contacts

#Open the database
db = contacts.open()

#Get a list of IDs of the available groups
ids = list(iter(db.groups))

#Remove the group whose ID is first in the list
del db.groups[ids[0]]
```

> **_Note_**
>
> Deleting a group will not delete its members, that is, the contacts that are in the group are not deleted from the contacts database, but remain in the phone's contact list.

Adding and removing contacts from a group

Calling the `append(id)` method of a Group object adds a contact with the corresponding ID to the group, as shown in the following code.

```
import contacts

#Open the database
db = contacts.open()

#Get a list of IDs of the available groups
group_ids = list(iter(db.groups))

#Open the first group in the list
group = db.groups[group_ids[0]]

#Get a list of all the contact IDs
contact_ids = contacts.open().keys()

#Add the first contact in the list
group.append(contact_ids[0])
```

To remove a contact from a group, we use the `del()` operator on the group.

5.2 Calendar overview

Calendar data is accessed in much the same way as contacts data. A calendar is represented by a `CalendarDb` object that contains `Entry` objects. Any new entries or changes saved to existing entries in a Python application appear in the device's native Calendar application, and vice versa.

The available entry types are classes derived from the main `Entry` class, as follows:

- `AppointmentEntry` - returned by the `add_appointment()` method
- `EventEntry` - returned by the `add_event()` method
- `AnniversaryEntry` - returned by the `add_anniversary()` method
- `ReminderEntry` - returned by the `add_reminder()` method
- `ToDoEntry` - returned by the `add_todo()` method

5.2.1 Adding entries

Creating a calendar entry is simple: open a database, call one of its methods (depending on what type of entry you opt for), optionally give values to the attributes of the entry and save the changes.

The following snippet demonstrates how to add an appointment that expires at a certain time. The content attribute of the Entry class is used to specify the subject of the appointment – a short description that will be shown in the phone's Calendar application. The location attribute is used to specify the location of the appointment. The `set_time()` function is used to specify the time frame during which the appointment entry will be valid.

After creating the entry it is important to save it using the `commit()` method.

```
import e32calendar, appuifw

#Open the database
db = e32calendar.open()

#Create an appointment entry
appointment = db.add_appointment()

#Add the regular information
appointment.content = appuifw.query(u"Enter subject", "text")
appointment.location = appuifw.query(u"Enter location", "text")

#Ask the user for the start and end time
t1 = appuifw.query(u"Enter start hour", "time")
d1 = appuifw.query(u"Enter start date", "date")
t2 = appuifw.query(u"Enter end hour", "time")
d2 = appuifw.query(u"Enter end date", "date")

start_time = t1 + d1
end_time = t2 + d2

#Set the start and end time
appointment.set_time(start_time, end_time)

#Save the entry
```

```
appointment.commit()
```

The following code creates a simple to do calendar entry and, after a few seconds, asks the user if it's been done, marking it as complete if it is.

```
import e32calendar, appuifw, e32, time

app_lock = e32.Ao_lock()
def quit():
      t.cancel()
      app_lock.signal()
appuifw.app.exit_key_handler = quit

#Open the database
db = e32calendar.open()

#Create a to do entry
todo = db.add_todo()

#Add information about the subject
todo.content = appuifw.query(u"Enter subject", "text")

#Ask the user for the start and end time
t1 = appuifw.query(u"Enter start hour", "time")
d1 = appuifw.query(u"Enter start date", "date")
t2 = appuifw.query(u"Enter end hour", "time")
d2 = appuifw.query(u"Enter end date", "date")
```

```
start_time = t1 + d1
end_time = t2 + d2

#Set the start and end time
todo.set_time(start_time, end_time)

appuifw.note(u"Entry created!")

#Create a function that asks if the user has completed the to do
def todo_handler():
      answer = appuifw.query(u"Have you finished the to do?", "que-
ry")
      if answer == True:
            #The user no longer needs the entry active in the
#calendar since it's been taken care of
            todo.cross_out = True
      #To check when the entry was crossed out we use the
#crossed_out_time attribute
      appuifw.note(u"Entry crossed out at " + time.ctime(todo.
cross_out_time))

#Instantiate a timer and use it to call the function after 10
#seconds
t = e32.Ao_timer()
t.after(10, todo_handler)

#Save the entry
todo.commit()
```

Calendar entries often have associated alarms for attracting the user's attention. Alarms are set using the entry's `alarm` attribute. Note that alarms can only be enabled for entries of type `AppointmentEntry` and `AnniversaryEntry`; on other event types the alarm will not go off. Note also that setting the alarm to `None` cancels it.

The following example code illustrates a calendar entry that is meant to remind to user to pick up a gift for an anniversary:

```
import e32calendar, time

#Open the database
db = e32calendar.open()

#Create an anniversary entry
anniversary = db.add_anniversary()

#Set the alarm for this time tomorrow, and give the entry highest
#priority
anniversary.set_time(time.time() + 86400)
anniversary.content = u"Pick up gift for Shelley"
anniversary.priority = 1
anniversary.alarm = time.time() + 86400

anniversary.commit()
```

Entries can also be repeated, which means they become active at regular intervals based on associated repeat rules (***pys60.garage.maemo.org/doc/s60/node96.html***). For example, a person can have a calendar entry to remind them of another person's birthday. This entry should repeat every year on the same day.

```
import e32calendar, time

#Open the database
db = e32calendar.open()

#Add an anniversary entry
anniversary = db.add_anniversary()

anniversary.content = u"Hannah's birthday!"
anniversary.set_time(time.time() + 86400)

#Define the repeat rule
repeat = {"type":"yearly_by_date",
          "start":time.time() + 86400,
          "end":None,
          "interval":1}

anniversary.set_repeat(repeat)

anniversary.commit()
```

5.2.2 Displaying and deleting entries

The `find_instances(...)` method, called on the database, can be used to find all the calendar entries within a time frame that match the search criteria.

`find_instances()` returns a list of dictionaries that have the IDs of the entries and, using the subscript notation, the actual `Entry` object can be retrieved and its information can be displayed.

```
import e32calendar, appuifw, time

db = e32calendar.open()

#Find all entries between two dates given by the user that contain
#the word "birthday"
start = appuifw.query(u"Enter start date", "date")
end = appuifw.query(u"Enter end date", "date")
entries = db.find_instances(start, end, u"birthday")

#Display their subject and date
for i in entries:
      print "Description: " + db[i["id"]].content
      print "Date: " + time.strftime("%H:%M %m/%d/%Y", time.
localtime(db[i["id"]].start_time))
```

Deleting an entry is similar to deleting a contact: once the ID is acquired, calling the `del()` operator on the object removes the entry.

5.3 Summary

This chapter has demonstrated how to perform operations on the device's contacts and calendar data, including:

- Adding and deleting contacts
- Retrieving information such as name and phone number
- Creating and removing calendar entries of various types.

6

Telephony and Messaging

Symbian supports many operations and has many features. But it is first and foremost a smartphone operating system. The word phone here is what is at the core of Symbian's functionality. Python directly supports the use of Symbian devices as phones.

Phone communication is usually split into two forms: voice and messaging. Python supports each of these in clear, intuitive ways. We handle both of these forms of communication in this chapter, along with a large example for each.

6.1 Introduction

If you think through the actions you perform to make or receive a phone call, or to send or receive a text message, they are very simple. The functionality built into the Python modules that support telephony and messaging reflect this. The functionality is implemented by callbacks, functions that are called by the operating system when the phone receives a phone call or a message.

Both telephony and messaging support are discussed in this chapter. We walk through the Python support, including callbacks, and we demonstrate this support with complete examples. We conclude the chapter by discussing how Python allows access to records (logs) that the phone keeps about calls and messages that have been made, sent and received.

6.2 Telephone Operations

Telephone operations, as humans perform them, are very simple. We can dial a phone. We can answer an incoming call. We can hang up on a call. Python support for telephony reflects this simplicity. Python adds the ability to monitor a phone for a call, an action we also perform when we expect an important call!

Python telephony functionality is built into the `telephone` module. This module needs to be imported before access to the functionality is possible.

6.2.1 Making a Phone Call

To dial a phone using the `dial()` function use the calling sequence:

```
telephone.dial(<number>)
```

The parameter `<number>` is a string that holds the phone number to dial. It will be dialed as given, so all parts of the number need to be included (country code, area code, etc). For example, this will dial a number in the United States:

```
telephone.dial(u"+15075551122")
```

The `<number>` must be encoded in unicode.

If there is already a phone call going on when the call to `dial()` is made, the existing phone call is placed on hold automatically and the new phone call is placed.

To hang up (terminate) a phone call use the `hang_up()` method without a parameter. Calling this method terminates the current call if that call was initiated by a `dial()` method call.

Let's consider some examples. Let's start by making a local call:

```
import telephone
telephone.dial("5551234")
```

This tells the phone make a phone call, as shown in Figure 6.1.

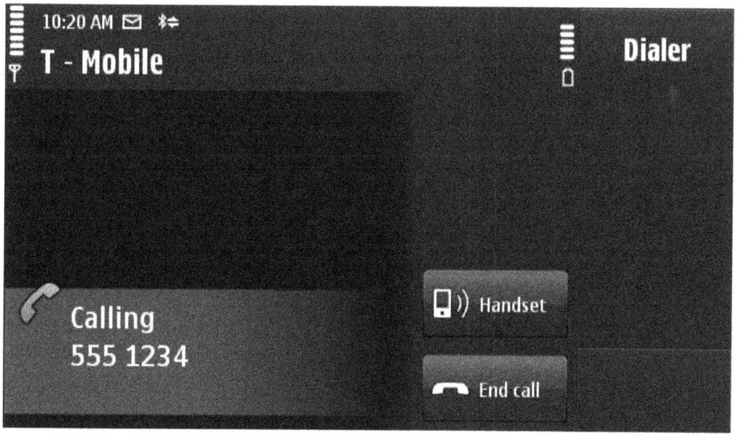

Figure 6.1: A Symbian phone making a call using `dial()`

At this point, the following call terminates the phone call:

```
telephone.hang_up()
```

Here are a few important notes about Python's understanding and use of phone calls:

- Python has its own idea of the pairing of call initiation and hanging up. For example, if you dial a phone number and start a phone call manually, then call `hang_up()`, you get the following error:

```
Traceback (most recent call last):
File "<console>", line 1, in <module>
  File "c:\resource\python25\python25.zip\telephone.py",
line 60, in hang_up
    _phone_answer.hang_up()
RuntimeError: no call to hang up
```

- Even though there is a phone call in progress, Python did not start the call so it cannot terminate it.
- Likewise, if you start a phone call with a call to `dial()`, you must use `hang_up()` before you call again, even if you hang up manually. Let's say we perform the sequence below:

```
>>> telephone.dial("5551234")
>>> # ...now we hang up the phone manually
>>> telephone.dial("5551234")
Traceback (most recent call last):
  File "<console>", line 1, in <module>
  File "c:\resource\python25\python25.zip\telephone.py",
line 53, in dial_phone.dial()
```

```
RuntimeError: call in progress, hang up first
```

6.2.2 Answering a Phone Call

Another simple operation that humans do is to answer the phone. The telephone module makes this easy with the `answer()` method call. Just as answering a phone call when the phone call is not ringing is a bit silly, simply calling `answer()` is also useless unless there is actually a call coming in. To properly answer a call, the phone must be prepared or configured to do so, then must be able to figure out when a call is coming in.

To prepare a phone, the `telephone` module supplies the `incoming_call()` method. Calling this function sets up the phone to receive a call. The call to this method returns immediately, but the Python runtime system is now listening for an incoming call. Once a call comes in, it can be answered by calling with the `answer()` method. There are several ways to make your application call the `answer()` method: for example in response to the user tapping a button on the application's user interface; or in response to a state change of the phone (see the next section for how to detect state changes).

Answering phone call implies nothing more than connecting the two sides of the call. There is no further application interaction after that.

6.2.3 Monitoring Phone Activity

The `telephone` module provides a way to monitor phone activity. The module identifies 12 states that a phone line can be in, as shown in the table 6.1.

Table 6.1 12 phone line states

Python Name	State Value	Description
`EStatusUnknown`	0	the state of calling is unknown
`EStatusIdle`	1	no active calls are taking place
`EStatusDialling`	2	dialing is taking place on a phone line
`EStatusRinging`	3	the phone is ringing
`EStatusAnswering`	4	the phone is being answered
`EStatusConnecting`	5	the phone call is connecting to the remote phone
`EStatusConnected`	6	the phone call has been connected to the remote phone
`EStatusReconnectPending`	7	something has caused a channel loss and the call is being reconnected
`EStatusDisconnecting`	8	the phone call is being disconnected
`EStatusHold`	9	the current call is on hold
`EStatusTransferring`	10	the current call is being transferred
`EStatusTransferAlerting`	11	the remote phone is being alerted to the call being transferred

The `telephone` module enables the state to be monitored through a callback function. An application must specify and register a function that the operating system is to call each time the phone changes between the states above.

Let's look at an example. The function below prints the new state whenever the state changes.

```
import telephone
def newphonestate (stateInformation):
    newState = stateInformation[0]
    if newState == telephone.EStatusUnknown:
        msg = "The new state is unknown"
    elif newState == telephone.EStatusIdle:
        msg = "The phone is idle"
    elif newState == telephone.EStatusDialling:
        msg = "The phone is dialling"
    elif newState == telephone.EStatusRinging:
        msg = "The new phone is ringing, call is from %s" %
stateInformation[1]
    elif newState == telephone.EStatusAnswering:
        msg = "A call is being answered"
    elif newState == telephone.EStatusConnecting:
        msg = "A call is connecting"
    elif newState == telephone.EStatusConnected:
        msg = "A call has been connected"
    elif newState == telephone.EStatusReconnectPending:
        msg = "The channel has been lost and a reconnect is being
attempted"
```

```
    elif newState == telephone.EStatusDisconnecting:
        msg = "A call is being disconnected"
    elif newState == telephone.EStatusHold:
        msg = "A call is being placed on hold"
    elif newState == telephone.EStatusTransferring:
        msg = "A call is being transferred"
    elif newState == telephone.EStatusTransferAlerting:
        msg = "The phone is alerting the remote phone about a
transferred call"

    print "The phone has changed states."
    print "    ",msg

telephone.call_state(newphonestate)
```

There are several things to note in this example:

- The function that will be called (the callback function) has a parameter: a tuple that carries information about the new state to which the phone has moved. This tuple has two items: the first is the new state value and the (optional) second item is the phone number for an incoming call.
- The function is registered by a call to the `call_state()` function.
- Every time the phone state is changed, a new call to `call_state()` is made.

The output of the code above is shown below for a call that comes to the phone, is answered by the phone's user, and is then terminated by the caller:

```
The phone has changed states.
    The new phone is ringing, call is from 15055551234
The phone has changed states.
    A call is being answered
The phone has changed states.
    A call has been connected
The phone has changed states.
    A call is being disconnected
The phone has changed states.
    The phone is idle
```

Code of this type can be used to replace `incoming_call()`. The disadvantage of using incoming_`call()` is that execution is suspended so, for example, it would not work in a program with a graphic user interface. Using `call_state()` with a callback follows the event-driven model of a GUI and is therefore better suited for this type of programming.

6.3 A Sample Application: Caller Information

Consider an example of the telephone interface. Let's say that a person in a sales position keeps notes about her clients in the contacts database on her phone. She thinks it would be nice to pull up that information automatically when a client calls her phone.

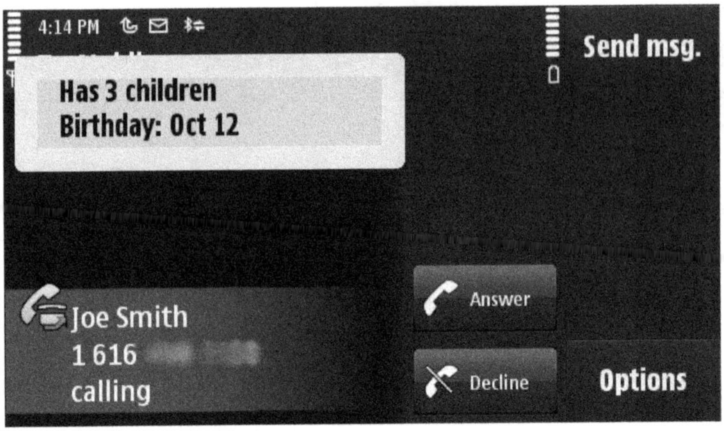

Figure 6.2 Example Screenshot of Sales Person App

This application is running in the background and pops up the information window when it can find information. You can put an application in the background by starting it, then pressing the applications key to display the application icons. The application keeps running in the Python runtime environment while allowing you to interact with other applications.

We can implement this example fairly easily. In fact, the code below is mostly contact searching rather than telephone call processing. Consider the code below.

```
import telephone, contacts
import appuifw, e32, graphics, topwindow
```

```
#-----------------------------------------------------------------------
---------------
#  This function is called when a phone call is made.  It does the
#  contact lookup and the display of the info window.
#-----------------------------------------------------------------------
---------------

def displayNotes(infoTuple):

    # Get the phone's state
    phoneState = infoTuple[0]

    # Only react when the phone is ringing
    if phoneState == telephone.EStatusRinging:

        # Start by opening the contacts database and looking up
the phone number
        db = contacts.open()
        contactList = db.find(infoTuple[1])

        # Build the list of notes in a string, separated by "\n"
        noteString = ""
        if contactList:
            try:
                for note in contactList[0].find(type='note'):
                    if len(noteString)>0:
                        noteString = noteString + "\n" + note.value
                    else:
```

```
                        noteString = note.value
            except:
                noteString = u"No notes available"
        else:
            noteString = u"The phone number was not found"

        # Now we build the topwindow window from the notes
        notes = noteString.split("\n")
        window = topwindow.TopWindow()
        window.size = (350, 40+(30*len(notes)))
        window.position = (10, 40)
        img = graphics.Image.new((310, 30*len(notes)))
        img.clear(0x99CCFF)
        position = 20
        for note in notes:
            img.text((20, position), unicode(note), font = 'title')
            position += 30
        window.add_image(img, (20, 20))
        window.background_color = 0xDDDDDD
        window.shadow = 4
        window.corner_type = 'corner5'

        # Display the window and sleep for 5 seconds.  Then hide it.
        window.show()
        e32.ao_sleep(5)
        window.hide()

# Finally, install the function as the phone callback
```

```
telephone.call_state(displayNotes)
```

Let's go through this code in pieces. The import statements reveal what we need to make this idea work:

```
import telephone, contacts
import appuifw, e32, graphics, topwindow
```

The bulk of the code is implemented in the `displayNotes()` function, which is the callback for the system when the state changes. As we discussed in the previous section, this function is defined with a parameter, called `infoTuple` here, that has information about the call. The first thing that we do is extract the state of the phone:

```
# Get the phone's state
phoneState = infoTuple[0]
```

We only want to do something when the phone is ringing, so this is the only state the function reacts to:

```
# Only react when the phone is ringing
if phoneState == telephone.EStatusRinging:
...
```

The code proceeds to open the contacts database and look up the contact using the phone number in the `infoTuple` variable:

```
# Start by opening the contacts database and looking up the phone
number
db = contacts.open()
contactList = db.find(infoTuple[1])
```

The remainder of the `displayNotes()` function retrieves the notes from the contact entry, then builds a `TopWindow` window to display it. You can examine how this code works yourself.

The code finally registers the `displayNotes()` function as the callback for phone calls:

```
# Finally, install the function as the phone callback
telephone.call_state(displayNotes)
```

Exercise: Extend This Code

The sales person would like to know how many times she has spoken with someone. You might change the code to (a) react to some different call status types (`EStatusAnswering` perhaps), (b) find a note with the count on it and (c) change that note. You have most of the code you need in the above example, except for code that adds a field to a contact and changes a field.

6.4 Messaging Operations

As with telephone operations, the operations when dealing with SMS and MMS messaging are simple. We can send messages; we can receive messages; and we can store messages. Each of these operations is handled through a Python module.

6.4.1 Sending SMS Messages

The `messaging` module handles the sending of SMS messages. The method used to send a SMS message in the `messaging` module is the `sms_send()` method, whose format is shown below:

```
sms_send(<number>, <message>,[<encoding>, <callback>, <name>])
```

The parameters are as follows:

- <number> is the telephone number of the recipient of the message.
- <message> is the body text of the message to be sent.
- <encoding> is a specification of the encoding of the message. It can can be 7-bit encoding ("`7bit`"), 8-bit encoding ("`8bit`") or Unicode ("`UCS2`"). The default setting is for 7-bit encoding.
- <callback> is the name of the function to call when the status of the message changes. This callback function is called with a single parameter: the state value of the message. The default value for this parameter is None (that is, no callback).
- <name> is the name to be given to the message when it is recorded. The default value of this parameter is the telephone number of the recipient.

A message can be in one of nine states, from created to sent. The messaging module has constants that represent each state, as shown in the table 6.2.

Table 6.2 Constants representing the nine message states

Python Name	State Value	Description
`ECreated`	0	the message has been created
`EMovedToOutBox`	1	the message has been moved to the Outbox
`EScheduled-ForSend`	2	the message is waiting for the phone to send it
`ESent`	3	the message has been sent
`EDeleted`	4	the message has been deleted from the Outbox
`ESchedule-Failed`	5	the message cannot be schedule for sending
`ESendFailed`	6	the message cannot be sent
`ENoServiceCen-tre`	7	a state for a message in a phone emulator, indicating no service is possible
`EFatalServer-Error`	8	the message has encountered an error from the phone service's message server

The relationships between these states is shown in Figure 6.3.

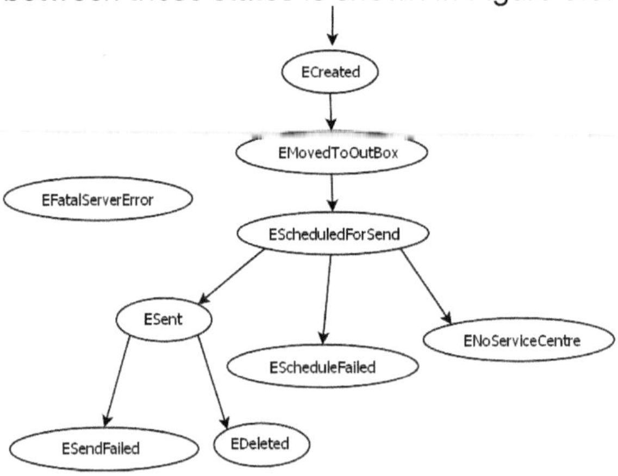

Figure 6.3 Relationships between message states

The lines through the diagram provide a path of state changes for messages. For example, a message could be created, moved to the Outbox, scheduled for sending, then sent. A message might also be created, moved to the Outbox, scheduled for sending, then deleted.

Consider this example of sending a message. As with the telephone example, our callback simply prints a string that shows the state of our message as it moves from creation to sending.

```
import messaging
def newmessagestate (newState):
    if newState == messaging.ECreated:
        msg = "A message has been created"
    elif newState == messaging.EMovedToOutBox:
        msg = "The message has been moved to the Outbox"
    elif newState == messaging.EScheduledForSend:
        msg = "The message has been scheduled for sending"
    elif newState == messaging.ESent:
        msg = "The message has been sent"
    elif newState == messaging.EDeleted:
        msg = "The message has been deleted"
    elif newState == messaging.EScheduleFailed:
        msg = "The message scheduling has failed"
    elif newState == messaging.EStatusConnected:
        msg = "Attempts to send the message have failed"
    elif newState == messaging.ENoServiceCentre:
        msg = "You are using an emulator; you cannot send from the
```

```
emulator"
    elif newState == messaging.EFatalServerError:
        msg = "A fatal error has occured with the messaging sys-
tem"

    print "The message has changed states."
    print "    ",msg

messaging.sms_send("15055551234", "This is a text message for
testing state changes", callback=newmessagestate)
```

Using this code with an actual phone number (a real recipient) produces the following output:

```
The message has changed states.
    A message has been created
The message has changed states.
    The message has been moved to the Outbox
The message has changed states.
    The message has been scheduled for sending
The message has changed states.
    The message has been sent
The message has changed states.
    The message has been deleted
```

There are several things to note about the sending procedure and the `sms_send()` method:

- Until a message has transitioned through all of the states that it can -- consider the paths through the diagram in Figure 6-2 -- the `sms_send()` method cannot be used again.
- The name given to the text message in the call to the `sms_send()` method has a maximum size of 60 characters.
- The behavior when no callback is specified is to block until the message has transitioned through all of the states that it can.

6.4.2 Sending MMS Messages

MMS messages resemble SMS messages. They have a short text body, but they also may contain attachments. These attachments are media attachments: images, video, sound files, and so on.

Sending an MMS message with Python is not nearly as detailed or as informative as sending an SMS message. The `messaging` module supports MMS messages through a single method, `mms_send()`, which has the format below:

```
mms_send(<number>, <message>, [<attachment>])
```

The parameters closely match those for `sms_send()`. The <number> is the telephone number of the recipient. The <message> is a string whose value is the message to send. The optional <attachment> is the pathname in the phone's file system for the file to be attached to the message.

For example, you might want to send a picture of yourself to your friend. You would take a picture with your phone, then send it using the following call:

```
messaging.mms_send("15055554321", "Here is picture of me.  Aren't
I beautiful?", "E:\Images\12262008038.jpg")
```

The `mms_send()` method only allows one attachment.

6.4.3 The Inbox Module

The inbox module supports mailbox management in Symbian. In a confusing naming twist, the inbox module defines an Inbox class that represents a folder in Symbian message store. It is confusing because an Inbox object (an instance of an `Inbox` class) can examine the contents of the Outbox, Sent and Drafts folders as well as the Inbox.

Objects created from the Inbox class can examine all four folders in the message storage:

Table 6.3 Folders in the message storage

Python Name	Description
`EInbox`	The Inbox folder on the Symbian OS device
`EOutbox`	The Outbox folder on the Symbian OS device
`ESent`	The folder of sent messages
`EDraft`	The folder of draft messages

An `Inbox` object is created like this:

```
inbox = Inbox([<foldertype>])
```

Here, <foldertype> is one of the names in the table above. If the <foldertype> is not specified `EInbox` is used.

Once you have created an Inbox object you can get a list of SMS messages by using the `sms_messages()` method. This returns a list of message IDs as integers. This code prints the number of SMS messages in your Inbox:

```
import inbox
box = inbox.Inbox(inbox.EInbox)
messages = box.sms_messages()
print "You have %d SMS messages waiting." % len(messages)
```

Most of the remaining methods in the inbox module operate on an individual messages, specified using <messageID>.

- content(<messageID>) returns the content of the message as a string
- time(<messageID>) returns the time that the message arrived (in seconds since the epoch - see Time Operations in Chapter 3)
- address(<messageID>) returns the address of the sender of the message. This may be a telephone number or a name in the device's contacts list.
- unread(<messageID>) returns the "read" status of the message. A status value of 1 means that the message is unread and a status of 0 means the message has been read.
- set_unread(<messageID>,<status>) sets the status of the message to unread (1) or read (0)
- delete(<messageID>) attempts to delete the message. If the message does not exist Python raises a (`SymbianError`) exception.

In the following example we pick a text message to examine by taking the first message id in the message list.

```
import inbox
box = inbox.Inbox(inbox.EInbox)
messages = box.sms_messages()
id = messages[0]
```

Now, let's examine this message's attributes. It was received via Twitter and it was posted by a Nokia enthusiast.

```
>>> box.content(id)
u'nokconv: Post: You say business phones need long haul batter-
ies... but do all phones? http://ow.ly/15RMSR'
>>> print time.strftime("Message received on %a, %d %b %Y
at %H:%M:%S", time.localtime(box.time(id)))
Message received on Tue, 29 Sep 2009 at 07:43:52
>>> print "Message received from %s" % box.address(id)
Message received from Twitter
>>> print box.unread(id)
1
```

Note

I have the phone number of the Twitter service entered into my contacts under "Twitter", so the system reported the source of the message as "Twitter", not a number. Also, although we printed the contents of the message, the message remains unread. The unread status of the message is a property of the user interface.

There is one more method in the Inbox class, which we discuss below.

6.4.4 Receiving Messages

The Inbox class uses a callback function to process received messages. A callback function must be registered using the `bind()` function as shown below.

```
inbox.bind(<function name>)
```

When a message arrives, the system calls the callback function with the message ID as the parameter. Consider the example below:

```
import inbox
import time

box = inbox.Inbox(inbox.EInbox)

def incomingMsg(messageID):
   print messageID
   print time.strftime("Message received on %a, %d %b %Y
at %H:%M:%S", time.localtime(box.time(messageID)))

box.bind(incomingMsg)
```

This code looks as though it should print the ID of the message and the time of arrival, nicely formatted. However, it throws an exception as shown below:

```
Traceback (most recent call last):
  File "<console>", line 3, in incomingMsg
SymbianError: [Errno -21] KErrAccessDenied
```

To understand the problem with this code we must understand what is going on in the phone. The phone's built-in Messaging application, the one that displays messages, is running and has also registered a callback with the operating system. When we run our Python code there are two programs competing for the same resource (the message store). The messaging application is designed to run fast and will almost always access the message store before our Python code. Our Python code cannot access the message store at the same time, hence our exception.

To solve this race condition we can add a call to `time.sleep()`. This pauses the code long enough for the messaging application to relinquish access to the message store. The example now looks like this:

```
import inbox
import time
box = inbox.Inbox(inbox.EInbox)

def incomingMsg(messageID):
   time.sleep(5)
   print messageID
   print time.strftime("Message received on %a, %d %b %Y
at %H:%M:%S", time.localtime(box.time(messageID)))

box.bind(incomingMsg)
```

The results of the code now look like this:

```
1051799
Message received on Tue, 06 Oct 2009 at 15:58:52
```

The above code works in most cases, but it is not guaranteed to work all the time. The best solution is to try to access the message store for a certain number of times and trap the exception as a way to count the number of access failures. Consider this code:

```
import inbox
import time

box = inbox.Inbox(inbox.EInbox)

def incomingMsg(messageID):
    print messageID
    times = 0
    while (times < 10):
        try:
            print time.strftime("Message received on %a, %d %b %Y
at %H:%M:%S", time.localtime(box.time(messageID)))
            break
        except:
            times += 1

box.bind(incomingMsg)
```

6.5 A Sample Application: SMS Autoreply

Let's consider a larger example. Here is an application that automatically responds to incoming SMS messages with a "nice" vacation message. That is, a message formatted with the name of the sender, which indicates that we will send a reply later. We only do this if we can find a name for the sender; we do not want our reply message to look tacky by using a telephone number as the name.

Consider the code below as version 1:

```
import messaging, inbox, time

box = inbox.Inbox(inbox.EInbox)

def any(string1, string2):
    for i in range(len(string2)-1):
        if string1.find(string2[i:i+1])>-1:
            return True
    return False

def autoreply(messageID):
    time.sleep(5)
    sender = box.address(messageID)
    text = box.content(messageID)
    if not any(sender, "0123456789"):
        reply = sender + \
```

```
            ", I am not able to read your message at this time." + \
            "  I will respond soon."
        print 'Sending "'+reply+'" to '+sender
        messaging.sms_send(sender, reply)

box.bind(autoreply)
```

This code uses the function `any()` to determine whether any of the characters from `string2` are present in `string1`. Admittedly, this is a very crude way of detecting whether `string1` is a (telephone) number. When we run this code and then receive a text message, the output looks like this:

```
Sending "Joe Smith, I am not able to read your message at this
time.  I will respond soon." to Joe Smith
```

However, the message is not sent. In fact, when we look at the Outbox, we see: And when we move the message to the Drafts folder and try to work on it, we get the following error:

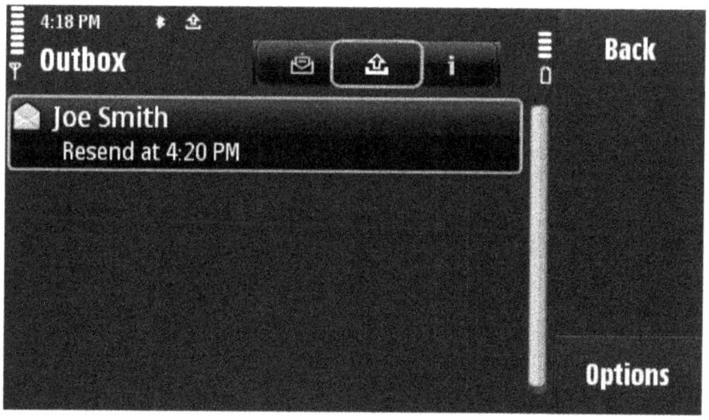

Figure 6.4: The message has not been sent.

We get this error because:

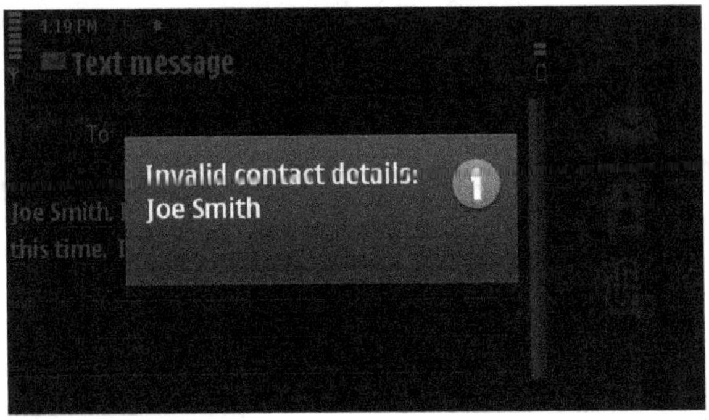

Figure 6.5: There's an error in contact details

the phone "filtered" the message through our contacts, which gave us a name ("Joe Smith") instead of a telephone number as the source of the message and we then tried to send the message to "Joe Smith" instead of a telephone number.

To correct this, we must retrieve the phone number from the contact in the Contacts database. Consider the code below:

```
import messaging, inbox, time, contacts

box = inbox.Inbox(inbox.EInbox)

def any(string1, string2):
    for i in range(len(string2)-1):
        if string1.find(string2[i:i+1])>-1:
            return True
```

```
    return False

def autoreply(messageID):
    time.sleep(5)
    sender = box.address(messageID)
    text = box.content(messageID)
    if not any(sender, "0123456789"):
        db = contacts.open()
        firstName = sender.split(" ")[0]
        lastName = sender.split(" ")[1]
        contactList = db.find(firstName)
        for contact in contactList:
            if contact.find("last_name")[0].value == lastName:
                phoneNumber = contact.find('phone_number')[0].value
                reply = sender + \
                        ", I am not able to read your message at
this time." + \
                        "  I will respond soon."
                print 'Sending "'+reply+'" to '+phoneNumber
                messaging.sms_send(phoneNumber, reply)
                break

box.bind(autoreply)
```

Let's walk through the `autoreply()` function. The first part of the function is the same: we sleep for 5 seconds and extract the sender and the text from the message. If there are no digits in the sender string we begin to process the message.

This fragment opens the contacts database, finds the first and last name, and finds all contacts in the database with the first name we extracted:

```
db = contacts.open()
firstName = sender.split(" ")[0]
lastName = sender.split(" ")[1]
contactList = db.find(firstName)
```

The contact is guaranteed to be in the database because the phone has already returned a name to this function rather than a phone number. It has already looked through the Contacts database and found the contact.

There could, however, be more than one contact entry with the same first name. So, we have to look through all them for the correct last name:

```
for contact in contactList:
    if contact.find("last_name")[0].value == lastName:
```

All that remains is to extract the phone number and to send the message:

```
phoneNumber = contact.find('phone_number')[0].value
reply = sender + \
        ", I am not able to read your message at this time." + \
        "  I will respond soon."
print 'Sending "'+reply+'" to '+phoneNumber
messaging.sms_send(phoneNumber, reply)
break
```

And, indeed, this code correctly sends a text message.

Extend This Code

This code is a bit simplistic:

- It assumes that the first name and the last name are separated by a space; names like "Frederik Siewertsz van Reesema" might not work.
- It assumes that "phone_number" is the number to use for text messages; on S60 3rd edition phones, "mobile_number" might be the better choice.
- There is no "guarantee" that this code will find the contact in the database; if the first name field is not used and the name appears in the last name field, this code will fail.
- How might you fix the code to make it more robust?

6.6 Accessing and using logs

All S60 devices keep a log of phone call and message activity. These logs are available through the logs Python module.

Log entries are seen as dictionaries in Python. For example, a phone call log entry as it might look to Python is shown below. Because of the large amount of data collected per entry this type of representation can be confusing so the data is separated into key/value pairs, one per line. Notice that the string value is represented with Unicode.

```
{
'status': u'No delivery',
```

```
'direction': u'Incoming',
'description': u'Voice call',
'duration type': 1,
'number': u'1616xxxxxxx',
'name': u'',
'contact': -1,
'flags': 0,
'time': 1254283601.7287519,
'duration': 80,
'link': 0,
'data': '',
'id': 8500,
'subject': u'6'
}
```

Here is a dictionary object depicting a text message entry. Each key is described in the table below.

```
{
'status': u'Delivered',
'direction': u'Incoming',
'description': u'Short message',
'duration type': -1,
'number': u'40404',
'name': u'',
'contact': -1,
'flags': 0,
'time': 1254333004.285248,
```

```
'duration': 0,
'link': 0,
'data': '\x00\x00\x00\x00\x01\x00\x00\x00\x00\x00\x00\x00\x00\x00\
x00\x00\x00\x00\x00\x00\x01\x00\x00\x00',
'id': 8576,
'subject': u'AAS: Ovi Developer Day  http://bit.ly/ImAiO'
}
```

Each of these entries has similar fields, described here.

Table 6.4 Text message entries

Python Name	Description
`status`	a brief depiction of the event
`direction`	the direction with respect to the phone of the event: either "Incoming" or "Outgoing"
`description`	a longer description of the event
`duration` `type`	a description of the type of event, such as a data event or a phone event
`number`	the remote phone number associated with the event
`name`	the name associated with the event
`contact`	the number ID of the contact associated with the event
`flags`	an indication of what cause the event; for example: the user checked for missed calls
`time`	time, in standard notation, when the event occurred

`duration`	number of seconds the event took
`link`	valid if this event was linked to another application
`data`	data associated with the event (for example, the message text)
`id`	the ID of the event in the log database
`subject`	the subject of the event; for example, the text of a message

Logs are kept for several different types of communication events. These types are: `call`, `sms`, `data`, `fax`, `email` and `scheduler`. The types are self-explanatory.

The methods in the logs module are quite straightforward. You can retrieve all log data, log data of a certain type, or log data of a certain type between specific times. When retrieving log entries, you can also filter the entries by mode, a descriptor of each message. Mode specifiers can be `in`, `out`, `fetched`, `missed`, `in_alt` or `out_alt`. Unless specified, the mode is the default value of in.

The methods of the logs module are as follows. Log data is returned as a list of dictionary objects.

- raw_log_data() returns all events of all types.
- log_data(<type>, [start_log=<start>, num_of_logs=<number of entries>, mode=<mode>]) returns log entries of a type specified by the <type> parameter. Optionally, you can specify where to start collecting the entries, the number of entries and the mode.
- log_data_by_time(<type>, <start time>, <end time>, [mode=<mode>]) retrieves entries of the type specified between <start time> and <end time>,

optionally of a specific mode. Times must be specified as standard Unix time in seconds from the epoch.

- calls([start_log=<start>, num_of_logs=<number of entries>, mode=<mode>])
- faxes([start_log=<start>, num_of_logs=<number of entries>, mode=<mode>])
- emails([start_log=<start>, num_of_logs=<number of entries>, mode=<mode>])
- sms([start_log=<start>, num_of_logs=<number of entries>, mode=<mode>])
- scheduler_logs([start_log=<start>, num_of_logs=<number of entries>, mode=<mode>])
- data_logs([start_log=<start>, num_of_logs=<number of entries>, mode=<mode>])

These calls retrieve specific types of log entries -- quite self-explanatory -- with the same optional parameters. You can specify the starting point of retrieval, the number of entries to retrieve, and the mode of entry to retrieve.

Here are a few examples. If we want to count the calls we missed in the last 24 hours, we could execute this code:

```
import logs

missed = logs.log_data_by_time('call', time.time()-86400, time.
time(), 'missed')
print 'You missed ' + str(len(missed)) + ' calls.'
```

If we want to show the senders of the last 10 messages received, we could execute this code:

```
import logs

for msg in logs.sms(num_of_logs=10):
    print msg['number']
```

With respect to the previous example, we should consider this question: is the first log entry the oldest one or the latest one? In other words, does the code above print the latest 10 messages received or the first 10 messages received? The answer is the latest, but it is left to you to write code to prove this.

6.7 Summary

Smartphones running Symbian are capable of many things, but fundamentally they are phones, which means they can make and receive phone calls, and send and receive SMS and MMS messages. This chapter discussed the support Python provides, through the `telephone` module, for making and answering phone calls; and, through the `messaging` module, for sending and receiving messages. We concluded the chapter by discussing how Python supports activity logs with the `logs` module, which works with information about calls and messages that have been made, sent and received.

Python support for telephony and messaging is provided mainly through callbacks, which are functions that are registered with the operating system and then called by the operating system when phone calls or messages are received by the phone. The use of callbacks was illustrated with several examples.

The modules described above provide a clean, convenient interface to the telephony and messaging functions of a phone. Platform services, which are covered in Chapter 12, also provide telephony and messaging functionality. Platform services are more difficult and less convenient to use, but access deeper and more powerful functionality.

7

Graphics and Multimedia

7.1 Introduction

Python supports operations for drawing basic primitives and text, capturing, displaying and editing images, and for recording and playing sound. With mobile devices becoming increasingly capable of advanced multimedia operations, the creative possibilities are almost endless.

This chapter demonstrates each of these operations through basic examples, and also provides worked examples of credible camera and music player applications.

7.2 Drawing on `Canvas`

The `canvas` is the most low-level UI control available in PyS60. It consists of a drawable area on the screen that other UI components can be displayed upon, including basic drawing primitives, text, images, and even camera viewfinder videos.

The `canvas` can intercept key events from the 5-way keypad present on many Symbian devices (it's a 5-way keypad because it can signal left, right, up, down, and has a central 'select' button). The `canvas` has a `bind()` method that can be used to associate a function with a key event.

```
canvas.bind(EKeyUpArrow, your_up_function)
canvas.bind(EKeyDownArrow, your_down_function)
canvas.bind(EKeyLeftArrow, your_left_function)
canvas.bind(EKeyRightArrow, your_right_function
canvas.bind(EKeySelect, your_select_function)
```

Some devices, such as those with touch screens, do not have physical softkeys or arrow keys. For these, you can use the canvas to display a virtual directional pad (if the application is in full screen mode, the directional pad is accompanied by two virtual softkeys, as shown in Figure 7.1). The pad can be enabled or disabled by setting `appuifw.app.directional_pad` to `True` or `False`, respectively.

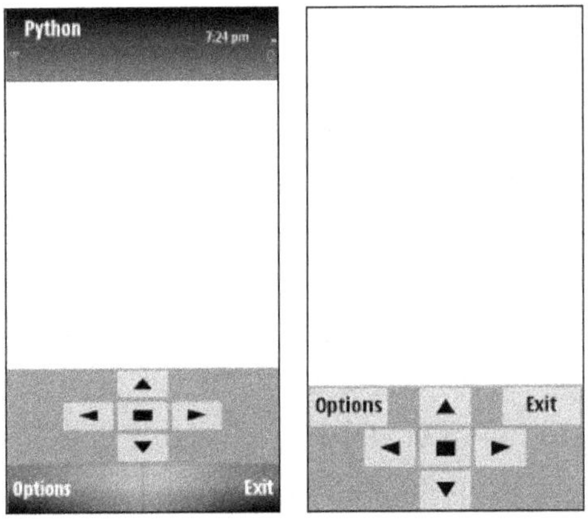

Figure 7.1 The virtual directional pad

Applications can draw to the Canvas using basic 'graphics primitives' or shapes. The available shapes include line, rectangle, polygon, ellipse, arc, pieslice and point. The methods used to draw shapes and their arguments have the general form method (coordseq[, <options>]) and are explained in detail in the PyS60 documentation.

The following example shows how to draw some shapes, and the resulting screen is shown in Figure 7.2.

```
import e32, appuifw

app_lock = e32.Ao_lock()
def quit():
      app_lock.signal()
appuifw.app.exit_key_handler = quit

appuifw.app.screen = 'full'

canvas = appuifw.Canvas()
appuifw.app.body = canvas

#line((x1,y1,x2,y2), width)
canvas.line((30,45,160,15), 0)

#rectangle((x1,y1,x2,y2), color)
canvas.rectangle((30,45,190,130), fill=0xCC55AA)

#ellipse((x1,y1,x2,y2), color)
canvas.ellipse((22,250,78,280), fill=0x337700)

#point((x,y), (R,G,B), width)
canvas.point((200,180), (243,46,113), width=6)

app_lock.wait()
```

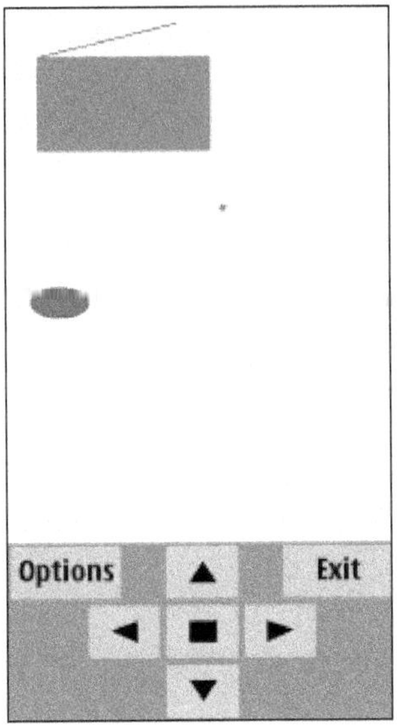

Figure 7.2 Some shapes drawn to the screen

The Canvas can also be used to draw text; this feature is often used to display text with customized font, size or colour, at arbitrary positions on the screen. The Canvas provides the `text()` method to set the text (font and colour) to be drawn, and `measure_text()` to determine the size and position that would be occupied by some given text if drawn in a specified font.

The following example shows how to draw the text 'Symbian' in a specified font, position and colour, which is shown in Figure 7.3.

```
import appuifw, e32


app_lock = e32.Ao_lock()
def quit():
    app_lock.signal()
```

```
appuifw.app.exit_key_handler = quit

canvas = appuifw.Canvas()
appuifw.app.body = canvas

#text((x,y), Unicode string, color, font=(name,size,style))
canvas.text((40,60), u"Symbian", 0x007F00, font=(u'Nokia Hindi
S60',45,appuifw.STYLE_BOLD))

app_lock.wait()
```

Figure 7.3 Customized text written on the canvas

We can define a special function to pass a redraw callback to the constructor for the `Canvas`. It specifies the operations to be performed when the canvas needs to be redrawn (which happens after it is obscured by something else on the screen). Here is a code fragment to illustrate.

```
...
def handle_redraw(rect):
      c.clear(0xFF0000)
c = appuifw.Canvas(redraw_callback=handle_redraw)
appuifw.app.body = c
...
```

7.3 Displaying and Handling Image Objects

The `Image` class, as defined in the `graphics` module, is used to create, edit and save images. Image objects are created with the `new()` method, specifying the desired size as follows:

```
import graphics

img = graphics.Image.new((360, 640))
```

An image can be edited in various ways. Text can be added to it, shapes can be drawn on it, and it can be transposed, rotated and resized. The following example shows how all these operations can be performed:

```
import graphics, appuifw, e32

app_lock = e32.Ao_lock()
def quit():
        app_lock.signal()
appuifw.app.exit_key_handler = quit
```

```
#Open an image
img = graphics.Image.open("C:\\Data\\my_image.jpg")

#Draw a rectangle on it
img.rectangle((30,45,110,100), fill=0xCC55AA)

#Rotate it by 90 degrees and resize it to a quarter of the origi-
nal size
#Other rotation options include ROTATE_180 and ROTATE_270
img = img.transpose(graphics.ROTATE_90)
img = img.resize((img.size[0]/2, img.size[1]/2))

#Display text on it
img.text((20, 45), u"Image editing", font="title")

#Save the image
img.save("C:\\Data\\my_edited_image.jpg", quality=100)

def handle_redraw(rect):
      canvas.blit(img)

#Show the result on the screen
canvas = appuifw.Canvas(redraw_callback=handle_redraw)
appuifw.app.body = canvas

app_lock.wait()
```

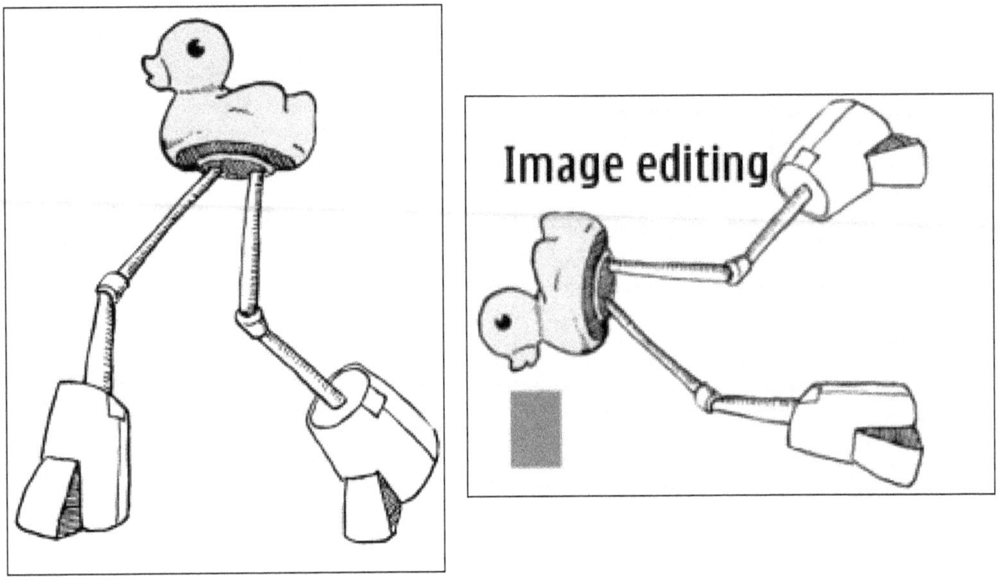

Figure 7.4 A “Before and After” example of editing an image

7.4 Screenshot capture

It is often useful to capture screenshots of your application for promotional, debugging or other purposes. This can be done from within a Python application using the graphics module’s `screenshot()` function.

The `screenshot()` function returns an image object, which can be used to save the image as a JPEG or PNG file (you can specify the type, or Python will work it out from the file name). By default, the image is saved synchronously; a callback can be specified as an optional parameter to save the file asynchronously.

The following example demonstrates capturing and synchronously saving a screenshot as a JPEG file:

```
import graphics

#Take the screenshot
img = graphics.screenshot()
#Save it to the specified path
img.save(u"C:\\Data\\screenshot.jpg")
```

7.5 Using the Camera

PyS60 offers access to the device's camera through the camera module and provides functions to capture and save photos and videos. The viewfinder can be used to display what is being captured. Once the camera is no longer needed, it must be released so that other applications may use it.

Using the Viewfinder

One of the most fundamental aspects of photography and videography is the ability to frame the subject as desired. The viewfinder allows us to do just that by showing the image that would be captured on the device's screen.

Figure 7.5 The viewfinder in action

The following code snippet demonstrates how to use the viewfinder. It defines a function that places the information received from the camera on the application's body (which is an instance of `Canvas`) and passes it as an argument to the `start_finder()` function. The size of the viewfinder can also be specified by passing a tuple of required width/height in pixels to the function's optional `size` argument.

```
import camera, appuifw, e32


app_lock = e32.Ao_lock()
def quit():
    #Close the viewfinder
    camera.stop_finder()
    #Release the camera so that other programs can use it
    camera.release()
    app_lock.signal()
```

```
appuifw.app.exit_key_handler = quit

#Define a for displaying the viewfinder; basically it just displays
an image on a Canvas
def vf(im):
      appuifw.app.body.blit(im)

#Set the application's body to Canvas
appuifw.app.body = appuifw.Canvas()

#Start the viewfinder and keep the backlight on
camera.start_finder(vf, backlight_on=1)

app_lock.wait()
```

Capturing Photos

Photos are captured with the `take_photo()` function. After capturing a photo, you can save it just as you would an ordinary image.

`take_photo()` has a number of (optional) arguments to specify various settings. The full form of the function is `take_photo([mode, size, zoom, flash, exposure, white_balance, position])`; the detailed meaning of each argument is described in the documentation.

Table 7.1 gives a brief description of each of the arguments.

Table 7.1: Arguments to `take_photo()`

Argument	Description	Possible values
`mode`	The display mode of the image	'RGB12', 'RGB16', 'RGB', 'JPEG_Exif', 'JPEG_JFIF'; returned by the Image_modes() function.
`size`	The resolution of the image	Two-element tuple returned by the image_sizes() function.
`zoom`	The zoom factor	From 0 to the value returned by the max_zoom() function.
`flash`	The flash mode setting	'none', 'auto', 'forced', 'fill_in', 'red_eye_reduce'; returned by the flash_modes() function.
`exposure`	The exposure adjustment level	'auto', 'night', 'backlight', 'center'; returned by the exposure_modes() function.
`white_balance`	The color temperature of the current light	'auto', 'daylight', 'cloudy', 'tungsten', 'fluorescent', 'flash'; returned by the white_balance_modes() function.
`position`	The camera used if the device has more than one	From 0 to the value returned by the cameras_available() function minus 1.

```
import camera, appuifw, e32

app_lock = e32.Ao_lock()
def quit():
      #Release the camera so that other programs can use it
      camera.release()
      app_lock.signal()
appuifw.app.exit_key_handler = quit

#Take the photo
photo = camera.take_photo('RGB', (1024, 768))

#Save it at maximum quality
photo.save("C:\\Data\\my_photo", quality=100)

app_lock.wait()
```

In some newer Symbian devices, in order to be able to capture images at the maximum resolution supported by the camera, one must:

- Switch to the landscape mode.
- Import the camera module.
- Take the picture in the 'JPEG_Exif' format.
- Save it by writing its information in a file, not as an Image object.

The following example illustrates how to capture a photo at maximum resolution. As was noted in the previous table, the {{icode|image_sizes()}} function returns a list of possible image resolutions. By calling it with a mode as an argument, in our case 'JPEG_Exif', it returns the list of all the resolutions compatible with that mode. The photo can be taken by selecting "Take photo" from the Options menu.

```
import appuifw, e32

#Switch to landscape mode
appuifw.app.orientation = "landscape"

import camera

app_lock = e32.Ao_lock()
def quit():
	#Release the camera so that other programs can use it
	camera.release()
	app_lock.signal()
appuifw.app.exit_key_handler = quit

#Function for taking the picture
def take_picture():
	#Take the photo
	photo = camera.take_photo('JPEG_Exif', camera.image_
sizes('JPEG_Exif')[0])
	#Save it
	f = open(savepath, "wb")
	f.write(photo)
	f.close()
```

```
savepath = u"C:\\Data\\photo.jpg"
#This is the path and name for storing the photo

appuifw.app.body = appuifw.Canvas()

appuifw.app.menu=[(u"Take photo", take_picture)]

app_lock.wait()
```

Capturing Videos

Capturing video is done through the `start_record()` function of the camera module. It's necessary to start the viewfinder prior to calling the function. The following code snippet uses a timer to record video for 10 seconds, after which time the recording stops.

```
import camera, appuifw, e32

app_lock = e32.Ao_lock()
def quit():
      #Cancel the timer when the user exits, if it has not expired
      timer.cancel()
      #Close the viewfinder
      camera.stop_finder()
      #Release the camera so that other programs can use it
      camera.release()
      app_lock.signal()
appuifw.app.exit_key_handler = quit
```

```
#Function for displaying the viewfinder
def vf(im):
      appuifw.app.body.blit(im)

#Function that will be passed as an argument to start_record; it
is used for
#handling possible errors and monitoring the current status
def video_callback(err, current_state):
      global control_light
      if current_state == camera.EPrepareComplete:
            control_light=1
      else:
            pass

#The path where the video file will be saved
video_savepath = u"C:\\Data\\video.mp4"

appuifw.app.body = appuifw.Canvas()

#Start the viewfinder
camera.start_finder(vf)

#Start recording
video = camera.start_record(video_savepath, video_callback)

#Create a timer
timer = e32.Ao_timer()
```

```
#Record for 10 seconds, then stop
timer.after(10, lambda:camera.stop_record())

app_lock.wait()
```

7.6 PySymCamera - a tabs interface camera example

Here is an example of an application that can take pictures and record video. It pulls together the image capture and video examples discussed in the previous section into a fully functional application and uses tabs to switch between photo and video mode.

```
import camera, appuifw, e32, os, graphics, sysinfo
from key_codes import *

app_lock = e32.Ao_lock()
def quit():
      appuifw.app.set_tabs([], None)
      camera.stop_finder()
      camera.release()
      app_lock.signal()
appuifw.app.exit_key_handler = quit

#The "recording" variable keeps track of whether a video is cur-
rently being recorded
recording = False

def number_of_files():
```

```
	#The photos and videos will be stored in C:\Data,
	#and the current number is added at the end of each file name
	global number_of_photos, number_of_videos
	number_of_photos = 0
	number_of_videos = 0
	for f in os.listdir("C:\\Data"):
		if os.path.isfile("C:\\Data\\" + f):
			if f.startswith("my_photo") and f.endswith(".
jpg"):
				number_of_photos += 1
			if f.startswith("my_video") and f.endswith(".
mp4"):
				number_of_videos += 1

#Define the function to be called when the select key is pressed,
for taking photos or videos
def take():
	global recording

	if mode == "photocamera":
		number_of_files()
		photo = camera.take_photo('RGB', camera.image_sizes()
[0], zoom, flash)
		photo.save("C:\\Data\\my_photo" + str(number_of_photos
+ 1) + ".jpg")
		photocamera()
	elif mode == "videocamera":
		if not recording:
```

```
                  number_of_files()
                  camera.start_record("C:\\Data\\my_video" +
str(number_of_videos + 1) + ".mp4", video_callback)
                  recording = True
            elif recording:
                  camera.stop_record()
                  recording = False

#The functions for increasing and decreasing the zoom level
def zoom_up():
      global zoom

      if mode == "photocamera":
            if zoom + camera.max_zoom() / 2 <= camera.max_zoom():
                  zoom += camera.max_zoom() / 2
                  photo = camera.take_photo('RGB', camera.image_
sizes()[-1], zoom, flash='none')
                  camera.stop_finder()
                  photocamera()

def zoom_down():
      global zoom

      if mode == "photocamera":
            if zoom  - camera.max_zoom() / 2 >=  0:
                  zoom -= camera.max_zoom() / 2
                  photo = camera.take_photo('RGB', camera.image_
sizes()[-1], zoom, flash='none')
```

```
                camera.stop_finder()
                photocamera()

def handle_tabs(index):
    global recording, zoom
    if index == 0:
        if recording:
            camera.stop_record()
            recording = False
        camera.stop_finder()
        zoom = 0
        photocamera()
    if index == 1:
        camera.stop_finder()
        videocamera()
appuifw.app.set_tabs([u"Photo", u"Video"], handle_tabs)

#Create a new, blank image to be used for double buffering
img = graphics.Image.new(sysinfo.display_pixels())

#Define a function for displaying the viewfinder
def vf(im):
    img.blit(im)
    handle_redraw(())

def handle_redraw(rect):
    global canvas
    canvas.blit(img)
```

```
canvas = appuifw.Canvas(redraw_callback=handle_redraw)
appuifw.app.body = canvas

canvas.bind(EKeyUpArrow, zoom_up)
canvas.bind(EKeyDownArrow, zoom_down)
canvas.bind(EKeySelect, take)

#Define a callback for video capturing
def video_callback(err, current_state):
      global control_light
      if current_state == camera.EPrepareComplete:
            control_light=1
      else:
            pass

#Zoom is 0 initially
zoom = 0
#Flash is disabled by default
flash = "none"
flash_enabled = "  "
flash_disabled = "x "

#A function for enabling and disabling the flash
def set_flash(option):
      global flash, flash_enabled, flash_disabled
      if option == True:
            flash = "forced"
```

```
        flash_enabled = "x "
        flash_disabled = "  "
    if option == False:
        flash = "none"
        flash_enabled = "  "
        flash_disabled = "x "
    appuifw.app.menu = [(u"Flash", ((flash_enabled + u"Enabled",
lambda:set_flash(True)),
                        (flash_disabled + u"Disabled", lambda:set_
flash(False))))]

#Define the 2 main functions, one for photo mode and one for video
mode
def photocamera():
    #Define a variable that stores the current mode, used to take
action when a key is pressed
    global mode
    mode = "photocamera"

    camera.start_finder(vf, backlight_on=1)

    appuifw.app.menu = [(u"Flash", ((flash_enabled + u"Enabled",
lambda:set_flash(True)),
                            (flash_disabled + u"Disabled",
lambda:set_flash(False))))]

def videocamera():
    #Define a variable that stores the current mode, used to take
```

```
action when a key is pressed
        global mode
        mode = "videocamera"

        camera.start_finder(vf, backlight_on=1)

        appuifw.app.menu = []

photocamera()

app_lock.wait()
```

Now let's analyze the code to see what it does and how it works:

```
app_lock = e32.Ao_lock()
def quit():
        appuifw.app.set_tabs([], None)
        camera.stop_finder()
        camera.release()
        app_lock.signal()
appuifw.app.exit_key_handler = quit
```

First, we handle what happens when closing the application. We create an active object-based synchronization service (`app_lock` and define the function to be called when the application is closed. On close, the function has to:

- Get rid of the tabs as discussed in the tabs section of Chapter 4

- Stop the viewfinder
- Release the camera
- Call the service's `signal()` method, telling the script to end.

We assign the function to the right softkey, to handle an exit request from the user.

```
recording = False
```

This flag keeps track of whether or not video is currently being recorded. We need this in order to know what to do when the selection key is pressed in video mode.

```
def number_of_files():
        #The photos and videos will be stored in C:\Data,
                #and the current number is added at the end of
each file name
        global number_of_photos, number_of_videos
        number_of_photos = 0
        number_of_videos = 0
        for f in os.listdir("C:\\Data"):
                if os.path.isfile("C:\\Data\\" + f):
                        if f.startswith("my_photo") and f.endswith(".
jpg"):
                                number_of_photos += 1
                        if f.startswith("my_video") and f.endswith(".
mp4"):
                                number_of_videos += 1
```

This is the function we use to determine the number with which to name new images and videos. The function simply counts how many photos and videos there are in the location where we save the photos and videos. If the name of a file in that location matches a certain format (in this case, if it starts with "my_photo"/"my video" and has the ".jpg"/".mp4" extension), a counter variable is increased. The value of that counter variable (`number_of_photos` or `number_of_videos`) is increased by 1 and appended to the name of the associated file type when it is saved.

```
def take():
    global recording
```

> ***Note***
>
> This method of calculating a unique file number is not robust; If any files are deleted the next count will be the same as a name that has already been used. Production-quality code should further analyze whether each file name exists and continue to increase the counter until a unique file name is reached.

```
    if mode == "photocamera":
        number_of_files()
        photo = camera.take_photo('RGB', camera.image_sizes()
[0], zoom, flash)
        photo.save("C:\\Data\\my_photo" + str(number_of_photos
+ 1) + ".jpg")
        photocamera()
    elif mode == "videocamera":
        if not recording:
```

```
                number_of_files()
                camera.start_record("C:\\Data\\my_video" +
str(number_of_videos + 1) + ".mp4", video_callback)
                recording = True
            elif recording:
                camera.stop_record()
                recording = False
```

This is the most important function in the entire program. It's called when the selection key is pressed, and acts differently depending on whether it was called in 'photocamera' mode or 'videocamera' mode. In the first case, it calculates the numer of photos inside the save directory, takes a photo, saves it and re-starts the camera. In the second case, it first checks if video is being recorded. If it isn't, it calculates the number of videos inside the save directory and starts recording. If video is being recorded, it simply stops recording.

```
def zoom_up():
    global zoom

    if mode == "photocamera":
        if zoom + camera.max_zoom() / 2 <= camera.max_zoom():
            zoom += camera.max_zoom() / 2
            photo = camera.take_photo('RGB', camera.image_
sizes()[-1], zoom, flash='none')
            camera.stop_finder()
            photocamera()


def zoom_down():
```

```
        global zoom

        if mode == "photocamera":
                if zoom - camera.max_zoom() / 2 >= 0:
                        zoom -= camera.max_zoom() / 2
                        photo = camera.take_photo('RGB', camera.image_
sizes()[-1], zoom, flash='none')
                        camera.stop_finder()
                        photocamera()
```

These two functions complement each other. They are used for zooming in and zooming out, respectively. Since setting a zoom level other than 0 only works for taking pictures, we first check if the application is running in photocamera mode. If it is, we check if the zoom level can be modified beyond the current level. If it can, the current level is modified by half of the maximum zoom level. After that, a dummy photo is taken and the camera is restarted in order to make the viewfinder display at the new zoom level.

```
def handle_tabs(index):
        global recording, zoom
        if index == 0:
                if recording:
                        camera.stop_record()
                        recording = False
                camera.stop_finder()
                zoom = 0
                photocamera()
        if index == 1:
```

```
            camera.stop_finder()
            videocamera()
appuifw.app.set_tabs([u"Photo", u"Video"], handle_tabs)
```

This piece of code handles tabs. The function is called whenever the user switches between the two tabs the application uses (one for photocamera mode and one for videocamera mode). If the photo tab is selected, any ongoing recording is stopped and the camera is restarted in photo mode. If the video tab is selected, since there is no recording to stop, the application simply switches to that tab by restarting in video mode. The last line creates the two tabs.

```
img = graphics.Image.new(sysinfo.display_pixels())
```

When displaying the viewfinder, the high rate at which data is sent from the camera to the screen can cause flickering. This is solved by applying the concept of double buffering. Instead of displaying the viewfinder data directly on the screen we first place it on `img` and then display that.

```
def vf(im):
      img.blit(im)
      handle_redraw(())
```

In the preceding code we define a function that takes the data from the camera in the form of an image and draws it onto another image (the first phase of double buffering). Then it calls the canvas' redraw callback which puts the image on the canvas, thus displaying it on the screen (the second phase of double buffering).

```
canvas.bind(EKeyUpArrow, zoom_up)
canvas.bind(EKeyDownArrow, zoom_down)
canvas.bind(EKeySelect, take)
```

Now, we associate certain keys with certain actions. The `bind()` method of the Canvas instance binds a function to a keycode. For example, when the up arrow button is pressed, the `take()` function is called.

```
#Define a callback for video capturing
def video_callback(err, current_state):
      global control_light
      if current_state == camera.EPrepareComplete:
            control_light=1
      else:
            pass
```

The callback function will be called with an error code and status information as parameters. It has to be present in order to know that the device is ready to begin recording video. A list of possible states is available in the PyS60 documentation.

```
#Zoom is 0 initially
zoom = 0
#Flash is disabled by default
flash = "none"
flash_enabled = "  "
flash_disabled = "x "

#A function for enabling and disabling the flash
```

```
def set_flash(option):
	global flash, flash_enabled, flash_disabled
	if option == True:
		flash = "forced"
		flash_enabled = "x "
		flash_disabled = "  "
	if option == False:
		flash = "none"
		flash_enabled = "  "
		flash_disabled = "x "
	appuifw.app.menu = [(u"Flash", ((flash_enabled + u"Enabled",
lambda:set_flash(True)),
				(flash_disabled + u"Disabled",
lambda:set_flash(False))))]
```

Here, we specify that the zoom level is initially 0 and that flash is disabled at first. Then we define the `set_flash(option)` function that enables or disables the flash. The important lines of the function are **flash = "forced"** and **flash = "none"** (remember, 'forced' and 'none' are flash modes) because they set the flash on or off, depending on the Boolean value passed as an argument.

```
def photocamera():
	#Define a variable that stores the current mode, used to take
action when a key is pressed
	global mode
	mode = "photocamera"

	camera.start_finder(vf, backlight_on=1)
```

```
    appuifw.app.menu = [(u"Flash", ((flash_enabled + u"Enabled",
lambda:set_flash(True)),
                                    (flash_disabled + u"Disabled",
lambda:set_flash(False))))]
```

This is the function that is called when the camera is switched into photo mode. It sets the current mode to photocamera, starts the viewfinder and sets the menu accordingly.

```
def videocamera():
    #Define a variable that stores the current mode, used to take
action when a key is pressed
    global mode
    mode = "videocamera"

    camera.start_finder(vf, backlight_on=1)

    appuifw.app.menu = []
```

This function does the same thing as `photocamera`, only for video mode.

```
photocamera()

app_lock.wait()
```

We simply start the camera application in photo mode and tell the script not to complete executing until the right softkey is pressed (and thus the `quit()` function is called).

7.7 Text to speech

The audio module's `say()` function can be used to speak Unicode text phonetically (in the current device language). This makes it trivially easy to add text to speech capability to your applications. The following example 'plays' the text 'Python on Symbian':

```
import audio

audio.say(u"Python on Symbian")
```

Recording and Playing Sound Files

Audio can be recorded and played using the `audio` module. The most commonly used methods of sound objects are:

- `open()`
- `record()`
- `play()`
- `stop()`
- `close()`.

The supported sound file formats may vary from one device to another. The following code snippet demonstrates how to record a sound file and then play it.

```
import appuifw, e32, audio

app_lock = e32.Ao_lock()
```

```
def quit():
    #Close the Sound object
    s.close()
    app_lock.signal()
appuifw.app.exit_key_handler = quit

file_path = u"C:\\Data\\my_sound_file.mp3"

#Open the sound file
s = audio.Sound.open(file_path)

#Record for 10 seconds
s.record()
e32.ao_sleep(10)
s.stop()

#Play it indefinitely
s.play(audio.KMdaRepeatForever)

app_lock.wait()
```

7.8 PyMPlayer - a music player example

The following example is a basic music player application. Its features include play/pause functionality, code to increase and decrease the volume, and to display information about the status of the playback. The implementation of pause and resume are noteworthy, since there are no standard methods for them.

```
import appuifw, e32, audio, graphics, os, sysinfo
from key_codes import *

app_lock = e32.Ao_lock()
def quit():
      app_lock.signal()
appuifw.app.exit_key_handler = quit

class PyMPlayer:
      def __init__(self, path):
            #The path where the player will look for sound files
            self.path = path
            #A variable that keeps track of the current state of
the player;
            #None means no song is open, False means playing is
paused, and True means a song is playing
            self.playing = None
            #We will use this when coming out of pause in order to
know from what point the song should play
            self.pickup_time = 0
            #Create an image the size of the screen
            self.img = graphics.Image.new(sysinfo.display_pix-
els())
            #Instantiate a Canvas and set it as the application's
body,
            #and bind the keys that control playback options
            self.canvas = appuifw.Canvas(redraw_callback=self.
handle_redraw)
```

```
        self.canvas.bind(EKeyUpArrow, self.volume_up)
        self.canvas.bind(EKeyDownArrow, self.volume_down)
        self.canvas.bind(EKeySelect, self.play_pause)
        appuifw.app.body = self.canvas
        appuifw.app.menu = [(u"Pick song", self.select_song)]
        #Instantiate a timer that will be used for updating
the info displayed on the screen
        self.timer = e32.Ao_timer()

    def handle_redraw(self, rect):
        self.canvas.blit(self.img)

    #This function finds all the sound files in a certain direc-
tory
    #and displays them as a list for the user to choose from
    def select_song(self):
        self.list_of_songs = []
        for self.i in os.listdir(self.path):
            #Check if the extension is that of a sound file
and if it is, add the name to the list
            if self.i[-4:] in [".mp3", ".wav", ".wma"]:
                self.list_of_songs.append(unicode(self.i))
        #Ask the user which file they want to play,if there are any
        f len(self.list_of_songs) > 0:

try:

self.file_name = self.list_of_songs[appuifw.selection_list(self.
```

```
list_of_songs)]

except TypeError: #Occurs when the user cancels the selection
pass
else:
appuifw.note(u"No appropriate sound files available", 'info')


      def volume_down(self):
            try:
                  self.s.set_volume(self.s.current_volume() - 1)
            except:
                  pass


      #Here we handle opening a song for the first time and play-
ing/pausing it
      def play_pause(self):
            if self.playing == False:
                  self.s.set_position(self.pickup_time)
                  self.playing = True
                  self.s.play()
                  self.show_info()
            elif self.playing == True:
                  self.pickup_time = self.s.current_position()
                  self.playing = False
                  self.s.stop()
                  self.timer.cancel()
            if self.playing == None:
                  try: #If play is used before a song is selected,
```

```
an error occurs
                    self.s = audio.Sound.open(self.path + "\\" + self.file_name)
                    appuifw.app.menu = [(u"Stop", self.stop)]
                    self.playing = True
                    self.s.play()
self.show_info()
except:
pass

      #This function takes care of stopping playback
      def stop(self):
             appuifw.app.menu = [(u"Pick song", self.select_song)]
             self.s.stop()
             self.s.close()
             self.playing = None
             self.timer.cancel()

      #A function that establishes and displays elapsed time
      #and the duration of the song as well as the name of the file
      def show_info(self):
             #Calculate the values
             self.min1, self.sec1 = divmod((self.s.current_posi-
tion() / 1000000), 60)
             self.min2, self.sec2 = divmod((self.s.duration() /
1000000), 60)
             #Give the values the standard format mm:ss
             if self.min1<10:
                    self.info = u"0" + unicode(self.min1)
```

```
        else:
            self.info = unicode(self.min1)
        self.info += u″:″
        if self.sec1<10:
            self.info += u″0″ + unicode(self.sec1)
        else:
            self.info += unicode(self.sec1)
        self.info += u″ - ″
        if self.min2<10:
            self.info += u″0″ + unicode(self.min2)
        else:
            self.info += unicode(self.min2)
        self.info += u″:″
        if self.sec2<10:
            self.info += u″0″ + unicode(self.sec2)
        else:
            self.info += unicode(self.sec2)
        #Clear the image so things don′t overlap
        self.img.clear()
        #Calculate where to display the info so that it′s in
the center of the screen
        self.text_size = self.img.measure_text(self.file_name,
font=′title′)[0]
        self.text_width = self.text_size[2] - self.text_
size[0]
        self.text_height = self.text_size[3] - self.text_
size[1]
        self.text_x = (sysinfo.display_pixels()[0] / 2) -
```

```
(self.text_width / 2)
            self.text_y = (sysinfo.display_pixels()[1] / 2) -
self.text_height
            self.img.text((self.text_x, self.text_y), self.file_
name, font='title')
            self.text_size = self.img.measure_text(self.info,
font='title')[0]
            self.text_width = self.text_size[2] - self.text_
size[0]
            self.text_height = self.text_size[3] - self.text_
size[1]
            self.text_x = (sysinfo.display_pixels()[0] / 2) -
(self.text_width / 2)
            self.text_y = (sysinfo.display_pixels()[1] / 2) -
self.text_height
            self.img.text((self.text_x, self.text_y + self.text_
height), self.info, font='title')
            self.handle_redraw(())
            #Update the info every second
            self.timer.after(1, self.show_info)

      #The class' destructor; here we close the currently open sound file, if any
      def __del__(self):
            try:
                  self.s.stop()
                  self.s.close()
            except:
                  pass
```

```
#Create an instance of the player, passing the path where the
sound files are as an argument
player = PyMPlayer(u"C:\\Data")

app_lock.wait()
```

Upon taking a close look at the code example, the first thing to notice is that the music player is implemented as a class, not as a series of functions (classes are discussed at length in Chapter 2). This approach allows the player to be used in other applications by simply importing it like any other class from a module.

```
def __init__(self, path):
        #The path where the player will look for sound files
        self.path = path
        #A variable that keeps track of the current state of the
player;
        #None means no song is open, False means playing is paused,
and True means a song is playing
        self.playing = None
        #We will use this when coming out of pause in order to know
from what point the song should play
        self.pickup_time = 0
        #Create an image the size of the screen
        self.img = graphics.Image.new(sysinfo.display_pixels())
        #Instantiate a Canvas and set it as the application's body,
        #and bind the keys that control playback options
        self.canvas = appuifw.Canvas(redraw_callback=self.handle_re-
draw)
```

```
        self.canvas.bind(EKeyUpArrow, self.volume_up)
        self.canvas.bind(EKeyDownArrow, self.volume_down)
        self.canvas.bind(EKeySelect, self.play_pause)
        appuifw.app.body = self.canvas
        appuifw.app.menu = [(u"Pick song", self.select_song)]
        #Instantiate a timer that will be used for updating the info
displayed on the screen
        self.timer = e32.Ao_timer()
```

This is the constructor. The data that is needed right after the player starts is defined here. The current sound object, however, is only defined in the `play_pause()` method after a sound file is selected.

```
#This function finds all the sound files in a certain directory and
displays them as a list for the user to choose from
def select_song(self):
        self.list_of_songs = []
        for self.i in os.listdir(self.path):
                #Check if the extension is that of a sound file and if
it is, add the name to the list
                if self.i[-4:] in [".mp3", ".wav", ".wma"]:
                        self.list_of_songs.append(unicode(self.i))
        #Ask the user which file they want to play, if there are any
        if len(self.list_of_songs) > 0:
try:

self.file_name = self.list_of_songs[appuifw.selection_list(self.
list_of_songs)]
```

```
except TypeError: #Occurs when the user cancels the selection

pass

else:

appuifw.note(u"No appropriate sound files available", 'info')
```

We use this function to select a song to be played. It searches the directory at the specified path for files whose extension is that of a sound file and, when it finds one, it adds it to the list. The list is then displayed using a selection list, the user chooses a file, and thus the file name of the song to be played is established.

```
def volume_up(self):
    try:
        self.s.set_volume(self.s.current_volume() + 1)
    except:
        pass

def volume_down(self):
    try:
        self.s.set_volume(self.s.current_volume() - 1)
    except:
        pass
```

The preceding two functions handle modifying the volume. They are called when the up or down arrow keys are pressed. The volume is increased/decreased by one unit until it reaches maximum/0. Exceptions that may arise from trying to set the volume beyond maximum or below minimum or from trying to modify the volume when no sound object is defined (the `set_volume()` method belongs to a sound object) are handled with try... except statements.

```
def play_pause(self):
        if self.playing == False:
                self.s.set_position(self.pickup_time)
                self.playing = True
                self.s.play()
                self.show_info()
        elif self.playing == True:
                self.pickup_time = self.s.current_position()
                self.playing = False
                self.s.stop()
                self.timer.cancel()
        if self.playing == None:
                try: #If play is used before a song is selected, an error
occurs
        self.s = audio.Sound.open(self.path + "\\" + self.file_name)
                self.s = audio.Sound.open(self.path + "\\" + self.file_
name)
                self.playing = True
                self.s.play()
```

The player can be in one of three states at any given time:

- No sound file is currently open (self.playing == None). This means that either the player has just been loaded or that playback has been stopped.
- Playback is paused (self.playing == False).
- A sound file is playing (self.playing == True).

The `play_pause()` function handles switching between these states. When pausing the playback, the number of microseconds that have already been played is accessed with the `current_position()` method and stored in `self.pickup_time`, and the playback is stopped. In order to resume, we specify from where the file should start playing using the `set_position()` method, and we start playing the file. This approach is used because there is no predefined way of pausing and resuming playback.

```
def stop(self):
        appuifw.app.menu = [(u"Pick song", self.select_song)]
        self.s.stop()
        self.s.close()
        self.playing = None
        self.timer.cancel()
```

As the name suggests, this function is used to stop the playback. The sound file is closed, the menu is set to allow the user to pick a different song, and the timer that is used to update the information on the screen is canceled (updating the info when no song is playing would be pointless).

```
def show_info(self):
    #Calculate the values
    self.min1, self.sec1 = divmod((self.s.current_position() /
1000000), 60)
    self.min2, self.sec2 = divmod((self.s.duration() / 1000000),
60)
    #Give the values the standard format mm:ss
    if self.min1<10:
        self.info = u"0" + unicode(self.min1)
    else:
        self.info = unicode(self.min1)
    self.info += u":"
    if self.sec1<10:
        self.info += u"0" + unicode(self.sec1)
    else:
        self.info += unicode(self.sec1)
    self.info += u" - "
    if self.min2<10:
        self.info += u"0" + unicode(self.min2)
    else:
        self.info += unicode(self.min2)
    self.info += u":"
    if self.sec2<10:
        self.info += u"0" + unicode(self.sec2)
    else:
        self.info += unicode(self.sec2)
    #Clear the image so things don't overlap
```

```
        self.img.clear()
        #Calculate where to display the info so that it’s in the
center of the screen
        self.text_size = self.img.measure_text(self.file_name,
font=’title’)[0]
        self.text_width = self.text_size[2] - self.text_size[0]
        self.text_height = self.text_size[3] - self.text_size[1]
        self.text_x = (sysinfo.display_pixels()[0] / 2) - (self.
text_width / 2)
        self.text_y = (sysinfo.display_pixels()[1] / 2) - self.text_
height
        self.img.text((self.text_x, self.text_y), self.file_name,
font=’title’)
        self.text_size = self.img.measure_text(self.info,
font=’title’)[0]
        self.text_width = self.text_size[2] - self.text_size[0]
        self.text_height = self.text_size[3] - self.text_size[1]
        self.text_x = (sysinfo.display_pixels()[0] / 2) - (self.text_width / 2)
        Self.text_y = (sysinfo.display_pixels()[1] / 2) - self.text_height
        self.img.text((self.text_x, self.text_y + self.text_height), self.info,
font=’title’)
        self.handle_redraw(())
        #Update the info every second
        self.timer.after(1, self.show_info)
```

Here, we simply calculate the duration of the song and how far into it we are, and display the information along with the name of the file. The function is called every second with the help of the timer’s `after()` method.

The `measure_text()` method is used to determine how much space (in pixels) a certain text would take up if written in a certain font. The returned result contains a 4-element tuple with the coordinates of the top-left and bottom-right corners of the rectangle that would contain the text. We use the information to determine where to draw the text so that it appears in the middle of the screen. A complete description of the `measure_text()` method is available in the PyS60 documentation.

```
def __del__(self):
    try:
        self.s.stop()
        self.s.close()
    except:
        pass
```

An object's `__del__` method is called when that object is about to be destroyed. Here we close any open sound file.

7.9 Summary

This chapter outlined Python's graphics and multimedia capabilities. It showed how to draw primitive shapes, text and images to the screen using the graphics module, how to use the camera module to capture images and record videos, and how to use the audio module recording and playing sound files and for text to speech. The accompanying examples include a camera application supporting both video and still images (similar to those used on some real mobile devices), and a simple but credible music player.

8

Touch User Interface

This chapter explains how to write touch-aware applications for Symbian devices in Python, and how to support touch and non-touch devices with the same script.

8.1 Introduction

Touch-enabled user interfaces are more natural than interfaces that rely solely on hardware buttons or a keypad. While some applications work well with both types of interfaces, some applications are improved or are only usable if they have a touch interface.

The Symbian platform supports devices with and without touch interfaces. At the time of writing, popular 'touch' devices, based on Symbian^1, include:

- Nokia 5800 XpressMusic
- Nokia N97
- Samsung i8910 HD
- Sony Ericsson Satio
- Sony Ericsson Vivaz

This chapter explains how to detect whether touch is supported on the device, how to handle touch events from different regions of the screen in your canvas, and how Python will handle the case where overlapping touch screen event handlers have been declared. It is accompanied by a number of worked example applications and games that demonstrate how to create your own custom touch-enabled UI elements.

8.2 Supporting both touch and non-touch devices

Python applications that use only the basic user interface elements (e.g. notifications, list boxes, dialogs and so on) should not require any changes in order to run on touch-enabled devices. This is because events generated when the user touches a UI element are mapped to the same events that the application receives from physical key presses on a non-touch device.

Python on Symbian v2.0 provides explicit support for touch pointer events in the appuifw module's Canvas object. Applications that use a canvas for drawing can easily be made to work sensibly for both touch and non-touch devices by using an on-screen virtual directional keypad to simulate the action of the physical keypad, as discussed in the chapter on Graphics and Multimedia.

The following example shows how the virtual keypad can be enabled on touch devices only.

```
import appuifw
...
if appuifw.touch_enabled():
    appuifw.app.directional_pad=True;
else:
    appuifw.app.directional_pad=False;
...
```

The code above uses the `touch_enabled()` function to determine if the device is touch enabled, and returns `True` if touch UI is supported and `False` if not.

Applications that support custom touch-enabled `Canvas` elements can use this method conditionally to enable the code for touch devices.

8.3 Detecting touch events in full-screen mode

Python can detect four different touch events, which are referenced using key codes below (from `key_codes.py`):

- **`EButton1Down`** - Touch down event, sent when finger/stylus touches the screen
- **`EButton1Up`** - Touch up event, sent when finger/stylus is lifted from the screen
- **`EDrag`** – Drag event, sent when finger/stylus is dragged on the screen
- **`ESwitchOn`** - Tap screen event, sent when finger/stylus taps or double clicks the screen

In order to detect touch events, the Canvas binds an event handler to the required key codes, which is called whenever the specified event occurs. The approach is much the same as that used to bind key presses to the Canvas as we discussed in Chapter 7.

The following code snippet shows an application that will display a notification whenever the screen is touched. The Canvas binds to the `EButton1Down` event, but you can bind to other touch events by replacing `EButton1Down` with `EButton1Up` , `EDrag` or `ESwitchOn`.

```
import appuifw
import graphics
import e32
import key_codes #import key_codes - required for touch event de-
tection

# define white colour constant
RGB_WHITE =(255, 255, 255)

# change application screen size to 'full'
```

```
appuifw.app.screen = 'full'

def quit():
      '''Define quit function'''
      app_lock.signal()

def down_event(event):
      '''Pen DOWN event handler'''
      appuifw.note(u"Down Event")

#prepare canvas for drawing
canvas = appuifw.Canvas()
appuifw.app.body = canvas

#define right soft key as exit key
appuifw.app.exit_key_handler = quit

#clear canvas with white colour
canvas.clear(RGB_WHITE)

#bind canvas for touch event
canvas.bind(key_codes.EButton1Down, down_event)
#EButton1Up, EDrag and ESwitchOn could be used similarly

#Wait for user to exit
app_lock = e32.Ao_lock()
app_lock.wait()
```

In the above snippet, the `EButton1Down` event is bound to the `down_event()` function. The callback function can be replaced by calling the `bind()` function again with a different handler, or it can be cleared by specifying `None` as shown.

```
canvas.bind(key_codes.EButton1Down, None)
```

8.4 Detecting touch on a specific area

In the previous section, we showed how touch events can be detected on the full canvas. Detecting events on a specific area of the canvas is achieved by passing the top left and bottom right co-ordinates of the required region as additional parameters to the `bind()` call.

PyS60 doesn't offer any dedicated UI controls for buttons, but they can be provided as shapes drawn onto the canvas, and can be rounded, or even circular. The `bind()` approach only allows us to specify rectangular areas, so at the end of this section, we'll explain how to detect touch events in arbitrarily shaped regions.

8.4.1 Detecting a touch event within a rectangle

In order to detect a touch down event in a rectangle with top left corner co-ordinates (x1, y1) and bottom right corner co-ordinates (x2, y2), we would use:

```
canvas.bind(key_codes.EButton1Down, down_event,
((x1,y1),(x2,y2)))
```

The code snippet below illustrates how we detect each of the different touch events in a different area of the canvas/screen:

```
'''Detecting touch over a specific area of screen'''

import appuifw
import graphics
import e32
import key_codes #import key_codes - required for touch event de-
tection
```

```
# define colour constants
RGB_RED = (255, 0, 0)
RGB_GREEN = (0, 255, 0)
RGB_BLUE = (0, 0, 255)
RGB_PURPLE = (100,0,255)
RGB_BLACK = (0,0,0)

# disable directional pad
appuifw.app.directional_pad = False

#prepare canvas for drawing
canvas = appuifw.Canvas()
appuifw.app.body = canvas

#obtaining canvas size (Total_x and Total_y)
Total_x, Total_y = canvas.size
y1 = Total_y/4

def blue_down(event):
    ''' Blue DOWN event handler '''
    appuifw.note(u"Blue Down")

def green_up(event):
    ''' Green UP event handler '''
    appuifw.note(u"Green Up")

def red_drag(event):
    ''' Red DRAG event handler '''
    appuifw.note(u"Red Drag")

def purple_tap(event):
    ''' Purple TAP event handler '''
```

```
    appuifw.note(u"Purple Tap")

# Blue rectangle - DOWN Event
'''Draw Blue rectangle and text'''
canvas.rectangle(((0,0), (Total_x,y1)), fill=RGB_BLUE, width=5)
canvas.text((Total_x/2,y1/2), u"DOWN", fill = RGB_
BLACK,font=(u'Nokia Hindi S60',40,appuifw.STYLE_BOLD))
'''Bind DOWN to Blue rectangle'''
canvas.bind(key_codes.EButton1Down, blue_down, ((0,0),
(Total_x,y1)))

# Green rectangle - UP Event
'''Draw Green rectangle and text'''
canvas.rectangle(((0,y1), (Total_x,2*y1)), fill=RGB_GREEN, width=5)
canvas.text((Total_x/2,3*y1/2), u"UP", fill = RGB_
BLACK,font=(u'Nokia Hindi S60',40,appuifw.STYLE_BOLD))
'''Bind UP to Blue rectangle'''
canvas.bind(key_codes.EButton1Up, green_up, ((0,y1),
(Total_x,2*y1)))

# Red rectangle - DRAG Event
'''Draw Red rectangle and text'''
canvas.rectangle(((0,2*y1), (Total_x,3*y1)), fill=RGB_RED, width=5)
canvas.text((Total_x/2,5*y1/2), u"DRAG", fill = RGB_
BLACK,font=(u'Nokia Hindi S60',40,appuifw.STYLE_BOLD))
'''Bind DRAG to Red rectangle'''
canvas.bind(key_codes.EDrag, red_drag, ((0,2*y1), (Total_x,3*y1)))

# Purple rectangle - TAP Event
'''Draw Purple rectangle and text'''
canvas.rectangle(((0,3*y1), (Total_x,4*y1)), fill=RGB_PURPLE,
width=5)
canvas.text((Total_x/2,7*y1/2), u"TAP", fill = RGB_
```

```
BLACK,font=(u'Nokia Hindi S60',40,appuifw.STYLE_BOLD))
'''Bind TAP to Red rectangle'''
canvas.bind(key_codes.ESwitchOn, purple_tap, ((0,3*y1),
(Total_x,4*y1)))

#wait for user to exit
app_lock = e32.Ao_lock()
app_lock.wait()
```

When run, the example application looks like the screenshot shown in Figure 8.1. Each area of the screen responds to its specified type of event by displaying an information note. Note: If a drag event goes outside of a bound area, no drag events will be received.

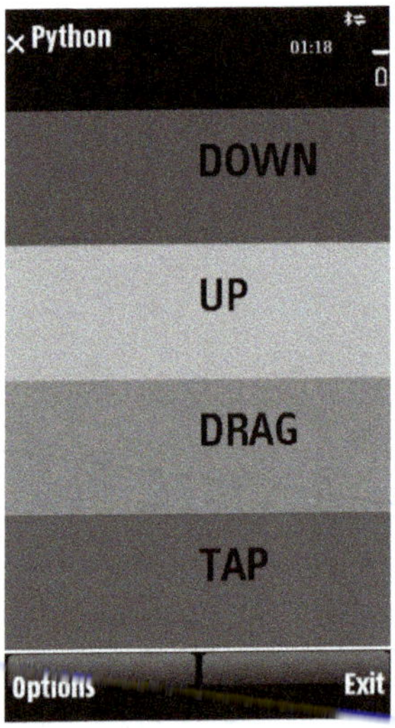

Figure 8.1 Event detection in four different canvas areas

8.4.2 Piano example (overlapping events)

Screen areas that bind to any oneparticular event keycode may overlap. Within the overlap region, only the callback function that was registered last will be called in response to an event. However, areas that bind to different event key-codes may overlap without issue, and both callbacks are invoked if both events occur in an overlap region.

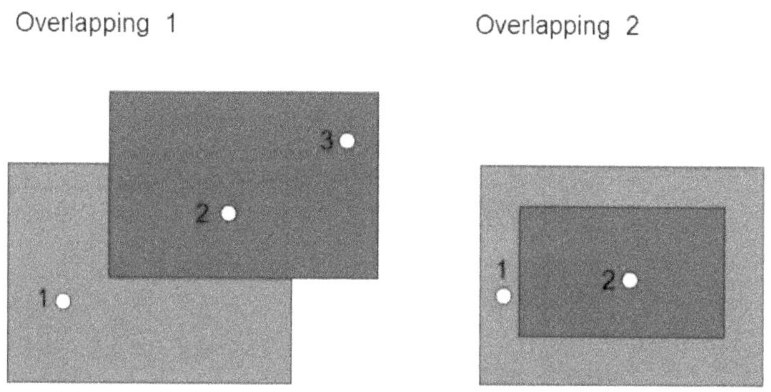

Figure 8.2 Overlapping areas

Consider the following examples:

For Overlapping 1:

- Touching on point 1 triggers the callback registered to the red rectangle.
- Touching on point 3 triggers the callback registered to the blue rectangle.
- Touching on point 2 (a region where overlap occurs) triggers the callback registered to the blue rectangle only.

For Overlapping 2:

- Touching on point 1 triggers the callback registered to the red rectangle.
- Touching on point 2 (a region where overlap occurs) triggers callback registered to the blue rectangle.

This is further illustrated with the example of a touch piano:

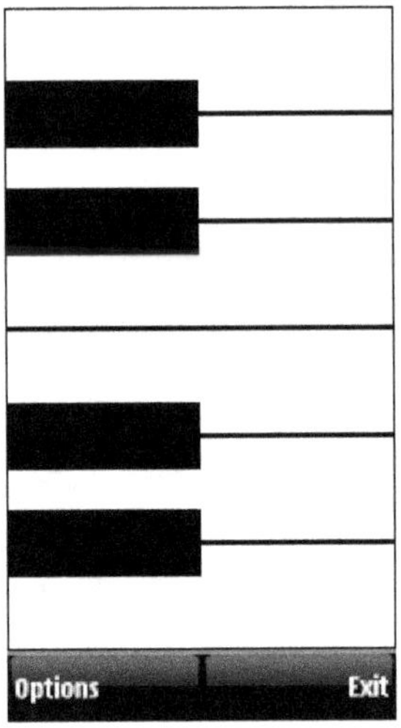

Figure 8.3 Touch Piano

The black keys overlap the white keys. To ensure that touching the overlapping area (black keys) triggers the callback functions registered to the respective black keys, we bind their event handlers last.

```
import appuifw
import graphics
import e32
import key_codes #import key_codes - required for touch event de-
tection
import audio

# define white colour constants
RGB_WHITE =(255, 255, 255)
RGB_BLACK =(0, 0, 0)

# define sound files
```

```
white1_sound= u"C:\\Data\\Sounds\\Digital\\white1.mp3"
white2_sound= u"C:\\Data\\Sounds\\Digital\\white2.mp3"
white3_sound= u"C:\\Data\\Sounds\\Digital\\white3.mp3"
white4_sound= u"C:\\Data\\Sounds\\Digital\\white4.mp3"
white5_sound= u"C:\\Data\\Sounds\\Digital\\white5.mp3"
white6_sound= u"C:\\Data\\Sounds\\Digital\\white6.mp3"
black1_sound= u"C:\\Data\\Sounds\\Digital\\black1.mp3"
black2_sound= u"C:\\Data\\Sounds\\Digital\\black2.mp3"
black3_sound= u"C:\\Data\\Sounds\\Digital\\black3.mp3"
black4_sound= u"C:\\Data\\Sounds\\Digital\\black4.mp3"

# change application screen size to 'full'
appuifw.app.screen = 'full'

# disable directional pad
appuifw.app.directional_pad = False

def quit():
	'''Define quit function'''
	app_lock.signal()
appuifw.app.exit_key_handler = quit

def white1(event):
	'''White1 callback function'''
	#The path of the file that is to be played when white1 is
touched
	s1 = audio.Sound.open(white2_sound)
	try: # Try to stop() - the file may be previously playing
		s1.stop()
		s1.play()
	except:
		s1.play()
```

```
def white2(event):
      '''White2 callback function'''
      #The path of the file that is to be played when white1 is
touched
      s2 = audio.Sound.open(white2_sound)
      try: # Try to stop() - the file may be previously playing
            s2.stop()
            s2.play()
      except:
            s2.play()

def white3(event):
      '''White3 callback function'''
      #The path of the file that is to be played when white1 is
touched
      s3 = audio.Sound.open(white3_sound)
      try: # Try to stop() - the file may be previously playing
            s3.stop()
            s3.play()
      except:
            s3.play()

def white4(event):
      '''White4 callback function'''
      #The path of the file that is to be played when white1 is
touched
      s4 = audio.Sound.open(white4_sound)
      try: # Try to stop() - the file may be previously playing
            s4.stop()
            s4.play()
      except:
            s4.play()
```

```
def white5(event):
	'''White5 callback function'''
	#The path of the file that is to be played when white1 is 
touched
	s5 = audio.Sound.open(white5_sound)
	try: # Try to stop() - the file may be previously playing
		s5.stop()
		s5.play()
	except:
		s5.play()

def white6(event):
	'''White6 callback function'''
	#The path of the file that is to be played when white1 is 
touched
	s6 = audio.Sound.open(white6_sound)
	try: # Try to stop() - the file may be previously playing
		s6.stop()
		s6.play()
	except:
		s6.play()

def black1(event):
	'''Black1 callback function'''
	#The path of the file that is to be played when white1 is 
touched
	s7 = audio.Sound.open(black1_sound)
	try: # Try to stop() - the file may be previously playing
		s7.stop()
		s7.play()
	except:
		s7.play()
```

```
def black2(event):
	'''Black2 callback function'''
	#The path of the file that is to be played when white1 is
touched
	s8 = audio.Sound.open(black2_sound)
	try: # Try to stop() - the file may be previously playing
		s8.stop()
		s8.play()
	except:
		s8.play()

def black3(event):
	'''Black3 callback function'''
	#The path of the file that is to be played when white1 is
touched
	s9 = audio.Sound.open(black3_sound)
	try: # Try to stop() - the file may be previously playing
		s9.stop()
		s9.play()
	except:
		s9.play()

def black4(event):
	'''Black4 callback function'''
	#The path of the file that is to be played when white1 is
touched
	s10 = audio.Sound.open(black4_sound)
	try: # Try to stop() - the file may be previously playing
		s10.stop()
		s10.play()
	except:
		s10.play()
```

```
#prepare canvas for drawing
canvas = appuifw.Canvas()
appuifw.app.body = canvas

#define right soft key as exit key
appuifw.app.exit_key_handler = quit

Total_x, Total_y = canvas.size
y1 = Total_y/6

#clear canvas with white colour
canvas.clear(RGB_WHITE)

#White Key #1 - Draw and bind touch Pen down event
canvas.rectangle(((0,0), (Total_x,y1)), outline=RGB_BLACK,
fill=RGB_WHITE, width=3)
canvas.bind(key_codes.EButton1Down, white1, ((0,0), (Total_x,y1)))

#White Key #2 - Draw and bind touch Pen down event
canvas.rectangle(((0,y1), (Total_x,2*y1)),outline=RGB_BLACK,
fill=RGB_WHITE, width=3)
canvas.bind(key_codes.EButton1Down, white2, ((0,y1),
(Total_x,2*y1)))

#White Key #3 - Draw and bind touch Pen down event
canvas.rectangle(((0,2*y1), (Total_x,3*y1)), outline=RGB_BLACK,
fill=RGB_WHITE, width=3)
canvas.bind(key_codes.EButton1Down, white3, ((0,y1),
(Total_x,2*y1)))

#White Key #4 - Draw and bind touch Pen down event
canvas.rectangle(((0,3*y1), (Total_x,4*y1)), outline=RGB_
BLACK,fill=RGB_WHITE, width=3)
```

```
canvas.bind(key_codes.EButton1Down, white4, ((0,3*y1),
(Total_x,4*y1)))

#White Key #5 - Draw and bind touch Pen down event
canvas.rectangle(((0,4*y1), (Total_x,5*y1)), outline=RGB_
BLACK,fill=RGB_WHITE, width=3)
canvas.bind(key_codes.EButton1Down, white5, ((0,4*y1),
(Total_x,5*y1)))

#White Key #6 - Draw and bind touch Pen down event
canvas.rectangle(((0,5*y1), (Total_x,6*y1)), outline=RGB_
BLACK,fill=RGB_WHITE, width=3)
canvas.bind(key_codes.EButton1Down, white6, ((0,5*y1),
(Total_x,6*y1)))

#Black Key #1 - Draw and bind touch Pen down event
canvas.rectangle(((0,y1-30), (Total_x/2,y1+30)), fill=RGB_BLACK,
width=3)
canvas.bind(key_codes.EButton1Down, black1, ((0,y1-30),
(Total_x/2,y1+30)))

#Black Key #2 - Draw and bind touch Pen down event
canvas.rectangle(((0,2*y1-30), (Total_x/2,2*y1+30)), fill=RGB_
BLACK, width=3)
canvas.bind(key_codes.EButton1Down, black2, ((0,2*y1-30),
(Total_x/2,2*y1+30)))

#Black Key #3 - Draw and bind touch Pen down event
canvas.rectangle(((0,4*y1-30), (Total_x/2,4*y1+30)), fill=RGB_
BLACK, width=3)
canvas.bind(key_codes.EButton1Down, black3, ((0,4*y1-30),
(Total_x/2,4*y1+30)))
```

```
#Black Key #4 - Draw and bind touch Pen down event
canvas.rectangle(((0,5*y1-30), (Total_x/2,5*y1+30)), fill=RGB_
BLACK, width=3)
canvas.bind(key_codes.EButton1Down, black4, ((0,5*y1-30),
(Total_x/2,5*y1+30)))

#Wait for user to exit
app_lock = e32.Ao_lock()
app_lock.wait()
```

8.4.3 Detecting touch events in arbitrary regions

The `bind()` function lets us receive touch events that occur in a rectangular area. But what do we do when we want to use other shapes, for example, buttons that have rounded edges, or some other arbitrary shape?

There are three basic approaches that we can use:

- We can approximate the area using a single rectangle, which not very nice, but may be acceptable for a slightly rounded rectangular button
- We can build up the required polygon using a number of overlapping or adjacent rectangles
- We can detect events in the bounding rectangle of our shape, and then, within the callback function, determine whether the touch event was inside the customized shape.

The following code snippet demonstrates the third approach, using the example of a circular area in which we want to detect touch events.

```
import appuifw
import graphics
import e32
import key_codes #import key_codes - required for touch event de-
tection
```

```
import math

# define colour constants
RGB_BLUE = (0, 0, 255)

# disable directional pad
appuifw.app.directional_pad = False

#prepare canvas for drawing
canvas = appuifw.Canvas()
appuifw.app.body = canvas

#obtaining canvas size (Total_x and Total_y)
Total_x, Total_y = canvas.size

# define circle centre co-ordinates and radius
circle_x=Total_x/2
circle_y=Total_y/2
radius=100

def calculate(centre, radius):
      '''Function to calculate co-ordinates of the circle'''
      return ((centre[0]-radius, centre[1]-radius),
(centre[0]+radius, centre[1]+radius))

def blue_down(pos):
    ''' Blue DOWN event handler '''
    global circle_x,circle_y, radius
      # Use the 'distance formula' to check if the touched posi-
tion is within the circle
    distance=math.hypot(pos[0]-circle_x, pos[1]-circle_y)
    if distance<=radius:
            appuifw.note(u"Circle touched")
```

```
# Blue rectangle - DOWN Event
'''Draw Blue rectangle and text'''
canvas.ellipse((calculate((circle_x, circle_y), radius)), fill=RGB_
BLUE)
canvas.bind(key_codes.EButton1Down, blue_down)

#wait for user to exit
app_lock = e32.Ao_lock()
app_lock.wait()
```

The `blue_down(pos)` function is called if a touch event is called anywhere within the bounding rectangle of the circle, and it uses the position of the touch and the radius of the circle to determine whether the touch occured inside the circle. If so, it displays an information note.

Figure 8.4 shows the code above in action.

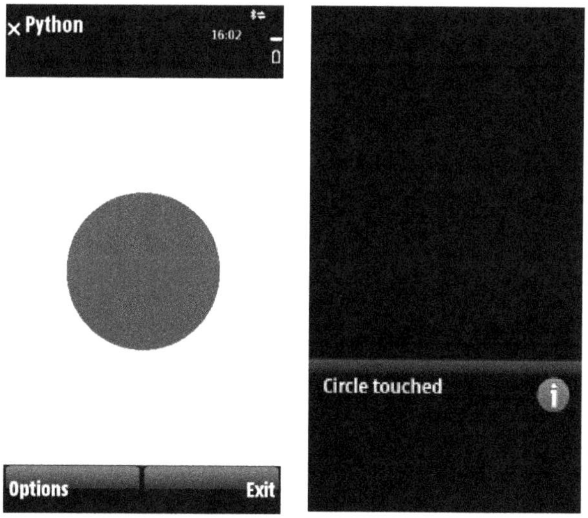

Figure 8.4 Circular touch areas

8.5 Painting with Touch

Using what we learned in this chapter and in the earlier chapters, let's make a simple application similar to 'Paint' on Windows.

First, we prepare a blank canvas (as in previous examples). Then we draw a point where we detect any touch event on the canvas. Since we need to detect more than one event type on the same area (full canvas) – we use the default `event_callback()` function of the canvas instead of binding to a single event.

```
canvas = appuifw.Canvas(event_callback=handle_event, redraw_
callback=handle_redraw)
appuifw.app.body = canvas
appuifw.app.exit_key_handler = quit
```

Whenever the canvas is touched, `handle_event` is called, and receives the event information passed as an argument. The event information is a dictionary containing the details related to the pointer event. It has the following format (which remains unchanged for non-touch devices):

- 'type': one of the several pointer events - `EButton1Down`, `EButton1Up`, `EDrag`, `ESwitchOn`
- 'modifiers': the modifiers that apply to this pointer event
- 'pos': a tuple containing the x-y pointer co-ordinates

In the `handle_event()` function, we detect the touch event and draw a point:

```
def handle_event(event):
    if event['type'] not in (key_codes.EButton1Up, key_codes.
EButton1Down,key_codes.EDrag):
        return
    canvas.point((event['pos'][0], event['pos'][1]),outline=RGB_
RED,width=10)
```

This first implementation of the paint application did not quite work as expected. Since we didn't get an event at every point, we didn't draw a continuous line, as shown in Figure 8.5.

Figure 8.5 Touchy Paint

In order to fix this, we modify the `handle_event()` function as shown below. This simply ensures that for a `EDrag` event we draw a line from the previous touched co-ordinate to the received dragged co-ordinate. We also draw two points when we detect touch to improve the resolution of drawing on the screen.

```
def handle_event(event):
      if event['type'] not in (key_codes.EButton1Up, key_codes.
EButton1Down,key_codes.EDrag):
            return
      if event['type'] in (key_codes.EButton1Down, key_codes.EBut-
ton1Up):
            canvas.point((event['pos'][0], event['pos']
[1]),outline=RGB_RED,width=10)
            canvas.point((event['pos'][0], event['pos']
[1]),outline=RGB_RED,width=10)
            prev_pos[0]=event['pos'][0]
```

```
            prev_pos[1]=event['pos'][1]

            #appuifw.note(u"Green Down")
      elif event['type'] ==key_codes.EDrag:
            rect=(prev_pos[0], prev_pos[1],event['pos'][0],
event['pos'][1])
            canvas.line(rect, outline=RGB_RED, width=10,fill=RGB_
RED)
            prev_pos[0]=event['pos'][0]
            prev_pos[1]=event['pos'][1]
```

The complete code of the paint application is as follows, with a screenshot in Figure 8.6.

```
import appuifw
import graphics
import e32
import key_codes #import key_codes - required for touch event de-
tection

# disable directional pad
appuifw.app.directional_pad=False;

# define colour constants
RGB_RED = (255, 0, 0)
RGB_GREEN = (0, 255, 0)
RGB_BLUE = (0, 0, 255)
RGB_WHITE =(255, 255, 255)

canvas=None
global prev_pos
prev_pos=[0,0]
```

```
# change application screen size to 'full'
appuifw.app.screen = 'large'

def handle_redraw(event):
'''Define redraw function'''
   pass

def handle_event(event):
        '''Define event callback function'''
      if event['type'] not in (key_codes.EButton1Up, key_codes.
EButton1Down,key_codes.EDrag):
            return
      if event['type'] in (key_codes.EButton1Down, key_codes.EBut-
ton1Up):
            canvas.point((event['pos'][0], event['pos']
[1]),outline=RGB_RED,width=10)
            canvas.point((event['pos'][0], event['pos']
[1]),outline=RGB_RED,width=10)
            prev_pos[0]=event['pos'][0]
            prev_pos[1]=event['pos'][1]
      if event['type'] ==key_codes.EDrag:
            rect=(prev_pos[0], prev_pos[1],event['pos'][0],
event['pos'][1])
            canvas.line(rect, outline=RGB_RED, width=10,fill=RGB_
RED)
            prev_pos[0]=event['pos'][0]
            prev_pos[1]=event['pos'][1]

canvas = appuifw.Canvas(event_callback=handle_event, redraw_
callback=handle_redraw)
appuifw.app.body = canvas
appuifw.app.exit_key_handler = quit
```

```
# Clear the canvas
canvas.clear(RGB_WHITE)

app_lock = e32.Ao_lock()
app_lock.wait()
```

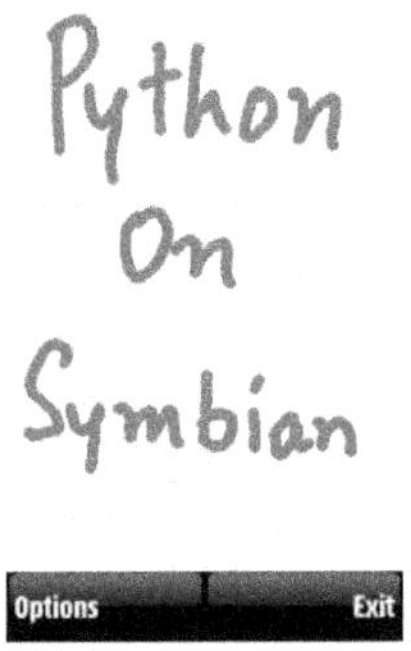

Figure 8.6 Touchy Paint

8.6 Touchy Tic-Tac-Toe

We finish up this chapter with a quick and easy game - Tic-Tac-Toe (***en.wikipedia.org/wiki/Tic-tac-toe***).

```
import appuifw
import graphics
import e32
import key_codes #import key_codes - required for touch event de-
tection

# define colour constants
RGB_RED = (255, 0, 0)
RGB_GREEN = (0, 255, 0)
RGB_BLUE = (0, 0, 255)
```

```
RGB_BLACK=(0,0,0)

# define board colour
board_colour=RGB_BLUE

# define flag variables
turn_flag="Cross"
flag_rect1=None
flag_rect2=None
flag_rect3=None
flag_rect4=None
flag_rect5=None
flag_rect6=None
flag_rect7=None
flag_rect8=None
flag_rect9=None

def handle_redraw(event):
      pass

# disable directional pad
appuifw.app.directional_pad = False

canvas = appuifw.Canvas(redraw_callback=handle_redraw)
appuifw.app.body = canvas

Total_x, Total_y = canvas.size

RectWidth=Total_x/3
RectHeight=Total_y/3
print RectWidth,RectHeight

def draw_cross(pos, cross_colour):
```

```
        '''Function to draw a cross - on the co-ordinates passed
as arguments'''
      cross_length=30
      cross_width=15
      a=pos[0]-cross_length
      b=pos[1]-cross_length
      while a<=pos[0]+cross_length:
            canvas.point((a,b), width=cross_width, outline=cross_
colour)
            a+=1
            b+=1
      a=pos[0]+cross_length
      b=pos[1]-cross_length
      while a>=pos[0]-cross_length and b<=pos[1]+cross_length:
            canvas.point((a,b), width=cross_width, outline=cross_
colour)
            a-=1
            b+=1

def check_winner():
        '''Function to check the winner after each turn'''
      global flag_rect1,flag_rect2,flag_rect3,flag_rect4,flag_
rect5,flag_rect6,flag_rect7,flag_rect8,flag_rect9
      if flag_rect1=="Cross" and flag_rect2=="Cross" and flag_
rect3=="Cross":
            appuifw.note(u"Cross wins!")
      elif flag_rect1=="Zero" and flag_rect2=="Zero" and flag_
rect3=="Zero":
            appuifw.note(u"Zero wins!")
      elif flag_rect1=="Cross" and flag_rect4=="Cross" and flag_
rect7=="Cross":
            appuifw.note(u"Cross wins!")
      elif flag_rect1=="Zero" and flag_rect4=="Zero" and flag_
```

```
rect7=="Zero":
            appuifw.note(u"Zero wins!")
      elif flag_rect1=="Cross" and flag_rect5=="Cross" and flag_
rect9=="Cross":
            appuifw.note(u"Cross wins!")
      elif flag_rect1=="Zero" and flag_rect5=="Zero" and flag_
rect9=="Zero":
            appuifw.note(u"Zero wins!")
      elif flag_rect2=="Cross" and flag_rect5=="Cross" and flag_
rect8=="Cross":
            appuifw.note(u"Cross wins!")
      elif flag_rect2=="Zero" and flag_rect5=="Zero" and flag_
rect8=="Zero":
            appuifw.note(u"Zero wins!")
      elif flag_rect3=="Cross" and flag_rect6=="Cross" and flag_
rect9=="Cross":
            appuifw.note(u"Cross wins!")
      elif flag_rect3=="Zero" and flag_rect6=="Zero" and flag_
rect9=="Zero":
            appuifw.note(u"Zero wins!")
      elif flag_rect3=="Cross" and flag_rect5=="Cross" and flag_
rect7=="Cross":
            appuifw.note(u"Cross wins!")
      elif flag_rect3=="Zero" and flag_rect5=="Zero" and flag_
rect7=="Zero":
            appuifw.note(u"Zero wins!")
      elif flag_rect1=="Cross" and flag_rect2=="Cross" and flag_
rect3=="Cross":
            appuifw.note(u"Cross wins!")
      elif flag_rect1=="Zero" and flag_rect2=="Zero" and flag_
rect3=="Zero":
            appuifw.note(u"Zero wins!")
      elif flag_rect4=="Cross" and flag_rect5=="Cross" and flag_
```

```
rect6=="Cross":
            appuifw.note(u"Cross wins!")
      elif flag_rect4=="Zero" and flag_rect5=="Zero" and flag_
rect6=="Zero":
            appuifw.note(u"Zero wins!")
      elif flag_rect7=="Cross" and flag_rect8=="Cross" and flag_
rect9=="Cross":
            appuifw.note(u"Cross wins!")
      elif flag_rect7=="Zero" and flag_rect8=="Zero" and flag_
rect9=="Zero":
            appuifw.note(u"Zero wins!")

def down(pos):
    ''' Event handler '''
    global turn_flag, flag_rect1,flag_rect2,flag_rect3,flag_rect4,flag_
rect5,flag_rect6,flag_rect7,flag_rect8,flag_rect9
    if 0<pos[0]<RectWidth and 0<pos[1]<RectHeight:

        if flag_rect1 not in ("Cross", "Zero"):
                 if turn_flag=="Cross":
                       draw_cross(pos, RGB_GREEN)
                       flag_rect1="Cross"
                       turn_flag="Zero"
                 else:
                       canvas.point(pos,0x00ff00,width=50)
                       flag_rect1="Zero"
                       turn_flag="Cross"
                 check_winner()
    elif RectWidth<pos[0]<2*RectWidth and 0<pos[1]<RectHeight:

        if flag_rect2 not in ("Cross", "Zero"):
                 if turn_flag=="Cross":
                       draw_cross(pos, RGB_GREEN)
```

```
                    flag_rect2="Cross"
                    turn_flag="Zero"
                else:
                    canvas.point(pos,0x00ff00,width=50)
                    flag_rect2="Zero"
                    turn_flag="Cross"
                check_winner()
    elif 2*RectWidth<pos[0]<3*RectWidth and 0<pos[1]<RectHeight:

        if flag_rect3 not in ("Cross", "Zero"):
                if turn_flag=="Cross":
                    draw_cross(pos, RGB_GREEN)
                    flag_rect3="Cross"
                    turn_flag="Zero"
                else:
                    canvas.point(pos,0x00ff00,width=50)
                    flag_rect3="Zero"
                    turn_flag="Cross"
                check_winner()
    elif 0<pos[0]<RectWidth and RectHeight<pos[1]<2*RectHeight:

        if flag_rect4 not in ("Cross", "Zero"):
                if turn_flag=="Cross":
                    draw_cross(pos, RGB_GREEN)
                    flag_rect4="Cross"
                    turn_flag="Zero"
                else:
                    canvas.point(pos,0x00ff00,width=50)
                    flag_rect4="Zero"
                    turn_flag="Cross"
                check_winner()
                print turn_flag, flag_rect4
    elif RectWidth<pos[0]<(2*RectWidth) and
```

```
RectHeight<pos[1]<2*RectHeight:

        if flag_rect5 not in ("Cross", "Zero"):
                  if turn_flag=="Cross":
                        draw_cross(pos, RGB_GREEN)
                        flag_rect5="Cross"
                        turn_flag="Zero"
                  else:
                        canvas.point(pos,0x00ff00,width=50)
                        flag_rect5="Zero"
                        turn_flag="Cross"
                  check_winner()
    elif 2*RectWidth<pos[0]<3*RectWidth and
RectWidth<pos[1]<2*RectHeight:

        if flag_rect6 not in ("Cross", "Zero"):
                  if turn_flag=="Cross":
                        draw_cross(pos, RGB_GREEN)
                        flag_rect6="Cross"
                        turn_flag="Zero"
                  else:
                        canvas.point(pos,0x00ff00,width=50)
                        flag_rect6="Zero"
                        turn_flag="Cross"
                  check_winner()
    elif 0<pos[0]<RectWidth and 2*RectHeight<pos[1]<3*RectHeight:

        if flag_rect7 not in ("Cross", "Zero"):
                  if turn_flag=="Cross":
                        draw_cross(pos, RGB_GREEN)
                        flag_rect7="Cross"
                        turn_flag="Zero"
                  else:
```

```
                canvas.point(pos,0x00ff00,width=50)
                flag_rect7="Zero"
                turn_flag="Cross"
            check_winner()

    elif RectWidth<pos[0]<2*RectWidth and 2*RectHeight<pos[1]<3*Re
ctHeight:

        if flag_rect8 not in ("Cross", "Zero"):
            if turn_flag=="Cross":
                draw_cross(pos, RGB_GREEN)
                flag_rect8="Cross"
                turn_flag="Zero"
            else:
                canvas.point(pos,0x00ff00,width=50)
                flag_rect8="Zero"
                turn_flag="Cross"
            check_winner()

    elif 2*RectWidth<pos[0]<3*RectWidth and 2*RectHeight<pos[1]<3*
RectHeight:

        if flag_rect9 not in ("Cross", "Zero"):
            if turn_flag=="Cross":
                draw_cross(pos, RGB_GREEN)
                flag_rect9="Cross"
                turn_flag="Zero"
            else:
                canvas.point(pos,0x00ff00,width=50)
                flag_rect9="Zero"
                turn_flag="Cross"
            check_winner()
```

```
# Draw rectangles #1 #2 and #3
canvas.bind(key_codes.EButton1Down, down, ((0,0),
(RectWidth,RectHeight)))
canvas.bind(key_codes.EButton1Down, down, ((RectWidth,0),
(2*RectWidth,RectHeight)))
canvas.bind(key_codes.EButton1Down, down, ((2*RectWidth,0),
(3*RectWidth,RectHeight)))
canvas.rectangle(((0,0), (RectWidth,RectHeight)), fill=board_co-
lour, width=5,outline=RGB_BLACK)
canvas.rectangle(((RectWidth,0), (2*RectWidth,RectHeight)),
fill=board_colour, width=5, outline=RGB_BLACK)
canvas.rectangle(((2*RectWidth,0), (3*RectWidth,RectHeight)),
fill=board_colour, width=5,outline=RGB_BLACK)

# Draw rectangles #4 #5 and #6
canvas.bind(key_codes.EButton1Down, down, ((0,RectHeight),
(RectWidth,2*RectHeight)))
canvas.bind(key_codes.EButton1Down, down, ((RectWidth,RectHeight),
(2*RectWidth,2*RectHeight)))
canvas.bind(key_codes.EButton1Down, down,
((2*RectWidth,RectHeight), (3*RectWidth,2*RectHeight)))
canvas.rectangle(((0,RectHeight), (RectWidth,2*RectHeight)),
fill=board_colour, width=5,outline=RGB_BLACK)
canvas.rectangle(((RectWidth,RectHeight)
, (2*RectWidth,2*RectHeight)), fill=board_colour,
width=5,outline=RGB_BLACK)
canvas.rectangle(((2*RectWidth,RectHeight),
(3*RectWidth,2*RectHeight)), fill=board_colour,
width=5,outline=RGB_BLACK)

# Draw rectangles #7 #8 and #9
canvas.bind(key_codes.EButton1Down, down, ((0,2*RectHeight),
(RectWidth,3*RectHeight)))
```

```
canvas.bind(key_codes.EButton1Down, down,
((RectWidth,2*RectHeight), (2*RectWidth,3*RectHeight)))
canvas.bind(key_codes.EButton1Down, down,
((2*RectWidth,2*RectHeight), (3*RectWidth,3*RectHeight)))
canvas.rectangle(((0,2*RectHeight), (RectWidth,3*RectHeight)),
fill=board_colour, width=5,outline=RGB_BLACK)
canvas.rectangle(((RectWidth,2*RectHeight),
(2*RectWidth,3*RectHeight)), fill=board_colour,
width=5,outline=RGB_BLACK)
canvas.rectangle(((2*RectWidth,2*RectHeight),
(3*RectWidth,3*RectHeight)), fill=board_colour,
width=5,outline=RGB_BLACK)

app_lock = e32.Ao_lock()
app_lock.wait()
```

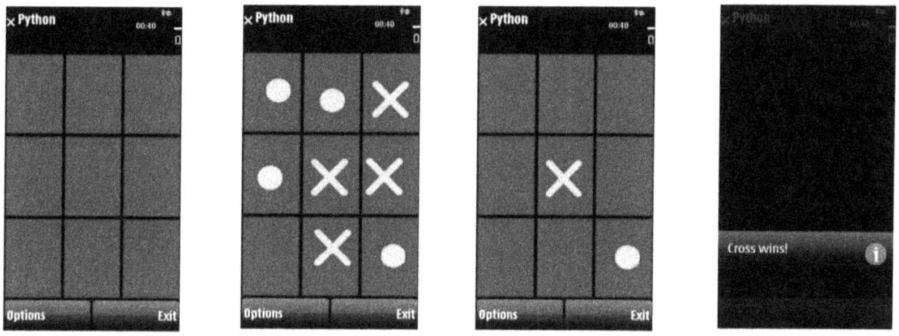

Figure 8.7 Tic-Tac-Toe

Let's go through this code in pieces. After importing the required modules, the color constants and flags used in the game are initialized.

```
# define colour constants
RGB_RED = (255, 0, 0)
RGB_GREEN = (0, 255, 0)
RGB_BLUE = (0, 0, 255)
RGB_BLACK=(0,0,0)

# define board colour
board_colour=RGB_BLUE

# define flag variables
turn_flag="Cross"
flag_rect1=None
flag_rect2=None
flag_rect3=None
flag_rect4=None
flag_rect5=None
flag_rect6=None
flag_rect7=None
flag_rect8=None
flag_rect9=None
```

In this example, we need to draw two shapes: a circle and cross. The circle is quite simple and can be achieved by a single line. Drawing a cross is a little more complex so we define a function to do this whenever needed, called `draw_cross(pos, cross_colour)`.

```
def draw_cross(pos, cross_colour):
        '''Function to draw a cross - on the co-ordinates passed
as arguments'''
      cross_length=30
      cross_width=15
      a=pos[0]-cross_length
      b=pos[1]-cross_length
```

```
    while a<=pos[0]+cross_length:
        canvas.point((a,b), width=cross_width, outline=cross_
colour)
        a+=1
        b+=1
    a=pos[0]+cross_length
    b=pos[1]-cross_length
    while a>=pos[0]-cross_length and b<=pos[1]+cross_length:
        canvas.point((a,b), width=cross_width, outline=cross_
colour)
        a-=1
        b+=1
```

down(pos) is the callback function that we bind to the down touch events. Here we check if the last shape drawn was a circle or a cross and accordingly draw the other one (since the players take turns to choose a square). A circle is drawn the first time the code is run because was initialized as 'Cross'.

```
def down(pos):
    ''' Event handler '''
    global turn_flag, flag_rect1,flag_rect2,flag_rect3,flag_rect4,flag_
rect5,flag_rect6,flag_rect7,flag_rect8,flag_rect9
    if 0<pos[0]<RectWidth and 0<pos[1]<RectHeight:

        if flag_rect1 not in ("Cross", "Zero"):
            if turn_flag=="Cross":
                draw_cross(pos, RGB_GREEN)
                flag_rect1="Cross"
                turn_flag="Zero"
            else:
                canvas.point(pos,0x00ff00,width=50)
                flag_rect1="Zero"
                turn_flag="Cross"
```

```
            check_winner()
    elif RectWidth<pos[0]<2*RectWidth and 0<pos[1]<RectHeight:

        if flag_rect2 not in ("Cross", "Zero"):
            if turn_flag=="Cross":
                draw_cross(pos, RGB_GREEN)
                flag_rect2="Cross"
                turn_flag="Zero"
            else:
                canvas.point(pos,0x00ff00,width=50)
                flag_rect2="Zero"
                turn_flag="Cross"
            check_winner()
    elif 2*RectWidth<pos[0]<3*RectWidth and 0<pos[1]<RectHeight:

        if flag_rect3 not in ("Cross", "Zero"):
            if turn_flag=="Cross":
                draw_cross(pos, RGB_GREEN)
                flag_rect3="Cross"
                turn_flag="Zero"
            else:
                canvas.point(pos,0x00ff00,width=50)
                flag_rect3="Zero"
                turn_flag="Cross"
            check_winner()
    elif 0<pos[0]<RectWidth and RectHeight<pos[1]<2*RectHeight:

        if flag_rect4 not in ("Cross", "Zero"):
            if turn_flag=="Cross":
                draw_cross(pos, RGB_GREEN)
                flag_rect4="Cross"
                turn_flag="Zero"
            else:
```

```
                        canvas.point(pos,0x00ff00,width=50)
                        flag_rect4="Zero"
                        turn_flag="Cross"
                check_winner()
                print turn_flag, flag_rect4
    elif RectWidth<pos[0]<2*RectWidth and
RectHeight<pos[1]<2*RectHeight:

        if flag_rect5 not in ("Cross", "Zero"):
                if turn_flag=="Cross":
                        draw_cross(pos, RGB_GREEN)
                        flag_rect5="Cross"
                        turn_flag="Zero"
                else:
                        canvas.point(pos,0x00ff00,width=50)
                        flag_rect5="Zero"
                        turn_flag="Cross"
                check_winner()
    elif 2*RectWidth<pos[0]<3*RectWidth and
RectWidth<pos[1]<2*RectHeight:

        if flag_rect6 not in ("Cross", "Zero"):
                if turn_flag=="Cross":
                        draw_cross(pos, RGB_GREEN)
                        flag_rect6="Cross"
                        turn_flag="Zero"
                else:
                        canvas.point(pos,0x00ff00,width=50)
                        flag_rect6="Zero"
                        turn_flag="Cross"
                check_winner()
    elif 0<pos[0]<RectWidth and 2*RectHeight<pos[1]<3*RectHeight:
```

```
        if flag_rect7 not in ("Cross", "Zero"):
                if turn_flag=="Cross":
                        draw_cross(pos, RGB_GREEN)
                        flag_rect7="Cross"
                        turn_flag="Zero"
                else:
                        canvas.point(pos,0x00ff00,width=50)
                        flag_rect7="Zero"
                        turn_flag="Cross"
                check_winner()

    elif RectWidth<pos[0]<2*RectWidth and 2*RectHeight<pos[1]<3*Re
ctHeight:

        if flag_rect8 not in ("Cross", "Zero"):
                if turn_flag=="Cross":
                        draw_cross(pos, RGB_GREEN)
                        flag_rect8="Cross"
                        turn_flag="Zero"
                else:
                        canvas.point(pos,0x00ff00,width=50)
                        flag_rect8="Zero"
                        turn_flag="Cross"
                check_winner()

    elif 2*RectWidth<pos[0]<3*RectWidth and 2*RectHeight<pos[1]<3*
RectHeight:

        if flag_rect9 not in ("Cross", "Zero"):
                if turn_flag=="Cross":
                        draw_cross(pos, RGB_GREEN)
                        flag_rect9="Cross"
                        turn_flag="Zero"
```

```
            else:
                  canvas.point(pos,0x00ff00,width=50)
                  flag_rect9="Zero"
                  turn_flag="Cross"
            check_winner()
```

After drawing each shape (Cross or Zero), we call the function. This checks if there are 3 correctly aligned zeros or crosses, and if so, declares the winner using a note.

```
def check_winner():
        '''Function to check the winner after each turn'''
      global flag_rect1,flag_rect2,flag_rect3,flag_rect4,flag_
rect5,flag_rect6,flag_rect7,flag_rect8,flag_rect9
      if flag_rect1=="Cross" and flag_rect2=="Cross" and flag_
rect3=="Cross"):
            appuifw.note(u"Cross wins!")
      elif flag_rect1=="Zero" and flag_rect2=="Zero" and flag_
rect3=="Zero":
            appuifw.note(u"Zero wins!")
      elif flag_rect1=="Cross" and flag_rect4=="Cross" and flag_
rect7=="Cross":
            appuifw.note(u"Cross wins!")
      elif flag_rect1=="Zero" and flag_rect4=="Zero" and flag_
rect7=="Zero":
            appuifw.note(u"Zero wins!")
      elif flag_rect1=="Cross" and flag_rect5=="Cross" and flag_
rect9=="Cross":
            appuifw.note(u"Cross wins!")
      elif flag_rect1=="Zero" and flag_rect5=="Zero" and flag_
rect9=="Zero":
            appuifw.note(u"Zero wins!")
```

```
    elif flag_rect2=="Cross" and flag_rect5=="Cross" and flag_
rect8=="Cross":
            appuifw.note(u"Cross wins!")
    elif flag_rect2=="Zero" and flag_rect5=="Zero" and flag_
rect8=="Zero":
            appuifw.note(u"Zero wins!")
    elif flag_rect3=="Cross" and flag_rect6=="Cross" and flag_
rect9=="Cross":
            appuifw.note(u"Cross wins!")
    elif flag_rect3=="Zero" and flag_rect6=="Zero" and flag_
rect9=="Zero":
            appuifw.note(u"Zero wins!")
    elif flag_rect3=="Cross" and flag_rect5=="Cross" and flag_
rect7=="Cross":
            appuifw.note(u"Cross wins!")
    elif flag_rect3=="Zero" and flag_rect5=="Zero" and flag_
rect7=="Zero":
            appuifw.note(u"Zero wins!")
    elif flag_rect1=="Cross" and flag_rect2=="Cross" and flag_
rect3=="Cross":
            appuifw.note(u"Cross wins!")
    elif flag_rect1=="Zero" and flag_rect2=="Zero" and flag_
rect3=="Zero":
            appuifw.note(u"Zero wins!")
    elif flag_rect4=="Cross" and flag_rect5=="Cross" and flag_
rect6=="Cross":
            appuifw.note(u"Cross wins!")
    elif flag_rect4=="Zero" and flag_rect5=="Zero" and flag_
rect6=="Zero":
            appuifw.note(u"Zero wins!")
    elif flag_rect7=="Cross" and flag_rect8=="Cross" and flag_
rect9=="Cross":
            appuifw.note(u"Cross wins!")
```

```
    elif flag_rect7=="Zero" and flag_rect8=="Zero" and flag_
rect9=="Zero":
        appuifw.note(u"Zero wins!")
```

Summary

This chapter has shown how to add touch support to your applications, and how to make conditional on whether touch is supported by the device.

It's also shown how you can register the whole Canvas or just specific areas for touch events, and how you can create custom touch-enabled UI elements, and used a number of examples, including a touch piano, paint application and a tic-tac-toe game, to illustrate the key points.

9

Basic Network Programming

This chapter provides an overview of basic IP networking concepts, including how to use the Python sockets API to set up ad-hoc, multicast and broadcast networks.

9.1 Introduction

Networked applications have fundamentally changed the way that people interact and perform their day to day tasks; we take it for granted that we can communicate, play, bank, collaborate, search for and share information, shop, and so on, without even needing to leave our computers. Mobile networked applications offer a further paradigm shift: not only can we do all of these things wherever we are, but we can share our location, presence and preferences to allow these (and other) services to offer us a much more personal and tailored experience. The mobile phone is already the most personal device that most people own; networked applications have the opportunity to make it even more so.

Python is a great runtime for writing networked applications, making it possible to construct network servers and clients with just few lines of code. Python on Symbian shares this benefit; there are a few different paradigms associated with mobile devices (and consequently some different socket options) but, in general, porting from the desktop or writing network code from scratch is a straightforward exercise.

This chapter is accompanied by worked examples showing how to set up simple ad-hoc networks with a client and server, and how to use multicast and broadcast networking. In addition, the chapter briefly covers how to use exception handling and other debugging techniques in your networked application.

9.2 Basic Network Principles

Network programming is difficult if you don't have at least a basic knowledge of IP addressing. The following sections discuss IP addressing schemes and unicast, multicast and broadcast addresses.

There are two main addressing schemes in use at time of writing: IPv4 (Internet Protocol version 4) and IPv6 (Internet Protocol version 6). IPv4 is by far the most common scheme used today, and is the one we'll discuss in this chapter.

9.2.1 IPv4 Addressing

There are three types of addresses in IPv4: *unicast*, *multicast* and *broadcast*:

- Unicast is the normal point-to-point connection between two devices on a network. Several protocols uses unicast addressing, including HTTP (Internet browsing), SMTP (email) and FTP (file transfer).
- Multicast is used to address messages to a specific group of machines, rather than a specific machine address. Machines that want to belong to a group must do it explicitly, joining the group via a socket API call. The group is, in fact, an IP address from a reserved range, as discussed later.
- Broadcast addresses are similar to multicast but less *selective*: messages are sent to all machines (no subscription required) in a specific subnet or

in the current local area network (if the subnet is not specified).

IPv4 uses a 32 bit number for the address of every networked device. The IP address is commonly represented as a sequence of four decimal numbers separated by dots, for example, 200.201.40.5 or 10.20.30.40. Each number represents one byte (8 bits) and can hence vary from 0 to 255.

The IP address is further broken down into the network ID and Host ID, which represent the network and the networked device (within the network) respectively. There have been a number of schemes used to allocate the 32 bit address space to networks. Historically, the network ID was just the first byte, meaning that there were only 256 possible networks. As the networks ran out, a new 'class'-based scheme was adopted, as shown in Figure 9.1.

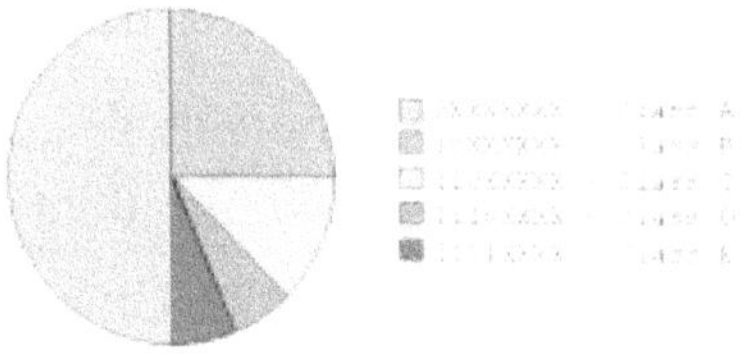

	Range for first byte
Class A	0 - 127
Class B	128 - 191
Class C	192 - 223
Class D	224 - 239
Class E	240 - 255

	1st Byte	2nd Byte	3rd Byte	4th Byte
Class A	Network ID	Host ID		
Class B	Network ID		Host ID	
Class C	Network ID			Host ID

Figure 9.1 New class based network scheme

The way this works is that the first bits are used to represent the 'class' of the address. Class A IP addresses start with 0 in the most significant bit of first byte - that is, they have the format `0XXXXXXXb` ("b" indicates that the number is in binary format, and 'X' indicates that the field can be either one or zero). Class

B, C, D and E addresses start with `10XXXXXXb`, `110XXXXXb`, `1110XXXXb`, and `1111XXXXb` respectively. Classes A, B, C are used for unicast, class D is used for multicast and class E is reserved.

The class of the address then determines how much of the rest of the number is used for the network ID and how much for the host. Class A addresses only use the first byte for the network address and the rest for host IDs, which implies that there are 127 class A networks (between `00000000b` and `01111111b`), each which have a very large number of computers in them. Class B addresses additionally use the second byte for the network ID while class C networks use both the second and third bytes. The result is that there are progressively more networks available to each of the address classes, each of which has fewer hosts (networked devices).

9.2.2 Subnet mask

The approach described is still a relatively inefficient method for allocating addresses to networks; it allows a lot more networks of varying sizes but still nowhere near enough. In order to extend the number of networks, a new partitioning scheme called Classless Inter-Domain Routing (CIDR) was created. In CIDR, a subnet mask is used to further subdivide networks, allowing us to arbitrarily specify which part of the IP address is the 'sub network ID' and which is the host ID.

The network mask is a 32-bit number that can be logically ORd with the IP address to get the network ID (it has 1 for all the left most bits that correspond to the network ID in the IP address). For example, consider the class A network address `10.0.0.0` with the network mask `255.255.255.0`. This mask has

1 in the first 24 bits (three consecutive bytes with 255) creating the network ID `10.0.0` and leaving one additional byte for host ID. The CIDR notation for this mask is /24, an abbreviated expression to say the amount of bits set.

Two host IDs are reserved: the first address (all bits in host ID reset) is the network address. The last address (all bits in host ID set) is used for sending messages to all machines in this subnet, and is known as the broadcast address.

In summary:

```
Network: 10.0.0.0
Mask: 255.255.255.0 or /24 (CIDR notation)
IP addresses range: 10.0.0.1 to 10.0.0.254 (to be used in your ma-
chines)
Broadcast: 10.0.0.255
```

Let's examine a more complex example. Suppose you received the following network/mask from your Internet Service Provider (ISP):

```
Network: 200.201.145.128
Mask: 255.255.255.192 or /26 (CIDR notation)
```

The first two significant bits in the last byte of the mask are set (`192d` - decimal or `11000000b`). This means that the first two significant bits of the last byte of the address (128 or 10b) are part of the network ID and only the last six bits are part of the host ID. Therefore, the network address is the value of the IP address with all the host ID bits reset to zero (`000000b` or `128d`), and the broadcast address is the value with the last 6 bits set to 1 (10111111b or 191d).

In summary:

```
Mask: 255.255.255.192 or /26 (CIDR notation)
Network: 200.201.145.128
IP addresses range: 200.201.145.129 to 200.201.145.190 (to be used
in your machines)
Broadcast: 200.201.145.191
```

9.2.3 Multicast addressing

IP multicast allows a networked application to communicate on a one-to-many basis, saving bandwidth and time.

Multicast IP addresses are special since they are not related to any specific network interface but instead to a group of machines. Networked devices that want to receive data on a multicast IP need to join to the group beforehand. Unfortunately, it is not possible understand multicast, and get the most out of the multicast sections later in this chapter, without first understanding how IP addresses are translated into physical addresses.

Each network interface has its own physical address called its MAC (Medium Access Control). The MAC is a 48-bit number that must be unique for each network interface within a subnetwork. This subnetwork may be understood as a physical network consisting of one or several network segments interconnected by layer one or layer two network devices such as repeaters and hubs (layer one) or bridges and switches (layer two). However, they may repeat if network segments are interconnected by IP routers (layer three). Typically, MAC address are represented as six hexadecimal numbers, with eight bits and separated by colons: `00:1E:68:BB:49:AB`.

MACs are essential to deliver packages that come from the IP layer, since network interfaces only deal with physical addresses, not IPs (see Figure 9.2). So, in order to translate IP addresses (IP layer) into MAC addresses (data link layer), the ARP protocol is employed. Using ARP requests, tables for translating IP into MAC addresses are created in all networked nodes (called ARP cache), allowing translations and posterior delivery.

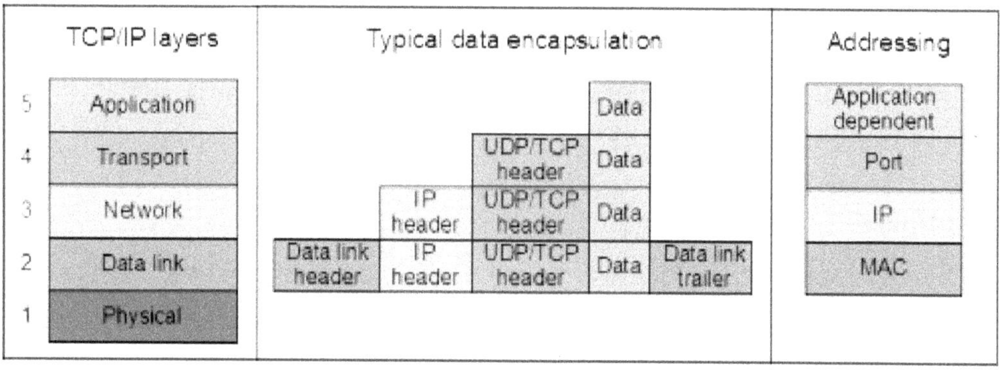

Figure 9.2 TCP layers

However, a question arises about multicast addressing: how to deliver a message if we have multiple destinations? In this case, a special MAC address not tied to any network interface is created using a common and fixed prefix (`01:00:5E`) and part of the original multicast IP. Moreover, all nodes that belong to that multicast group must program their network interface to receive messages addressed to that specific MAC address and not only to their own MAC address. Figure 9.3 shows how the multicast IP `224.202.20.30` is mapped to the MAC address `01:00:5E:4A:14:1E`.

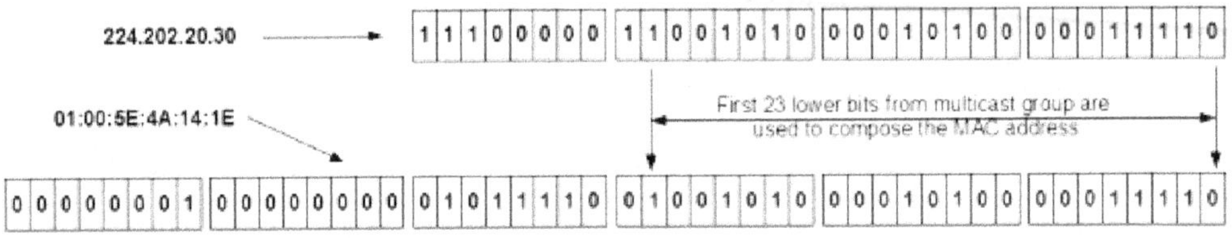

Figure 9.3 Multicast IP mapping

Special socket options are used to join multicast groups, creating special filters for corresponding MAC addresses in the network interface.

9.2.4 Ports

The IP address is used to locate a machine within a specific network, while the port is used to access the specific service. A single machine may run a number of IP based services (e.g. an FTP or web server), using a different port for each one.

The common analogy used to describe the relationship between IP addresses and ports is a company switchboard. You dial the company phone number to get the switchboard (which is analogous to the IP address), and then the extension number (Port) is used to get a specific person.

In a URL, the port is usually specified after the address, preceded by a colon:

```
http://www.example.com:8000
```

9.2.5 TCP and UDP

IP networking uses a transport protocol to define how the communication will be performed. TCP (Transmission Control Protocol) and UDP (User Datagram Protocol) are the most common transport methods:

- TCP is a connection oriented protocol - it provides a reliable and ordered byte stream between two addresses (it's similar to making a telephone call to someone).
- UDP uses a simpler "connection-less" model based on messages. UDP does not have any order or delivery guarantee (it's similar to sending several letters to someone).
- TCP manages the reliable and ordered delivery of packets, making it the obvious protocol in many cases. UDP is a more lightweight protocol, and may be a good choice where reliable delivery is not an issue, or where reliability can be easily implemented in an application-specific protocol.

9.3 The Python Socket API

This section provides an overview of the socket API, showing how to set up mobile clients and servers and how to detect and connect to access points.
The discussion is illustrated with the aid of two examples:

- The fortune client and server example shows a mobile client that receives random messages from a PC based server.

- The 'homebrew' example shows a mobile Python client that waits for files sent from a PC based server.

9.3.1 Fortune client/server

> ***Tip***
>
> In this example, our server is running on a PC with an IP address of `10.0.0.100`. You need to modify the client and server scripts to use the IP address of your local network - which can find out by starting a command prompt/terminal and typing ipconfig (Windows) or ifconfig (Linux).

The fortune server sends random messages from the Zen of Python to the fortune client over an ad-hoc unicast network. The example assumes that you have a Symbian device and a PC connected to a WiFi router, as shown in Figure 9.4. The client application runs on the device and the server runs on the PC. The server could also run on a device, but this way you get to see how similar Python network programming is on the PC and on Symbian.

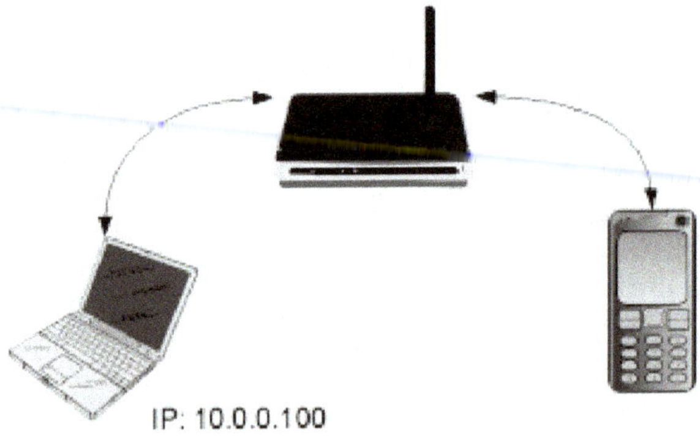

Figure 9.4 Fortune client/server example hardware configuration

The fortune client code is as follows (note that some details, including exception handling and network configuration are omitted for the sake of clarity).

The script first imports the socket module in order to access all socket networking functions. It then defines the address of the server and the port where the service is running (these must be published by the server).

The socket() function creates a network file descriptor, very similar to the one received when a file is opened. The function sets the address family and the transport protocol to IPv4 and TCP using socket options. Common address families are `AF_INET` IPv4 addresses) and `AF_INET6` (IPv6 addresses). TCP can be selected with `SOCK_STREAM` and `UDP` with `SOCK_DGRAM`. All of these constants are located inside the socket module.

```
# Fortune client
from socket import *
from appuifw import note

HOST = "10.0.0.100"
PORT = 54321

s = socket(AF_INET,SOCK_STREAM)
s.connect((HOST,PORT))

fortune = u""
while True:
    data = s.recv(1024)
```

```
    if not data:
        break
    fortune += data

s.close()

note(fortune,"info")
```

After socket creation, we call `connect()` to initiate the connection to the fortune server, specifying a tuple with IP (or host domain name such as symbian.org) and port. Since the transport protocol was set when we created the socket, all elements for accessing the server are now prepared. At this point an access point selection dialog is presented to the client, and connection will take place once an access point is selected.

> ***Tip***
>
> If you have a firewall running on the PC side, it is necessary to open the incoming port 54321. Otherwise your mobile client will not be able to connect to the server.

The `recv()` function is called within a loop to wait for a message. The bytes received each time `recv()` returns are added to the fortune buffer. When the server has finished sending the message it terminates the connection; the client `recv()` returns with an empty string, which causes the loop to terminate. The client then closes the connection to its socket and displays the received message to the user (closing the socket is not strictly necessary, because it would otherwise be automatically closed when garbage-collected).

> **Note**
>
> The `recv()` function specifies at least one argument - the maximum number of bytes that may be received when the function returns. A common misunderstanding is that each `recv()` will receive a complete message, or that it will receive the amount of bytes specified in the call. Network and operating system conditions (delay, buffers, throughput and so on) may change the amount of bytes received at each `recv()` call. Even though the streaming is guaranteed by TCP, the programmer must still check for protocol integrity.

The server code shown as follows is relatively straightforward - it creates a TCP/IP socket, binds to the address and port and waits (listens) for connections. When a connection is received it selects a random message, sends it, then closes the connection.

```
# Fortune server
from socket import *
from random import choice

# Fortune database from The Zen of Python, by Tim Peters (import
this)
PHRASES =[ u"Beautiful is better than ugly.",
           u"Explicit is better than implicit.",
           u"Simple is better than complex.",
           u"Complex is better than complicated.",
           u"Flat is better than nested.",
           u"Sparse is better than dense.",
           u"Readability counts.",
```

```
            u"Special cases aren't special enough to break the
rules.",
            u"Although practicality beats purity.",
            u"Errors should never pass silently.",
            u"Unless explicitly silenced.",
            u"In the face of ambiguity, refuse the temptation to
guess.",
            u"There should be one-- and preferably only one --obvi-
ous way to do it.",
            u"Although that way may not be obvious at first unless
you're Dutch.",
            u"Now is better than never.",
            u"Although never is often better than *right* now.",
            u"If the implementation is hard to explain, it's a bad
idea.",
            u"If the implementation is easy to explain, it may be a
good idea.",
            u"Namespaces are one honking great idea -- let's do
more of those!" ]

HOST = "10.0.0.100"
PORT = 54321

s = socket(AF_INET,SOCK_STREAM)
s.bind((HOST,PORT))
s.listen(5)

while True:
```

```
    (cs,addr) = s.accept()
    fortune = choice(PHRASES)
    cs.sendall(fortune)
    cs.close()
```

The server script is run on the PC and the client script in the Python shell on the device. Screen shots of messages being received on the mobile device are shown in Figure 9.5 as follows:

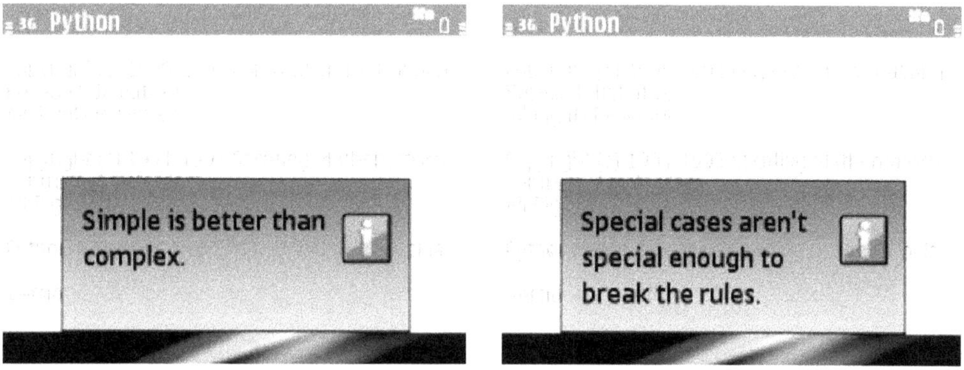

Figure 9.5 Screen shots of messages being received on the mobile device

9.3.2 Access point selection

On a mobile device there may be a number of potential connections to the Internet: via the phone network, WiFi, or a tethered connection to a PC. By default, Python will pop up a dialog when a socket calls `connect()` to allow users to choose which connection they want to use.

Python also provides a number of functions to allow applications to query the set of available access points and set a default connection. This allows access points to be stored and reused (reducing the number of prompts received by the user):

- `access_points()`: Returns a list of all the available access point ids and their names
- `set_default_access_point(ap_name)`: Sets the default access point to be used when the socket is opened and starts the connection.

These methods make it easy to create a custom access point selection dialog. The code and a screenshot of such a dialog are shown as follows and in Figure 9.6 respectively.

```
# Selecting access point
from appuifw import *
import socket

def sel_access_point():
    """ Select the default access point.
        Return True if the selection was done or False if not
    """
    aps = socket.access_points()
    if not aps:
        note(u"No access points available","error")
        return False

    ap_labels = map(lambda x: x['name'], aps)
    item = popup_menu(ap_labels,u"Access points:")
```

```
    if item is None:
        return False

    socket.set_default_access_point(aps[item]["name"])

    return True

if sel_access_point():
    note(u"Connect!","info")
```

Figure 9.6 Custom access point selection dialog

Once you have connected to your destination it is possible to get your own IP address and port by calling the socket method `getsockname()`:

```
>>> s = socket.socket(socket.AF_INET,socket.SOCK_STREAM)
>>> s.connect(("10.0.0.100",54321))
>>> s.getsockname()
('10.0.0.102', 54838)
```

If you need to know this IP address prior to connecting to your destination, you can use the `btsocket` module. This module provides much the same functionality as socket but adds support for sockets over Bluetooth connections. For most operations the modules can be used interchangeably. Unfortunately `btsocket` cannot be used as a direct replacement for socket in all cases because it does not expose all of the socket options (this causes problems when creating a multicast server). In addition, it does not support the socket time-outs (`settimeout()`, discussed later).

If you want to use `btsocket`, the following code can be used to select the access point (this function will be used in other examples, copy it when necessary).

```
# Selecting access point
from appuifw import *
import btsocket

def sel_access_point_bt():
    """ Select the default access point.
        Return the acess point if the selection was done
        or None if not
    """
    aps = btsocket.access_points()
    if not aps:
        note(u"No access points available","error")
        return None

    ap_labels = map(lambda x: x['name'], aps)
```

```
    item = popup_menu(ap_labels,u"Access points:")
    if item is None:
        return None

    apo = btsocket.access_point(aps[item]['iapid'])
    btsocket.set_default_access_point(apo)

    return apo

apo = sel_access_point_bt()
if apo:
    apo.start()
    note(u"Connect! IP "+apo.ip(),"info")
```

This function returns an access point object, which has three interesting methods:

```
>>> dir(apo)
['ip', 'start', 'stop']
```

The `start()` function can be used to activate the access point, and you can interrupt it with `apo.stop()`. If you are using DHCP, the IP address will be negotiated in this phase and may be retrieved using the `apo.ip()` function. These functions are used when sending/receiving datagrams (UDP, multicast or broadcast messaging), and with these types of messages there is no connection phase so you manage the access point directly.

When the access point is running, the phone will show the connection icon on the phone home screen as shown in Figure 9.7.

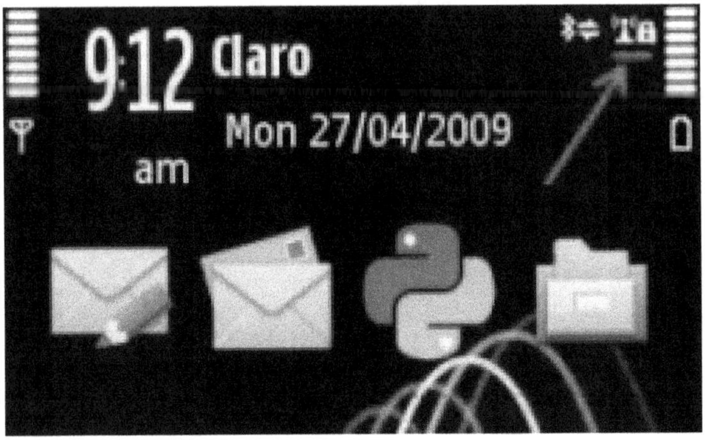

Figure 9.7 Phone in which a connection is active

Take care when mixing `btsocket` and `socket`:

- If you want to fix the access point you will need to select the access points for both modules.
- Some Python standard modules will import socket instead of `btsocket`, resulting in unexpected behavior. In this case, we recommend that you add the following lines to the beginning of your first script:

```
import sys
try:
    # Try to import btsocket as socket
    sys.modules['socket'] = __import__('btsocket')
```

```
except ImportError:
    pass
```

This ensures that any further script that tries to import socket will import `bt-socket` instead.

9.3.3 Protocols and TCP servers

In this section, we create a single-thread server to receive files over a WiFi network. Initially, we define a PC client script to send the files, and we then demonstrate a client that can be hosted on a mobile device.

The client and server rely on a simple communication protocol (a communication protocol is a set of agreed rules for data representation, signaling, authentication and error detection that can be used to share information between two end points). The protocol doesn't need to be complicated or based on any particular standard, it just needs to be understood by both the server and the client.

Our 'homebrew file transfer protocol' has three fields, separated by \n:

- A string representing the file name (maximum of 32 characters)
- The size of the file, specified to be big endian (most significant byte first in memory).
- Endian-ness is important when exchanging data between machines with different architectures to ensure it can be unpacked properly (PCs are little endian while the processors on mobile devices are usually big endian).
- The size can be used for providing progress notification or confirming that

there is enough space for the received file (we don't actually use it in this example).

- File contents.

The protocol is shown in Figure 9.8:

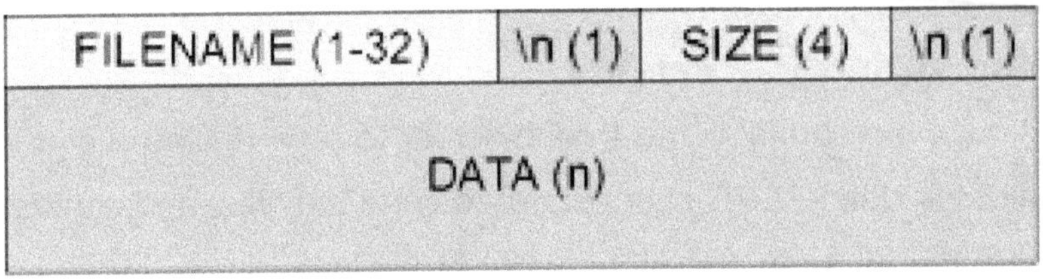

Figure 9.8 File format of a "homebrew" file message

TCP servers use the following sequence of calls to set up the connection with a client:

1. `socket()`: Creates a socket object to provide the sockets API
2. `bind()`: Binds the socket (server) to a specific IP address and port where clients will expect to find the service (binding tells the operating system that events on the specified IP address and port should be directed to the application). For multi-homed machines (machines with several IP addresses), we can specify an IP address of 0.0.0.0 to tell the operating system that we want to bind the server to all available local IP addresses (but the same port).
3. `listen()`: Reserves resources in the device, telling it how many simultaneous connection requests it must be able to handle on the current socket, after which new connection requests must be dropped. Once a connection is established its reserved resources are released, allowing further connection requests. The number should be the same as the

likely number of simultaneous connection requests, noting of course that larger numbers will consume more resources. The number doesn't affect how many connections a server may have active, just how many may be established at the same time.

4. `accept()`: Blocks the thread waiting on incoming connections. At this point everything is defined and the server is up and running. When a connection arrives, the program continues its normal execution flow just after the `accept()` call.

Note that it is possible to make `accept()` non-blocking with additional socket options.

`accept()` returns two important parameters:

- a socket for describing the incoming connection.
- client IP address and port, as a tuple.

From this point, all further communication with the client must be done using the returned socket. Data may be exchanged using `recv()` and `send()`. Multi-threaded servers will create a new thread and pass the socket to it, then call `accept()` again to wait for more clients.

The server code is as follows. The server is a Python application that creates a custom access point selection dialog (as discussed in the preceding section), and an 'About' dialog. The code to set up the connection follows the pattern described.

```
# File upload server
import sys
try:
    # Try to import btsocket as socket
    sys.modules['socket'] = __import__('btsocket')
except ImportError:
    pass
import socket
from appuifw import *
import os
import e32
import struct

class FileUpload(object):
    """ File upload server class
    """
    def __init__(self):
        self.lock = e32.Ao_lock()
        self.dir = "e:\\file_upload"
        if not os.path.isdir(self.dir):
            os.makedirs(self.dir)
        self.apo = None
        self.port = 54321
        self.new_line = u"\u2029"
        app.title = u"File upload"
        app.screen = "normal"
        app.menu = [(u"About", self.about)]
        self.body = Text()
```

```
        app.body = self.body
        self.lock.wait()

    def recv_file(self,cs,addr):
        """ Given a client socket (cs), receive a new file
            and save it at self.dir
        """
        data = ""
        name = ""
        size = 0
        # waiting for file name
        while True:
            n = data.find("\n")
            if n >= 0:
                name = data[:n]
                data = data[n+1:]
                break
            buf = cs.recv(1024)
            data += buf

        # waiting for file size (may be useful for limits checking)
        while True:
            n = data.find("\n")
            if n >= 0:
                # unpack one long (L) using big endian (>) endian-
ness
                size = struct.unpack(">L",data[:n])[0]
                data = data[n+1:]
```

```
                break
            buf = cs.recv(1024)
            data += buf

        self.body.add(u"Uploading %s (%d bytes)" % (name,size) +
self.new_line)
        # waiting for file contents
        fname = os.path.join(self.dir,name)
        f = open(fname,"wb")
        while True:
            f.write(data)
            data = cs.recv(1024)
            if not data:
                break
        self.body.add(u"Finished." + self.new_line)
        cs.close()
        f.close()

    def server(self,ip,port):
        """ Starts a mono thread server at ip, port
        """
        s = socket.socket(socket.AF_INET,socket.SOCK_STREAM)
        s.bind((ip,port))
        s.listen(1)

        while True:
            (cs,addr) = s.accept()
            self.body.add(u"Connect to %s:%d" % (addr[0],addr[1])
```

```
+ self.new_line)
            self.recv_file(cs,addr)

    def sel_access_point(self):
        """ Select and set the default access point.
            Return the access point object if the selection was
done or None if not
        """
        aps = socket.access_points()
        if not aps:
            note(u"No access points available","error")
            return None

        ap_labels = map(lambda x: x['name'], aps)
        item = popup_menu(ap_labels,u"Access points:")
        if item is None:
            return None

        apo = socket.access_point(aps[item]['iapid'])
        socket.set_default_access_point(apo)

        return apo

    def about(self):
        note(u"File upload for PyS60","info")

    def run(self):
        self.apo = self.sel_access_point()
```

```
        if self.apo:
            self.apo.start()
            self.body.add(u"Starting server." + self.new_line)
            self.body.add(u"IP = %s" % self.apo.ip() + self.new_
line)
            self.body.add(u"Port = %d" % self.port + self.new_
line)
            self.body.add(u"Repository = %s" % (self.dir) + self.
new_line)
            self.server(self.apo.ip(),self.port)
            self.lock.wait()
        app.set_tabs( [], None )
        app.menu = []
        app.body = None
        app.set_exit()

if __name__ == "__main__":
    app = FileUpload()
    app.run()
```

When compared to the fortune client-server example, the code to process a 'homebrew' message is relatively complicated. This is because the data does not arrive in one go and we need to parse it as it arrives in order to get the filename and size. As discussed in the section 'File-like sockets' the `makefile()` function can make processing easier by reading a specified amount of data or a whole 'line'.

Finally, the small PC script shown as follows may be used to send the file:

```
# File upload client
import struct
import sys
import os
import socket

if len(sys.argv) < 4:
    print "%s server_addr server_port file_to_upload" % sys.argv[0]
    sys.exit(1)

ip = sys.argv[1]
port = int(sys.argv[2])
full_name = sys.argv[3]
base_name = os.path.basename(full_name)
size = os.path.getsize(sys.argv[3])

print "Sending %s to %s:%d ..." % (base_name,ip,port)

s = socket.socket(socket.AF_INET,socket.SOCK_STREAM)
s.connect((ip,port))
f = open(full_name,"rb")
header = "%s\n%s\n" % (base_name,struct.pack(">L",size))
s.sendall(header)
while True:
    data = f.read(1024)
    if not data:
        break
```

```
    s.sendall(data)


s.close()
f.close()
```

Run it from command line, specifying the server IP address, port, and the file to be sent:

```
script_name.py server_ip server_port file_to_send
```

Figures 9.9 and 9.10 show these programs running. The command ping was used to test the ad-hoc connection between PC (10.0.0.100) and mobile phone (10.0.0.103), before transferring files.

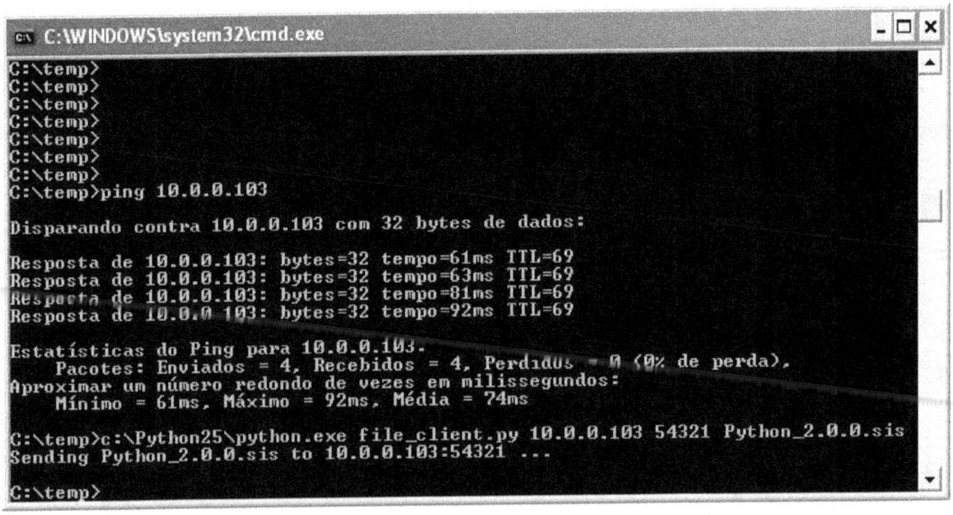

Figure 9.9 PC client sending file

Figure 9.10 Mobile server receiving file

Finally, the following code is for a client that you can run on the device to send the files. It is similar to the PC script but the main difference is that it adds a UI wrapper and a class for selecting files (`FileSel`).

Take a look in the source code and try to understand how it works. Some socket calls are surrounded by try... catch statements (exceptions) and we will talk about them later.

```
# File upload client
import sys
try:
    # Try to import btsocket as socket
    sys.modules['socket'] = __import__('btsocket')
except ImportError:
    pass
import socket
from appuifw import *
```

```
import os
import e32
import struct
import time
import re

class FileSel(object):
    """
    Open a selection file dialog. Returns the file selected or None.
    Initial path and regular expression for filtering file list may
be provided.

    Examples:
    sel = FileSel().run()
    if sel is not None:
        ...

    sel = FileSel(mask = r"(.*\.jpeg|.*\.jpg|.*\.png|.*\.gif)").
run()
    if sel is not None:
        ...

    """
    def __init__(self,init_dir = "", mask = ".*"):
        self.cur_dir = unicode(init_dir)
        if not os.path.exists(self.cur_dir):
            self.cur_dir = ""
        self.mask = mask
```

```
        self.fill_items()

    def fill_items(self):
        if self.cur_dir == u"":
            self.items = [ unicode(d + "\\") for d in e32.drive_
list() ]
        else:
            entries = [ e.decode('utf-8')
                        for e in os.listdir( self.cur_dir.
encode('utf-8') ) ]
            d = self.cur_dir
            dirs  = [ e.upper() for e in entries
                      if os.path.isdir(os.path.join(d,e).
encode('utf-8'))  ]

            files = [ e.lower() for e in entries
                      if os.path.isfile(os.path.join(d,e).
encode('utf-8')) ]

            files = [ f for f in files
                      if re.match(self.mask,f) ]
            dirs.sort()
            files.sort()
            dirs.insert( 0, u".." )
            self.items = dirs + files

    def run(self):
        while True:
```

```
        item = selection_list(self.items, search_field=1)
        if item is None:
            return None
        f = self.items[item]
        d = os.path.abspath( os.path.join(self.cur_dir,f) )
        if os.path.isdir( d.encode('utf-8') ):
            if f == u".." and len(self.cur_dir) == 3:
                self.cur_dir = u""
            else:
                self.cur_dir = d
            self.fill_items()
        elif os.path.isfile( d.encode('utf-8') ):
            return d

class TxFile(object):
    """ TxFile client class
    """
    def __init__(self):
        self.lock = e32.Ao_lock()
        self.apo = None
        self.dir = ""
        self.port = 54321
        self.ip = ""
        self.new_line = u"\u2029"
        app.title = u"TX File"
        app.screen = "normal"
        app.menu = [(u"Send file", self.send_file),
                    (u"Set AP", self.set_ap),
```

```
                (u"Exit", self.close_app)]
        self.body = Text()
        app.body = self.body
        self.lock.wait()

    def close_app(self):
        self.lock.signal()

    def set_ap(self):
        """ Try to set an access point, return True or False to
indicate the success.
            If True, sets self.apo to choosen access point.
        """
        apo = self.sel_access_point()
        if apo:
            self.apo = apo
            return True
        else:
            return False

    def send_file(self):
        """ Send a file to server
        """
        # at leat one access point is necessary
        if not self.apo:
            if not self.set_ap():
                return
```

```
        # use our own IP as initial guess
        self.apo.start()
        if not self.ip:
            self.ip = self.apo.ip()

        # get server address
        ip = query(u"Server addr", "text", unicode(self.ip))
        if ip is None:
            return
        self.ip = ip

        # get filename
        full_name = FileSel(init_dir=self.dir).run()
        if full_name is None:
            return

        # transmitt file
        full_name = full_name.encode('utf-8')
        self.dir = os.path.dirname(full_name)
        base_name = os.path.basename(full_name)
        size = os.path.getsize(full_name)


        self.body.add(u"Connecting to %s:%d ..." % (self.ip,self.
port) + self.new_line)
        s = socket.socket(socket.AF_INET,socket.SOCK_STREAM)
        try:
            s.connect((self.ip,self.port))
```

```
        except socket.error, (val,msg):
            self.body.add(u"Error %d: %s" % (val,msg) + self.new_
line)
            return

        self.body.add(u"Sending %s (%d bytes)" % (base_name,size)
+ self.new_line)
        f = open(full_name,"rb")
        header = "%s\n" % (base_name) + struct.pack(">L",size) +
"\n"
        s.sendall(header)
        n = 0
        ta = time.time()
        while True:
            data = f.read(1024)
            if not data:
                break
            s.sendall(data)
            n += len(data)
            if n % 100 == 0: # a mark at each 100k
                self.body.add(u".")
        s.close()
        f.close()
        tb = time.time()
        self.body.add(self.new_line + u"Finished (%0.2f
kbytes/s)." % ((n/1024.0)/(tb-ta)) + self.new_line)

    def sel_access_point(self):
```

```
        """ Select and set the default access point.
            Return the access point object if the selection was
done or None if not
        """
        aps = socket.access_points()
        if not aps:
            note(u"No access points available","error")
            return None

        ap_labels = map(lambda x: x['name'], aps)
        item = popup_menu(ap_labels,u"Access points:")
        if item is None:
            return None

        apo = socket.access_point(aps[item]['iapid'])
        socket.set_default_access_point(apo)

        return apo

    def run(self):
        self.lock.wait()
        app.set_exit()

if __name__ == "__main__":
    app = TxFile()
    app.run()
```

9.4 Exception handling and debugging

The last section raised the issue of exception handling: the socket API on Python on Symbian makes extensive usage of exceptions to indicate errors like connection timeouts, unexpected closed connections and so on.

> ***Tip***
>
> You can use the `settimeout()` socket method to set the time out value for any socket operation, including the connection time. Note that this method is available only in the `socket()` module and not in `btsocket`.

For instance, the following code fragment shows how to use exception handling when connecting to a server.

```
# btsocket can be used as well
import socket
s = socket.socket(socket.AF_INET,socket.SOCK_STREAM)
try:
    s.connect(('nokia.com',2222))
except:
    print "Can´t connect"
```

Since port 2222 does not have a server listening on it, an exception will be raised and the script will print `Can't` connect.

The code catches every exception, but doesn't tell us very much about the problem. We can obtain more information by using the socket-specific exception:

`socket.error`. In the following example, if there is an exception we get the more useful message `ERROR: timed out`.

```
# btsocket can be used as well
import socket
s = socket.socket(socket.AF_INET,socket.SOCK_STREAM)
try:
    s.connect((‘nokia.com’,2222))
except socket.error, e:
    print “ERROR: %s” % e
```

Another useful exception is `socket.gaierror`, related to address resolution problems. In the next example an invalid address is used (‘nokiacom’), generating an exception. Note how we use several except statements.

```
# btsocket can be used as well
import socket
s = socket.socket(socket.AF_INET,socket.SOCK_STREAM)
try:
    s.connect((‘nokiacom’,2222))
except socket.gaierror, e:
    print “ADDR ERROR: %s” % e
except socket.error, e:
    print “ERROR: %s” % e
except:
    print “Can’t connect”
```

The output is as shown, with the most specific exception displayed first:

```
ADDR ERROR: (11001, 'getaddrinfo failed')
```

Following the 'Zen of Python', 'explicit is better than implicit' and 'errors should never pass silently', it is better to handle exceptions individually. However, the 'lazy approach' (first example) may be enough in many situations.

Exception handling can be used to help your program deal with unexpected and environmental errors. To deal with programmatic errors you're going to need the techniques discussed in Chapter 17, which include guidance on how to use the emulator and how to use file logging.

9.5 Advanced Socket API

9.5.1 Multicast

The previous examples demonstrated unicast networking with TCP. Multicast and broadcast networking uses UDP, because it is inherently message-based rather than data-stream based. This section explains how to send multicast messages in your applications and, as a bonus, provides an overview of UDP networking.

The following Python code sends ten 'hello world' messages every two seconds to the multicast address 224.202.20.30. The screenshot in Figure 9.11 shows the multicast frame, addressed to MAC `01:00:5e:4a:14:1e`:

```
# Sending multicast from mobile
```

```
import e32
import btsocket
from appuifw import note, popup_menu

GROUP = "224.202.20.30"
PORT = 54321

apo = sel_access_point_bt()
if apo is not None:
    apo.start()
    sock = btsocket.socket(btsocket.AF_INET, btsocket.SOCK_DGRAM)
    for i in range(10):
        n = sock.sendto('hello world',(GROUP,PORT))
        print "Message sent (%d bytes)" % n
        e32.ao_sleep(2)
```

It is possible to use the `socket` module as well, by changing the access point selection routine:

```
# Sending multicast from mobile
import e32
import socket
from appuifw import note, popup_menu

GROUP = "224.202.20.30"
PORT = 54321

if sel_access_point():
```

```
sock = socket.socket(socket.AF_INET, socket.SOCK_DGRAM)
for i in range(10):
    n = sock.sendto('hello world',(GROUP,PORT))
    print "Message sent (%d bytes)" % n
    e32.ao_sleep(2)
```

The code is fairly straightforward:

- Select an access point, set it as the default access point. For those running `btsocket`, use the `apo` object to start the access point. UDP is a connection-less protocol, so we need to set the access point directly.
- Create a UDP socket (the transmission control protocol is set with `SOCK_DGRAM` instead of `SOCK_STREAM`).
- Call `sendto()` in a loop to send the "hello world" message to the specified group and port.

`sendto()` allows us to specify the message destination in the format (address, port). We use this instead of the more familiar `send()` function because there is no mandatory connection phase in UDP networking. Note that you can use the `send()/recv()` primitives instead non-connected versions `sendto()/recvfrom()` if you want, but you'll first need to connect the UDP socket.

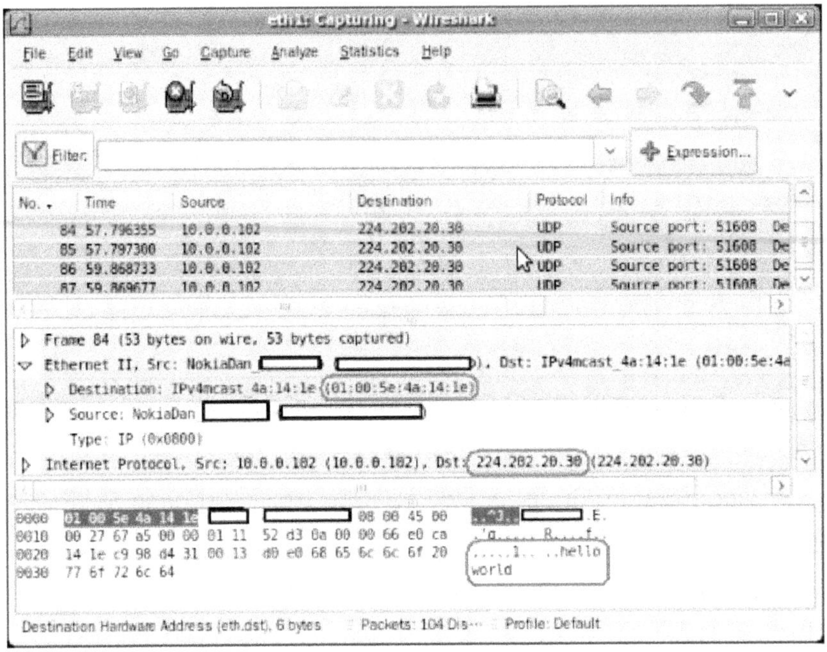

Figure 9.11 Wireshark screenshot showing multicast frame

To receive multicast messages, we first create a socket and bind it to the interface. We then join the desired group, as discussed in the Multicast Addressing section at the beginning of this chapter. This can be done using two calls to `setsockopt()` function. The first call enables multicast reception for the interface and the second tells the network card which IP we are waiting for.

After joining the group, the last step is to call `recvfrom()` to wait for a message. Again, `recvfrom()` is similar to `recv()` but it additionally returns the address of the incoming package.

> ***Note***
>
> At time of writing Python on Symbian v2.0 allows applications to send but not receive multicast messages using `btsocket` or even `socket`. While a group of options `SOL_IP` is not present in the `btsocket` module, socket returns a Error 17: File exists when you call `setsockopt` using multicast parameters.

As Python on Symbian does not enable multicast messages to be received, the following code is run on the PC:

```
# PC multicast server
import time
import sys
import socket

GROUP = "224.202.20.30"
PORT = 54321
ITF_ADDR = '10.0.0.101'

def join_grp(sock,grp,itf):
    # enabling multicasting option for interface itf
    sock.setsockopt(socket.SOL_IP,
                    socket.IP_MULTICAST_IF,
                    socket.inet_aton(itf))
    # joining to multicast group grp in interface itf
    sock.setsockopt(socket.SOL_IP,
                    socket.IP_ADD_MEMBERSHIP,
                    socket.inet_aton(grp)+socket.inet_aton(itf))
```

```
def leave_grp(sock,grp,ITF_ADDR):
    # removing
    sock.setsockopt(socket.SOL_IP,
                    socket.IP_DROP_MEMBERSHIP,
                    socket.inet_aton(grp)+socket.inet_aton(ITF_ADDR))

sock = socket.socket(socket.AF_INET,socket.SOCK_DGRAM)
sock.bind((ITF_ADDR,PORT))
join_grp(sock,GROUP,ITF_ADDR)

for n in range(10):
    (data,addr) = sock.recvfrom(1500)
    print "Received ",data,"from",addr

leave_grp(sock,GROUP,ITF_ADDR)
```

The code may at first appear a little opaque. It may help to know that the `inet_aton()` method converts an IPv4 address to 32-bit packed binary format as a string of four characters (see Python documentation). Also, that `Setsockoption()` has three parameters:

- `level`: used to select a group of options, like `SOL_SOCKET` for socket options and `SOL_IP` for options related to IP layer.
- `option name`: the current value of the option
- `option value`: the new value of the option

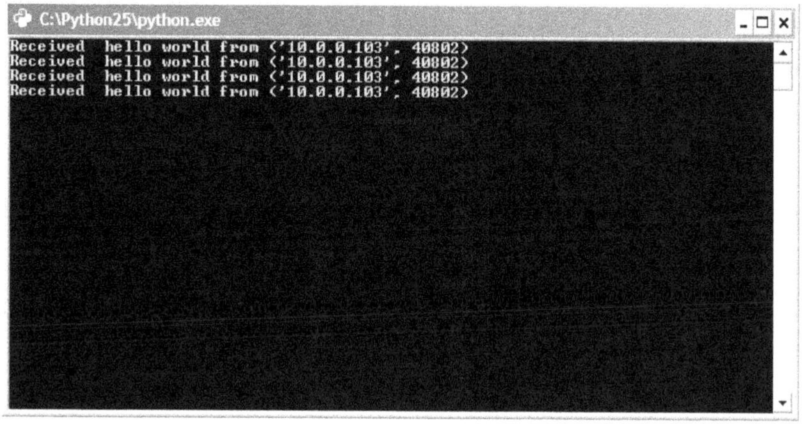

Figure 9.12 Received messages displayed on PC python console

9.5.2 Broadcast

Broadcast messaging allows programs to send UDP messages to all machines in a subnet by specifying the destination as a specific broadcast address. All machines in the subnet will receive these broadcast messages without need to register.

There are four types of broadcast (the first two are the most common):

- Limited broadcast: A special broadcast where the destination address is 255.255.255.255. It is limited because only machines in the local subnet will receive this message - messages are never forwarded to other networks.
- Subnet directed broadcast: The subnet broadcast IP address is used to specify the target subnet. Routers may forward this message but they need to know the subnet mask. For instance, the broadcast address for network 172.16.10.0 with mask 255.255.255.0 is 172.16.10.255.

- Net-directed broadcast: The broadcast address is calculated using the default mask for class A, B or C addresses. Class A will have a broadcast address like <netid>.255.255.255, for instance. Routers will forward these messages, but it is possible to disable them.
- All subnets directed broadcast: Quite similar to net directed broadcast, but in this approach all subnets are grouped. For example, 172.16.255.255 is the broadcast address for all subnets-directed to network 172.16.10.0.

In the data link layer, broadcast messages use the special MAC address `FF:FF:FF:FF:FF:FF` regardless the type of broadcast IP address used. The screenshot shown in Figure 9.13 shows this MAC used for the subnet broadcast address 10.0.0.255 for network 10.0.0.0/24.

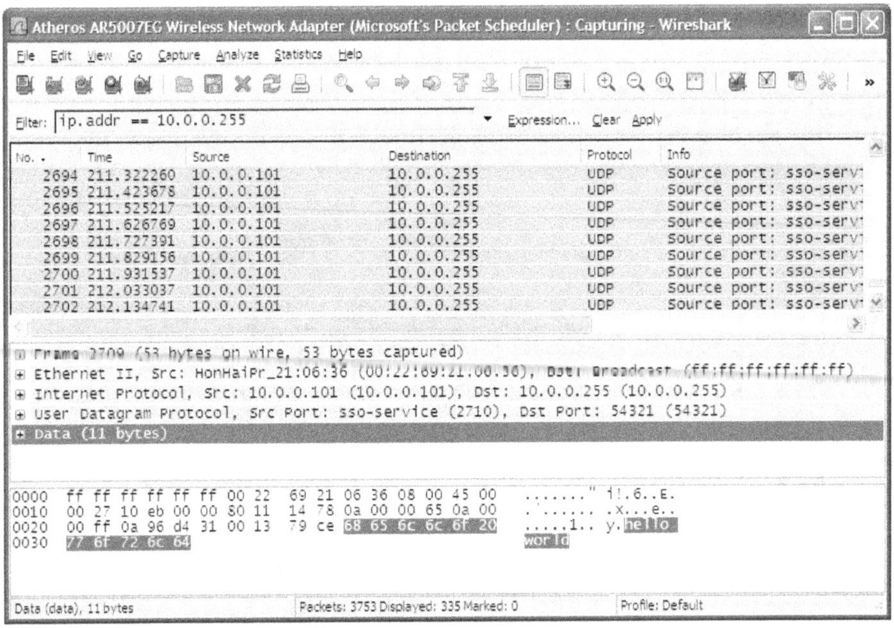

Figure 9.13 Wireshark showing frame for broadcast message

The following code sends broadcast messages. We set the socket option SO_BROADCAST to true in SOL_SOCKET. Note that the code will also run on the PC if you replace `e32.ao_sleep(2)` by `time.sleep(2)`.

> ***Note***
> This example will work only for the socket module since the SOL_SOCKET group of options is not present in the `btsocket` module.

```
# Sending broadcast messages
import socket
import e32

BCIP = "255.255.255.255"
PORT = 54321

sock = socket.socket(socket.AF_INET,socket.SOCK_DGRAM)
sock.setsockopt(socket.SOL_SOCKET,socket.SO_BROADCAST, True)
for i in range(10):
    n = sock.sendto('hello world',(BCIP,PORT))
    print "Message sent (%d bytes)" % n
    e32.ao_sleep(2)
```

The following example shows a code snippet for receiving broadcast messages.

```
# Receiving broadcast messages
import socket
from appuifw import popup_menu
```

```
PORT = 54321
sock = socket.socket(socket.AF_INET,socket.SOCK_DGRAM)
sock.bind(('0.0.0.0',PORT))

if sel_access_point():
    for i in range(10):
        (data,addr) = sock.recvfrom(1500)
        print "Received ",data,"from",addr
```

It is possible to use the `socket` module as well, changing the access point selection routine:

```
# Receiving broadcast messages
import btsocket
from appuifw import popup_menu

PORT = 54321
sock = btsocket.socket(btsocket.AF_INET,btsocket.SOCK_DGRAM)
sock.bind(('0.0.0.0',PORT))

apo = sel_access_point_bt()
if apo:
    apo.start()
    for i in range(10):
        (data,addr) = sock.recvfrom(1500)
        print "Received ",data,"from",addr
```

9.5.3 File-like sockets

TCP sockets return an arbitrary amount of data with every `recv()` call. As a result, we end up either buffering the whole message in memory before parsing it (resulting in less memory efficient code) or parsing it on-the-fly (resulting in more complicated code).

Python's socket API provides methods that make processing streamed data a lot easier. The `makefile()` function transforms a standard socket object in an object with file-like behavior. With this file-like socket you can `read()` a fixed amount of bytes or `readline()` to receive a complete line. Being able to read a known size of data significantly reduces the complexity of the data.

> ***Note***
> While frequently used in Python applications, this object not is common in other socket APIs.

The first example is a line-oriented client-server. The client code (displayed first) sends five lines to the server through the file-like object. The newline character is appended to each line of text - this is what is used to detect lines of data by the receiver. A call to `flush()` is added before calling `time.sleep()` to flush any pending bytes.

```
# File-like sockets - client
# btsocket can be used as well
import socket
import e32
```

```
sock = socket.socket(socket.AF_INET,socket.SOCK_STREAM)
sock.connect(('127.0.0.1',54321))
fsock = sock.makefile()

for i in range(5):
    msg = u"Sending line %d ...\n" % i
    fsock.write(msg)
    print msg
    # call flush to send pending bytes
    fsock.flush()
    # slow down for better comprehension
    e32.ao_sleep(1)

sock.close()
```

The server is simple:

```
# File-like sockets - server
# btsocket can be used as well
import socket

s = socket.socket(socket.AF_INET,socket.SOCK_STREAM)
s.bind(('127.0.0.1',54321))
s.listen(1)

while True:
    sock,addr = s.accept()
    fsock = sock.makefile()
```

```
    print "New connection from",addr
    while True:
        line = fsock.readline()
        if not line:
            print "Connection closed"
            break
        print "=> ",line
```

File-like sockets are even more useful when we need to decode headers or other protocol information. Suppose we have created a protocol in which we send the version and size as two four-byte integers (big endian format) followed by the data. The following client and server code shows how makefile makes this easy:

```
# File-like sockets - proto client
# btsocket can be used as well
import socket
import struct
import random

sock = socket.socket(socket.AF_INET,socket.SOCK_STREAM)
sock.connect(('127.0.0.1',54321))

fsock = sock.makefile()
# creating a random header
version = random.randint(0,5)
size = random.randint(0,10)
header = struct.pack('>LL',version,size)
print "Version:",version
```

```
print "Size:",size
fsock.write(header)
data = 'X'*size
print "Data:",data
fsock.write(data)
fsock.flush()
sock.close()
```

> ***Note***
>
> The `struct` module is useful when handling data stored in files or from network connections.

The server is similar:

```
# File-like sockets - proto server
# btsocket can be used as well
import socket
import struct

s = socket.socket(socket.AF_INET,socket.SOCK_STREAM)
s.bind(('127.0.0.1',54321))
s.listen(1)
while True:
    sock,addr = s.accept()
    fsock = sock.makefile()
    print "New connection from",addr
    # decoding header
```

```
header = fsock.read(8)
(version,size) = struct.unpack('>LL',header)
print "Version:",version
print "Size:",size
data = fsock.read(size)
print "Data:",data
sock.close()
```

9.6 Further reading

The following books use C as a programming language to explain the socket API. The behavior of Python sockets is similar because the C socket API has become a de facto standard across most programming languages.

Beej's Guide to Network Programming
Concise and straight to the point, this guide remains a great reference.
TCP/IP Illustrated, Volume 1, 1994, by W. Richard Stevens
Despite being quite old, this is still a fantastic book. It covers in details several important protocols, including: TCP, UDP, IP, ICMP and others.

TCP/IP Illustrated, Volume 2
This provides implementation information and source code for BSD 4.4, the starting point for many network stack implementations.

UNIX Network Programming, Third edition, 2004, by W. Richard Stevens, Bill Fenner and Andrew M.Rudoff.
This book was originally written by Stevens, but after he passed away in 1999, it was released in a new edition. The book discusses both the socket API and

more recent protocols, like IPv6 and SCTP. It is a book for programmers and a great reference.

Several books have been written specifically for Python developers, for example:

Foundations of Python Network Programming, 2004, by John Goerzen. This book covers not only the socket API but also several important modules found in Python.

Source Code
All examples shown in this chapter are available for download from ***croozeus.com/PythonOnSymbianBookExampleCode_Ch09BasicNetProg.zip.***

9.7 Summary

This chapter shows how to program networked applications on Symbian devices using Python's socket APIs. Covering both the fundamental principles of IP networking and also aspects of sockets programming that are specific to mobile devices, the text is complemented by simple but illustrative examples of Python network clients and servers. The topic also covers more advanced IP networking topics, including multicast and broadcast networks, and debugging networking code.

Chapter 14, which covers advanced network programming, extends the concepts in this chapter to discuss higher level networking protocols (e.g. HTTP, XML-RPC), and to cover the essentials of multi-threaded network programming.

10

Location Based Services

This chapter explains the location and positioning technologies available on Symbian mobile devices, and demonstrates how position information can be combined with information from online services to create a simple mapping application.

10.1 Introduction

GPS enabled mobile devices are already replacing dedicated hardware for mapping, search and navigation. This trend is likely to continue as more devices have integrated positioning modules, and companies such as Nokia and Google provide free mapping solutions as part of their standard offering. This is good news for developers. The world might not need another mapping application but there are still endless opportunities for compelling location-aware applications. One of the most powerful ways to personalize mobile applications is to make them location aware. An application that tells you when the next train you want to catch is leaving is very useful: One that tells you how far it is to walk to the train, and wakes you up when you're about to sleep though your station is even more useful!

In this chapter we demonstrate how to add location context sensitivity to Python applications.

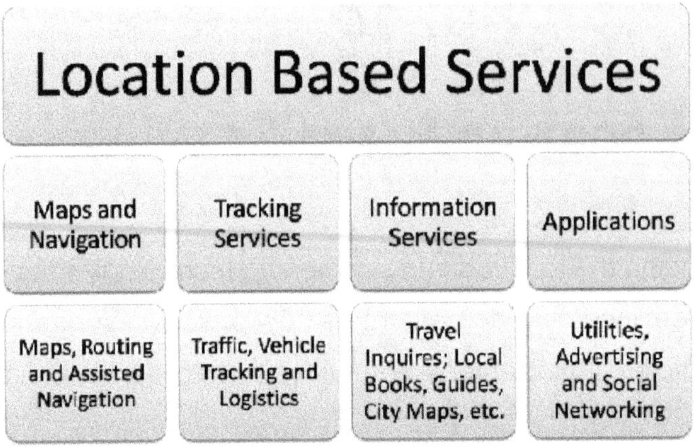

Figure 10.1 Basic classification of location based services

10.2 Getting location information

Python on Symbian allows the location of a mobile device to be determined based on information from the telephone network or from GPS receivers. There are other sophisticated methods for determining location (for example, indoor positioning using WLAN or Bluetooth) but these methods are beyond the scope of this book.

10.2.1 Network-based location

Network-based location tracking techniques use the service provider's network infrastructure to get the approximate position of the mobile device. The accuracy of network-provided location information is relatively poor when compared to GPS positioning (at best several hundred meters, and decreasing in suburban and rural areas where cells are more widely spaced). However, network-provided information has the advantage of being available indoors and on low end mobile handsets.

The following location information can be obtained from the mobile network:

- Mobile Country Code (MCC) - Represents the user's home country, as described by the SIM card's IMSI number. A list of MCCs is available on ***en.wikipedia.org/wiki/List_of_mobile_country_codes***.
- Mobile Network Code (MNC) - Identifies a mobile phone operator/carrier within a country (is used in conjunction with the MCC to identify the carrier globally)
- Location Area Code (LAC) - Uniquely represents a small geographical location.
- Cell ID (CID) - The unique number of a GSM cell for a given service provider.

The network information above is provided by the location module . The module is very simple: It has a single function, `gsm_location()`, that returns a tuple containing the GSM location information for the device.

> ***Note:***
> The Location capability is needed in order to use the location module. If the application (or the Python shell) does not have the capability, `gsm_location()` returns `None`.

The following example shows how to access and print the location information, and is followed by a screenshot of the script running on a phone.

```
import location
print location.gsm_location()
MCC, MNC, LAC, CID = location.gsm_location()
print "MCC =" + str(MCC)
print "MNC =" + str(MNC)
print "LAC =" + str(LAC)
print "CID =" + str(CID)
```

Figure 10.2 Results from `gsm_location()`

Note that the values above are all codes, not positioning co-ordinates that you can use directly in your application. There are a number of databases which map LAC/CIDs to location. Some of them, such as Google, provide web services that allow you to access the information over an Internet connection using the techniques discussed in Chapter 14. For more information, search the Internet using the term 'Mapping cell ID to location' or look for an open source project providing a cell ID database, ***www.opencellid.org***.

10.2.2 GPS positioning

The Global Positioning System (GPS) is a space-based global navigation system. A commercial GPS receiver can locate its position to within 3 to 15 metres,

95% of the time, by precisely timing the signals sent from a number of GPS satellites. GPS receivers can only be used outside as they require line of sight to at least 3 satellites.

Symbian platform mobile devices often include an integrated GPS receiver and support for Assisted GPS (A-GPS)- a GSM network based system that improves GPS startup performance. Symbian devices can also use positioning information from Bluetooth-enabled external GPS receivers. The Symbian platform UI includes applications for navigation, position, trip distance calculation and satellite status (showing the signal strength for each detected satellite). Screenshots are given below:

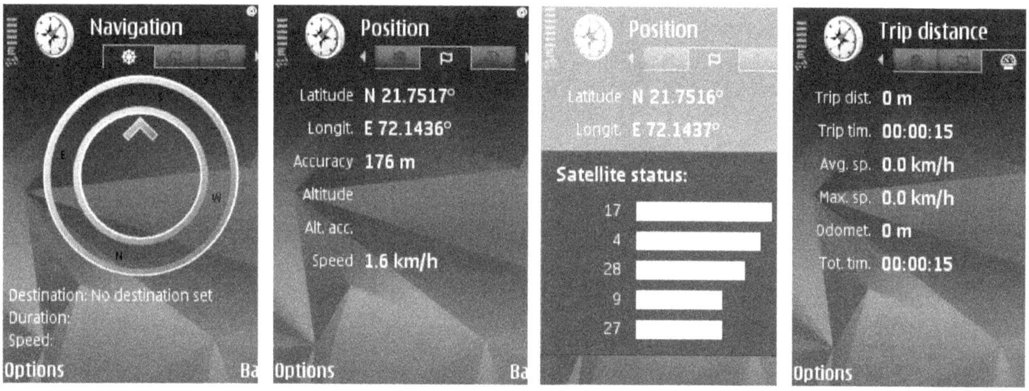

Figure 10.3 Symbian UI screenshots

Python applications use the positioning module to get information from both built in and external Bluetooth GPS receivers. Like the location module, it is simple to use.

The following code shows how to import the positioning module and how to use the `modules()` function to list the available modules.

```
>>> import positioning
>>> positioning.modules()
[{'available': 0, 'id': 270526873, 'name': u'Bluetooth GPS'}, {'available':
1,  id': 270526858, 'name': u'Integrated GPS'}, {'available': 1, 'id':
270559509, 'name': u'Network based'}]
```

The function returns a dictionary object for each supported module. The object indicates whether the module is available (a value of '1'), and contains its ID and a human readable name (description). By reformatting the list returned by the code above, we can see that this device supports an integrated GPS receiver, an AGPS module and a module for working with external Bluetooth GPS receivers, but that only the integrated GPS and AGPS are currently available:

```
{'available': 0, 'id': 270526873, 'name': u'Bluetooth GPS'}
{'available': 1, 'id': 270526858, 'name': u'Integrated GPS'}
{'available': 1, 'id': 270559509, 'name': u'Network based'}
```

We select the GPS module that we want to use by specifying its `id` with the `select_module(id)` function as follows: (In a real application we'd first check whether the module is available).

```
>>> positioning.select_module(270526850)
```

We can get detailed characteristics for a specific module using the `module_info(id)` function.

```
>>> positioning.module_info(270526858)
{'available': 1, 'status': {'data_quality': 3, 'device_status': 7},
'version': u '1.00(0)', 'name': u'Integrated GPS', 'position_quality':
{'vertical_accuracy':10.0, 'time_to_first_fix': 1000000L, 'cost': 1,
```

```
'time_to_next_fix': 1000000L, 'horizontal_accuracy': 10.0,
'power_consumption': 3}, 'technology': 1, 'id': 270526858, 'capabilities':
127, 'location': 1}
```

These characteristics can be used to compare the available GPS hardware at runtime and select the most appropriate for a specific use case.

In many cases we just want to use the device's default module (usually the integrated GPS receiver). We can fetch its id using the `default_module()` function. The code fragment shows how to use this function to get the default module and information about the default module.

```
>>> positioning.default_module() #returns the default GPS module id
270526858
>>> positioning.module_info(default_module()) # returns the module
details for the default GPS module
{'available': 1, 'status': {'data_quality': 3, 'device_status':7},
'version': u'1.00(0)', 'name': u'Integrated GPS', 'position_quality':
{'vertical_accuracy':10.0, 'time_to_first_fix': 1000000L, 'cost': 1,
'time_to_next_fix': 1000000L, 'horizontal_accuracy': 10.0,
'power_consumption': 3}, 'technology':1, 'id': 270526858, 'capabilities':
127, 'location': 1}
```

> ***Tip***
> The Emulator can be used to test positioning functions. On the Emulator menu do: **SimPSYConfigurator | Select Config File| some config files or Tools | Position**. After we have selected a positioning module, we can call `position()` to get the current position (the default module is used if no positioning module has been specified). The syntax of `position()` is:

```
position( course=0, satellites=0, callback=None,
interval=positioning.POSITION_INTERVAL, partial=0 )
```

When called without any parameters (all parameters are optional), the function blocks until positioning information is available and then returns a dictionary with the format below.

Before using the `position()` function we must first call `set_requestors()` on the service. The `set_requestors()` function specifies the type of requestor (a service or a contact), requestor data (e.g. telephone number) and the format of the requestor data. Most applications use the following (unfortunately the API is very thinly documented):

```
>>> positioning.set_requestors([{"type":"service","format":"application","data"
:"gps_app"}]
>>> positioning.position()
{'satellites': None, 'position': {'latitude': 19.120155602532, 'altitude':
16.0, 'vertical_accuracy': 7.5, 'longitude': 72.895265188042,
'horizontal_accuracy': 80.956672668457}, 'course': None}
```

Though 'satellites' are listed as `None` in the code above there is, in fact, a satellite signal. If there were no satellite signal there would be no data available and the function would return `NaN}` (not a number) as shown below:

```
>>> positioning.position()
{'satellites': None, 'position': {'latitude': NaN, 'altitude':NaN,
'vertical_accuracy': NaN, 'longitude': NaN, 'horizontal_accuracy': NaN},
'course': None}
```

To get 'satellites' and 'course' information we must specify the value 1 in the satellite parameters passed in. The function then returns information about course and satellites if it is available. If we set the `partial` parameter to 1 the function may return with incomplete information before the final fix is calculated.

```
>>> positioning.set_requestors([{"type":"service","format":"application","data"
:"gps_app"}]
>>> positioning.position(course=1,satellites=1, partial=1)
{'satellites': {'horizontal_dop': 2.86999988555908, 'used_satellites': 4,
'vertical_dop': 0.980000019073486, 'time': 1253539177.0, 'satellites': 11,
'time_dop': 1.69000005722046}, 'position': {'latitude': 19.1201448737,
'altitude': 16.0, 'vertical_accuracy': 6.5, 'longitude': 72.89526787025,
'horizontal_accuracy': 121.031242370605}, 'course': {'speed': NaN,
'heading': NaN, 'heading_accuracy': NaN, 'speed_accuracy': NaN}}
```

Some applications require occasional position fixes and use `position()` as shown above. Other applications require a continuous feed of position information at fixed intervals. In this case, we specify an `interval` in microseconds and a `callback` function. If a callback is passed as an argument, the `position()` function completes immediately. The callback function is called immediately with the current position, and is then called repeatedly at the specified time interval. The `stop_position()` function can be used to stop an on-going positioning request. Note that the callback function is called with the current position information as parameter; therefore you **must** ensure your callback function definition has a parameter.

The example here shows a script which uses a callback function to display the position every three seconds.

```
import positioning, appuifw

#callback function
def cb_pos(info):
    appuifw.note(unicode(info))

#start polling
positioning.set_requestors([{"type":"service","format":"applicatio
n","data":"gps_app"}]
positioning.position(course=1,satellites=1, callback=cb_pos, in-
terval=3000000, partial=0)
```

The last function in the positioning module is `last_position()`. This returns the cached value of the most recent GPS data received (which might be useful if you've started your application inside).

The simple example below demonstrates the use of the positioning module in more detail. The example prints `gps_data` every second for ten minutes, using a while loop and is well documented in the in-source comments. The main functions are:

- `initialize_gps()` - Initializes the GPS by selecting the GPS module, setting requestors and requesting for a fix every 0.5 seconds
- `cb_gps(event)` - Call back function which is called every 0.5 second
- `stop_gps()` - Stops the GPS

```
import e32, appuifw, positioning

def initialize_gps():
```

```
    '''This function initializes the GPS. The select_
module(module_id) can be used to select the GPS module in this
function.
    In this case we are using the default GPS (integrated GPS)
hence we do not need to select it.'''
    appuifw.note(u'Intializing GPS')
    global gps_data
    #Intitialize the global dictionary with some initial dummy
value (0.0 in this case)
    gps_data = {
    'satellites': {'horizontal_dop': 0.0, 'used_satellites': 0,
'vertical_dop': 0.0, 'time': 0.0,'satellites': 0, 'time_dop':0.0},
    'position': {'latitude': 0.0, 'altitude': 0.0, 'vertical_ac-
curacy': 0.0, 'longitude': 0.0, 'horizontal_accuracy': 0.0},
    'course': {'speed': 0.0, 'heading': 0.0, 'heading_accuracy':
0.0, 'speed_accuracy': 0.0}
    }
    try:
        # Set requesters - it is mandatory to set at least one
        positioning.set_requestors([{"type":"service","format"
:"application","data":"gps_app"}])
        # Request for a fix every 0.5 seconds
        positioning.position(course=1,satellites=1,callback=
cb_gps, interval=500000,partial=0)
        # Sleep for 3 seconds for the intitial fix
        e32.ao_sleep(3)
    except:
        appuifw.note(u'Problem with GPS','error')

def cb_gps(event):
    global gps_data
    gps_data = event

def stop_gps():
    '''Function to stop the GPS'''
    try:
        positioning.stop_position()
        appuifw.note(u'GPS stopped','error')
```

```
        except:
                appuifw.note(u'Problem with GPS','error')

#initialize GPS
initialize_gps()

#Set time for the script to run. 10 minutes in this case.
time_to_run=10
minutes=time_to_run*60

# Print the GPS data for 10 minutes.
while (minutes > 0):
        print gps_data['satellites']['used_satellites'], gps_
data['position']['latitude'], gps_data['position']['longitude'],
gps_data['course']['speed']
        minutes=minutes-1
        e32.ao_sleep(1)

# Stop the on-going request
stop_gps()
```

Symbian devices can also use the positioning module, exactly as described above, to access an external Bluetooth GPS receiver, for example, where the device doesn't have an integrated receiver, or where the external device is more accurate.

Using a socket to access an external receiver

This is a method for accessing GPS data from an external device over Bluetooth. We can use a Bluetooth socket connection to communicate directly with the receiver using "NMEA sentences": www.gpsinformation.org/dale/nmea.htm. The format of an NMEA sentence is as shown below:

```
$GPGGA,123519,4807.038,N,01131.000,E,1,08,0.9,545.4,M,46.9
,M,,*47
```

```
Where:
     GGA          Global Positioning System Fix Data
     123519       Fix taken at 12:35:19 UTC
     4807.038,N   Latitude 48 deg 07.038' N
     01131.000,E  Longitude 11 deg 31.000' E
     1            Fix quality: 0 = invalid
                               1 = GPS fix (SPS)
                               2 = DGPS fix
                               3 = PPS fix
                         4 = Real Time Kinematic
                         5 = Float RTK
                               6 = estimated (dead reckoning) (2.3
feature)
                         7 = Manual input mode
                         8 = Simulation mode
     08           Number of satellites being tracked
     0.9          Horizontal dilution of position
     545.4,M      Altitude, Meters, above mean sea level
     46.9,M       Height of geoid (mean sea level) above WGS84
                      ellipsoid
     (empty field) time in seconds since last DGPS update
     (empty field) DGPS station ID number
     *47          the checksum data, always begins with *
```

First, we establish a connection with the Bluetooth GPS receiver using the socket module (the Bluetooth GPS receiver must first be paired with the mobile device).

```
>>> import socket
>>> address, services = socket.bt_discover() # search for the
Bluetooth device
>>> gps_receiver = (address, services.values()[0]) # select the
external Bluetooth GPS receiver
>>> connection = socket.socket(socket.AF_BT, socket.SOCK_STREAM)
>>> connection.connect(gps_receiver) # establish connection
```

Next, we listen to the NMEA sentences transmitted by the external GPS receiver. We split the sentence to obtain the latitude and longitude. Note that Python's "file like sockets" API makes this very easy by providing each sentence as a single line (see Chapter 9 for more information).

```
>>> gps_data = connection.makefile("r", 0)
>>> if (gps_data.startswith("$GPGGA"): # check if gps_data is a
valid NMEA sentence. Refer to the sentence syntax above.
            gps_data = gps_data.split(",") # string handling
            latitude = gps_data[2] # define Latitude
            longitude = gps_data[4] # define Longitude

>>> print latitude, longitude
```

10.2.3 Other positioning technologies

In addition to using the location and positioning module, there are online web services which return the location information for the handset based on its IP address. This information can be obtained using the urllib module as described in Chapter 14. The accuracy of these services varies enormously - care should be taken because even though these services may return very detailed information, it is not uncommon for them to be incorrect even at the city level. To find more information on these services, use the term 'geo ip' in your preferred search engine.

10.3 Maps with GPS information: Where am I?

In the previous section, we discussed how to get the position of the mobile handset. We can be combined this information with mapping information to create applications that provide a personalized, contextual and compelling experience for the end-user. Not only can we show the user where they are, but we can add features such as custom descriptions, URLs, labels, groups, icons and so on.

This section demonstrates a simple mapping application called Where Am I? (originally contributed by Herb Jellinek). The application determines the location of the user and maps it on Google Maps. Where Am I? is compatible with devices with an integrated GPS receiver. The application could be made to work with an external Bluetooth GPS receiver or with another web service, such as Yahoo Maps or Ovi Maps with minor code modifications.

The application has a minimal user interface which allows us to focus on the positioning and mapping features. It demonstrates good exception handling, default access point selection techniques and debug logging which should provide a useful reference for new Python programmers on the Symbian platform.

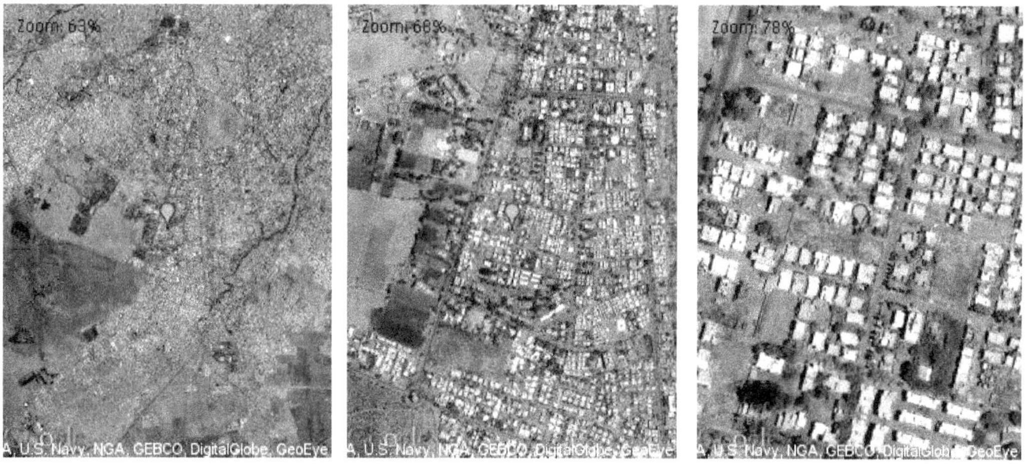

Figure 10.4 Where Am I application

Let's dive into the code now! The Where Am I? application is comprised of five files as shown in the following diagram.

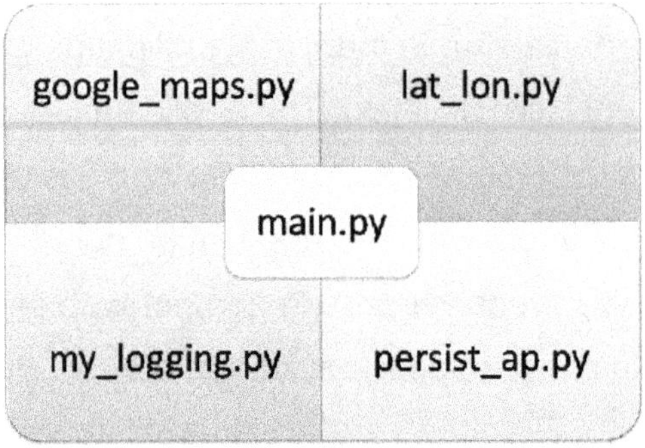

Figure 10.5 Where Am I application files

An overview of each file is given in the table below, and their implementations are discussed individually in the following sections.

Table 10.1: Where Am I Source Code Files

File Name	Function
main.py	The main application script that uses other libraries and displays the map.
lat_lon.py	Obtains the latitude and longitude of the current location using the positioning module.
google_maps.py	Plots the current location on Google maps.
persist_ap.py	Saves the access point for future use.
my_logging.py	Adds entries to the debug log.

10.3.1 Obtaining latitude and longitude co-ordinates

The lat_lon.py module provides a wrapper around the positioning module initialization sequence and reduces its API to a few key functions:

- hasPositioning() returns True if the device can get position information, and False otherwise.
- getLatLon() returns a tuple containing the latitude and longitude (or (None, None) if positioning isn't supported)
- getPos() returns a dictionary containing the following attributes (or None if positioning isn't supported):
  - time: <float, Unix time>
  - latitude: <float>
  - longitude: <float>
  - altitude: <float>
  - horizontal_accuracy: <float>
  - vertical_accuracy: <float>

The code is much the same as discussed earlier in this chapter and should be straightforward to understand.

```
# lat_lon.py
# A simple module that wraps the positioning module to hide its
initialization
# sequence and simplify its API to a couple of simple calls.

import positioning

modules = positioning.modules()
if len(modules) == 0:

    # There's no way to get our position, so don't try.
```

```
    def getPos():
        return None
    # There's no way to get our position, so don't try.
    def getLatLon():
        return None, None
    # There's no way to get our position.
    def hasPositioning():
        return False

else:

    # select a positioning module (a device might have several)
    positioning.select_module(positioning.default_module())

    # The documentation is completely opaque
    # regarding the meanings of the argument to set_requestors.
    positioning.set_requestors([{"type":   "service",
                                 "format": "application",
                                 "data":   "loc"}])

    # Return the current position of the device.
    def getPos():
        return positioning.position()['position']
    # Return the current position of the device as a simple lat/
lon tuple.
    def getLatLon():
        pos = getPos()
        return (pos['latitude'], pos['longitude'])
    # Yes, we can do positioning.
    def hasPositioning():
        return True
```

10.3.2 Retrieving Google Maps

The google_maps.py module is used to retrieve a Google map for a specified latitude and longitude in a specified image format, and to save it in a temporary file.

Google requires an API key in all requests to the Google Maps API. If you do not have an API Key, you can obtain one from ***code.google.com/apis/maps/signup.html***. This API key should be assigned the GMAPS_KEY variable in the example below.

> ***Warning***
> The Google Maps web API used in Where Am I? is available free for non-commercial use only. You should always read the terms of use carefully before using any web API in your application.

The source code below is well documented. The `GoogleMaps` class creates a URL (`GMAPS_URL`) in the correct format for the Google Maps web services API and includes the API Key `GMAPS_KEY`. It then uses the urllib module to retrieve the map and saves it to a temporary file. The urllib module is discussed in Chapter 14.

```
# google_maps.py
# Module for retrieving and displaying Google Maps.
#
import urllib
from graphics import Image
# for generating temp file names
import random

from my_logging import log

# The "key" that lets the Google Maps service know who is
# accessing its service. Treat this as confidential information.
#
# You must obtain your own Google Maps key from
```

```
# http://code.google.com/apis/maps/signup.html
#
GMAPS_KEY = "not set yet"

if GMAPS_KEY == "not set yet":
    print "You must obtain a Google Maps key."
    print "See the google_maps.py source code for details."

# The format of the images we retrieve.  Legal values are gif,
jpg,
# jpg-baseline, png8, png32
GOOGLE_IMAGE_FORMAT = "jpg"

# Mapping from Google image format name to file extension.
EXTENSIONS = {"gif": "gif", "jpg": "jpg", "jpg-baseline": "jpg",
              "png8": "png", "png32": "png"}

# Where to store the images we retrieve.  Keep it on D:, the temp
device.
# We pass this to urllib.urlretrieve, which should have the abil-
ity
# to generate its own temp file names, but which is broken in Py-
thon on the Symbian platform.
TEMP_FILE = u"D:\\temp"+str(random.randint(0,
10000))+"."+EXTENSIONS[GOOGLE_IMAGE_FORMAT]

# The minimum zoom factor
MIN_ZOOM = 0

# The maximum zoom factor.
MAX_ZOOM = 19

# Base URL to be used to retrieve map images from Google.  It's a
format
# string with the following fields, in order from left to right:
#
# %f - latitude of center of map
# %f - longitude of center of map
```

```
# %d - zoom factor to use, an integer from 0 (entire Earth) to
#        19 (individual buildings)
# %d - image width, in pixels
# %d - image height, in pixels
# %s - map type, a string equal to one of "roadmap" (a standard
roadmap image),
#        "mobile" (a mobile roadmap map image, with larger fea-
tures and text),
#        "satellite" (a satellite image),
#        "terrain" (a physical relief map, showing terrain and
vegetation),
#        "hybrid" (a hybrid of the satellite and roadmap image).
# %s - markers, a set of marker descriptors as described at
#        http://code.google.com/apis/maps/documentation/
staticmaps/#Markers
#
GMAPS_URL = "http://maps.google.com/staticmap?center=%f,%f&format=
"+GOOGLE_IMAGE_FORMAT+
"&zoom=%d&size=%dx%d&maptype=%s&markers=%s&key="+GMAPS_KEY


#
# An object that can produce a map of the area surrounding a given
location.
#
class GoogleMaps:
    # Create a new Google Maps map factory.  We pass in the de-
sired image
    # width and height and map type, as those are likely to be
common across
    # successive requests.  map type is optional and defaults to
"mobile".
    # marker color is optional and defaults to "green".  marker
size is
    # optional and defaults to "small".
    def __init__(self, (width, height), mapType="mobile",
markerColor="green",
                 markerSize="small"):
```

```
        self.width = width
        self.height = height
        self.mapType = mapType
        self.markerColor = markerColor
        self.markerSize = markerSize

    # Given a sequence of lat-lon pairs, return a string contain-
ing
    # map markers in the Google Maps format.  We use a fixed marker
color,
    # size, and no character labels.
    #
    # The string will look like
    # markers=markerDescriptor1|markerDescriptor2|markerDescript
or3|... etc.
    # where a markerDescription looks like
    # latitude,longitude,{size}{color}{alphanumeric-character}
    #
    # latitude - a latitudinal value with precision to 6 decimal
places
    # longitude - a longitudinal value with precision to 6 decimal
places
    # size - the size of marker, one of "tiny", "mid", "small"
    # color - a color from the set {black, brown, green, purple,
yellow,
    #         blue, gray, orange, red, white}.
    # alphanumeric-character - a single lowercase alphanumeric
character
    # from the set {a-z, 0-9}. Default and mid sized markers are
the
    # only ones capable of displaying an alphanumeric-character
parameter.
    #
    # Only the latitude and longitude parameters are required.
The others
    # are optional.
    def makeMarkerString(self, positions):
        str = ""
```

```
        for (lat, lon) in positions:
            str = str + ("%f,%f,%s%s|" % (lat, lon, self.marker-
Size,
                                                  self.markerColor))
        return str

    # Set the width and height for all subsequent requests.
    def setImageSize(self, pos):
        width, height = pos
        log("setImageSize(%d,%d)" % (width, height))
        self.width = width
        self.height = height

    # Get the map centered at centerLatLon, at zoom factor zoom,
    # with markers at positions markerPositions, which may be
empty.
    def getMapImage(self, centerLatLon, zoom, markerPositions):
        lat, lon = centerLatLon
        url = (GMAPS_URL % (lat, lon, zoom, self.width, self.
height,
                self.mapType, self.makeMarkerString(markerPosition
s)))
        log("url = "+url)
        file, ignoredHeaders = urllib.urlretrieve(url, TEMP_FILE)
        return Image.open(file)
```

10.3.3 Saving the access point

The Google Maps API is accessed over the Internet, which requires an access point to be specified by the user. In order to minimize the number of times the application has to prompt the user the persist_ap.py module saves the user's preferred access point to a database and, while it remains valid, reuses it for subsequent connections.

The access point selection and persistence logic is as follows (in pseudo code).

```
Open the access point database.
If it doesn't exist:
   Get list of available access points.
   If none available:
       Display error message.
       After user confirms, abort program.
   Otherwise:
       Display list of available access points.
       Get user's selection.
       Store it in DB.
       Set it as default.
If it does exist:
   Get name of access point from DB.
   Look up name of access point in list of available ones.
   If not found:
       (duplicate logic of "If it doesn't exist" case above)
   Otherwise:
       Set this access point as the default.
```

We don't reproduce the whole of the persist_ap.py module here. However, we do briefly discuss two important functions: `selectAP()` and `removePersistentAP()`.

`selectAP()` allows the user to select a valid access point and saves it in a database (`CONN_DB_NAME`).

```
# Database containing connection info
CONN_DB_NAME = u"e:\\python\\conninfo.db"

# DB key for the Internet Access Point
IAPID_KEY      = u"iapid"

def terminalError(msg):
    appuifw.note(msg, 'error')
```

```
#
# Let the user select an AP from the system's list.
# Write it to the DB and return the ID and access point object.
#
def userChooseAndSelectAP(db):
    accessPoints = socket.access_points()
    if accessPoints and len(accessPoints) > 0:
        apID = socket.select_access_point()
        ap = socket.access_point(apID)
        socket.set_default_access_point(ap)
        db[IAPID_KEY] = str(apID)
        return apID, ap
    else:
        terminalError(u"No access points available")
        return (None, None)
```

`removePersistentAP()` clears the saved access point from the database (`CONN_DB_NAME`).

```
#
# Open the connection info DB in the given mode.
# Return the DB object, or return None if it was not possible to
open it
# in that mode.
#
def openDB(mode="w"):
    try:
        db = e32dbm.open(CONN_DB_NAME, mode)
        log("opened DB %s mode %s" % (str(db), mode))
        return db
    except:
        log("openDB %s returns None" % mode)
        return None

# Remove the Access Point info stored in the database.
# Note that this doesn't affect the application's current default
```

```
access point.
# A subsequent call to selectAP should pop up the Access Point
menu and
# then set the default AP.
#
def removePersistentAP():
    db = openDB(mode="w")
    try:
        del db[IAPID_KEY]
    finally:
        if db:
            db.close()
```

10.3.4 Debug logging

my_logging.py provides a very simply interface for writing debug statements to a file (`gFile`). It is similar to the logging mechanism described in Chapter 17, except that it can be turned off, and provides a dedicated method for logging exceptions and it does not flush pending bytes to the file.

The four logging functions are:

- `disableLogging()` - disable logging
- `logException()` - log an exception
- `getLogFile()` - return path of the log file
- `log(msg)` - log msg to the log file

```
# my_logging.py
# Tiny logging module.
# This abstracts away the means for adding entries to the debug
log,
# allowing us to turn it off, for example.
#
```

```
import time

# Log file name - use the .txt extension so Symbian's File Manager
app knows
# how to open it, should you want to do that on the handset.
LOG_FILE_NAME = 'e:/Python/my-log.txt'

gFile = open(LOG_FILE_NAME, 'w')

gEnabled = True

def disableLogging():
    global gEnabled
    gEnabled = False

def logException():
    import traceback
    traceback.print_exc(None, gFile)

def getLogFile():
    return gFile

def log(msg):
    global gEnabled
    if gEnabled:
        logStr = time.strftime('%I:%M:%S: ', time.
localtime())+str(msg)+'\n'
        gFile.write(logStr)
```

10.3.5 Using the above libraries in main.py

main.py uses the simple APIs we've created to get the device's latitude and longitude, retrieve a map and then create a canvas to display the map to the user. We also allow the user to zoom in and out using up and down keys and update the map accordingly.

Again, the code is well documented in-source, and is in any case quite straight-forward:

```
# main.py
# Repeatedly fetch our position and display a map of it. Zoom in
and out
# using the up and down rocker keys.
#

import e32, appuifw
from graphics import Image
from key_codes import *

import sys
sys.path.append('e:\Python\lib')

import persist_ap
import lat_lon, google_maps

from my_logging import log, logException

APP_LOCK = e32.Ao_lock()

DEFAULT_ZOOM = 17

def main():
    # Select a network access point
    persist_ap.selectAP()

    appuifw.app.screen='full'
    appuifw.exit_key_handler = lambda:APP_LOCK.signal()

    # This will create our map images.
    mapFactory = google_maps.GoogleMaps((240, 320),
mapType="satellite")

    image = None
```

```
    canvas = None

    # Make zoom a list so we can set the zoom value from within
handleEvent.
    # The outer zoom list is available globally because we are us-
ing indices and there is no local list.
    # We could alternatively have made zoom global
    zoom = [DEFAULT_ZOOM]

    # Set the zoom value.  See note above regarding why we do it
this way.
    def setZoom(newValue):
        zoom[0] = newValue

    # Get the zoom value.  See note above regarding why we do it
this way.
    def getZoom():
        return zoom[0]

    # Draw the map image.
    def drawImage(rect):
        canvas.blit(image)
        canvas.text(((10, 20)),
                    u"Zoom: %d%%" % ((100.0 * getZoom()) / google_
maps.MAX_ZOOM))

    # Handle keyboard events, like the zoom keys.
    def handleEvent(event):
        log("handleEvent %s" % event)
        try:
            if event["type"] == appuifw.EEventKeyUp:
                if event["scancode"] == EScancodeUpArrow:
                    # zoom in (larger factor)
                    setZoom(min(google_maps.MAX_ZOOM, getZoom() +
1))
                elif event["scancode"] == EScancodeDownArrow:
                    # zoom out (smaller factor)
                    setZoom(max(google_maps.MIN_ZOOM, getZoom() -
```

```
1))
        except:
            logException()

    canvas = appuifw.Canvas(redraw_callback=drawImage,
                            event_callback=handleEvent)
    appuifw.app.body = canvas

    oldLatLon = None
    while True:
        latLon = lat_lon.getLatLon()
        if oldLatLon == latLon:
            continue
        oldLatLon = latLon
        image = mapFactory.getMapImage(latLon, getZoom(), (lat-
Lon,))
        drawImage(())

    APP_LOCK.wait()

if __name__ == "__main__":
    main()
```

10.4 Summary

This chapter illustrated various techniques of getting location information from the device using location and positioning modules. The chapter also highlights a sample application 'Where am I?', which maps the current location of the device on Google Maps.

11

Sensor Framework

The Symbian sensor framework provides access to sensor information on Symbian devices (most Nokia S60 3rd Edition, FP2 devices or later products). This chapter explains how to check for sensor support and monitor sensor data using the framework. It also gives some real-world examples of how you can use sensors to control your applications, and provides a very brief overview of the legacy sensor API used in earlier platforms.

11.1 Introduction

Mobile devices may contain many sophisticated sensors including, but not limited to, accelerometers, light sensors, proximity sensors, magnetometers, and magnetic north sensors! These sensors may be used for any number of purposes, such as to turn off touch screen sensitivity when a user's face is close to the screen, to dim the display in dark room to save power, and to use gesture and motion control in an application. Applications are already using sensors in ways that were not imagined when they were first included in mobile devices.

The Symbian platform provides access to all sensors through a "sensor framework". The framework provides a common generic mechanism for applications to query the platform for sensor availability and to obtain sensor data. It can be extended using plug-ins as new sensors are added, ensuring that a consistent interface is available to applications moving forward.

This chapter explains how to use the Symbian sensor framework through Python. At the end of the chapter there is a brief discussion of the legacy sensor-specific APIs used in older versions of the Symbian/S60 platform.

11.2 Sensor channels

Python provides access to the Symbian platform's sensor framework through the **sensor** module.

The sensor framework (and module) makes sensor data available through 'channels', where each channel represents a single type of information from a sensor. Some sensors will provide multiple channels; for example, an accelerometer can supply data to both a three-dimensional positioning channel and to a channel that detects double-taps on the screen.

In PyS60 v2.0.0, the following channels are currently supported:

- Accelerometer XYZ sensor
- Rotation sensor
- Orientation sensor
- Accelorometer double-tap sensor
- Proximity monitor sensor
- Ambient light sensor
- Magnetic North sensor
- Magnetometer XYZ sensor.

Programmers can use the `list_channels()` function to list all the channels available on a device. The function returns a list of dictionary objects, which contain channel information including:

- `id`: system id of the channel
- `type`: channel type, useful in access function calls
- `name`: system name of the channel.

For example, a Python shell session on the Nokia N97 lists 10 channels:

```
>>> import sensor
>>> sensor.list_channels()
[{'type': 536929669L, 'id': 7L, 'name': 'ProximityMonitor'},
{'type': 536919830L, 'id': 8L, 'name': 'AmbientLightData'},
{'type': 270553214L, 'id': 9L, 'name': 'AccelerometerXYZAxisDa-
ta'},
{'type': 270553217L, 'id': 10L, 'name': 'AccelerometerDoubleTap-
pingData'},
{'type': 270553215L, 'id': 11L, 'name': 'TSensrvTappingData'},
{'type': 536919776L, 'id': 12L, 'name': 'MagnetometerXYZAxisDa-
ta'},
{'type': 536957243L, 'id': 13L, 'name': None},
{'type': 536919775L, 'id': 14L, 'name': 'MagneticNorthData'},
{'type': 270553224L, 'id': 15L, 'name': 'OrientationData'},
{'type': 270553225L, 'id': 16L, 'name': 'RotationData'}]
```

The name of each channel is human-readable, for example, MagnetometerXYZAxisData is a magnetometer that provides three-dimensional spatial information. As you'll see in the rest of the chapter, I tend to use the name in our scripts rather than the type or id because this results in more readable code. Note too that not every sensor is useful - the one with name 'None' doesn't do anything, and the AccelerometerDoubleTappingData sensor and the TSensrvTappingData provide the same information.

11.3 Checking sensor availability

The sensor framework is not present on every Symbian device that supports Python, and not every device where it is present has the same set of sensors/channels. Well-written applications will either restrict their installation to devices and platform that support the full set of functionality, or selectively enable functionality based on the presence of specific sensors. Applications can check for the presence of the sensor module as follows:

```
try:
    import sensor
    SENSOR_AVAILABLE = True
except ImportError:
    SENSOR_AVAILABLE = False
```

The easiest way to determine if a particular sensor is available is to iterate through the available channels (use list_channels()) and compare the channel name to the name of the required channel. The following code shows how this may be done:

```
def sensorPresent(testSensor):
    sensors = sensor.list_channels()
    for sense in sensors:
        if sense['name'] == testSensor:
            return True
    return False
```

11.4 Channel classes and attributes

Each sensor channel is represented by a separate class. The classes have different attributes that are used to provide data from the sensor. For example, the accelerometer XYZ data channel class, called `AccelerometerXYZAxisData`, has x, y, and z attributes that give values along the X-, Y-, and Z-axes, respectively.

Table 2.1 lists each sensor channel, the name of the class the represents it, and the class attributes that are used to reference values of the sensor channel data.

Table 2.1:Sensor channels

Sensor Channel	Class Name	Class Attributes
Accelerometer XYZ sensor channel	`AccelerometerXYZAxisData`	x gives X-axis value y gives Y-axis value z gives Z-axis value
Accelerometer double-tap sensor channel	`AccelerometerDoubleTappingData`	direction gives the tap direction
Magnetometer XYZ sensor channel	`MagnetometerXYZAxisData`	x gives X-axis value y gives Y-axis value z gives Z-axis value calib_level is an integer giving the level of calibration: • 0 means the device is not calibrated • 1 indicates low calibration • 2 indicates a medium level of calibration • 3 indicates highly accurate calibration
Magnetic North sensor channel	`MagneticNorthData`	azimuth gives the degrees clockwise from magnetic north; values 0 to 359 are possible

<table>
<tr><td>Ambient light sensor channel</td><td><code>Ambient-LightData</code></td><td>ambient_light gives the light level as an integer percentage value, ranging from 0 to 100:
• 0 means very dark
• 100 means sunny</td></tr>
<tr><td>Proximity monitor sensor channel</td><td><code>Proximity-Monitor</code></td><td>proximity_state gives one of three values:
• 0 means that the proximity is not determined
• 1 means that the proximity of another object is not close
• 2 means that the proximity of another object is close
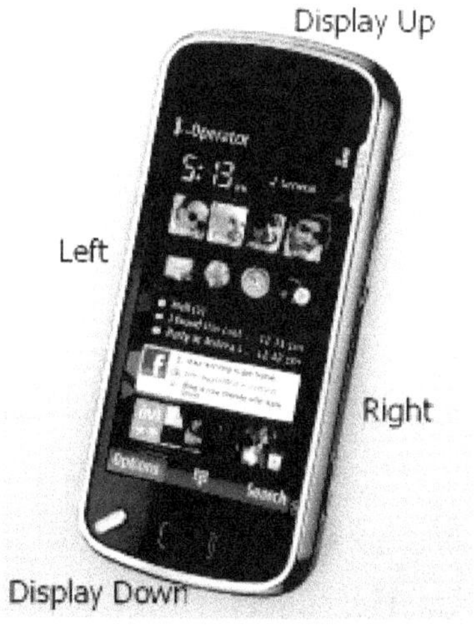

Figure 11.1 Labelling of sides on a phone</td></tr>
</table>

Orientation sensor channel	`OrientationData`	device_orientation gives the orientation of the device in a range of integer values from -1 to 6. The orientation is from the user's perspective, when the phone is held in "portrait" mode: • -1 means the sensor has not been initialized • 0 means the orientation is undefined • 1 means that the "display up" side is up • 2 means that the "display down" side is up • 3 means that the left side is up • 4 means that the right side is up • 5 means that the display itself is up • 6 means that the back of the device is up
Rotation sensor channel	`RotationData`	x gives X-axis value y gives Y-axis value z gives Z-axis value

Most of the information in the table is self-explanatory, although it's worth pointing out the following: Several of the sensors give a three-dimensional result as (x, y, z) axis data. It is important to remember that each three-dimensional sensor is different. The "accelerometer XYZ sensor channel" gives data on the movement on each axis; the "magnetometer XYZ sensor channel" gives data about the geomagnetic fields on each axis - the "rotation sensor channel" - gives the degree of rotation about each axis.

Some sensors return integer data where a descriptive string might be more useful. For example, an ambient light level of 40 may not be as meaningful as "`AmbientLightTwilight`". The `sensor.get_logicalname()` function allows you to get the string for a particular value, as follows:

```
# Format is:  get_logicalname(<classLookupName>, <value>)
# For example
sensor.get_logicalname(sensor.SensrvAmbientLightData, 40)
```

- There is more data available for the accelerometer double-tap sensor channel than just the "direction" value. The data is available from other functions in the `AccelerometerDoubleTappingData` class:
- `get_axis_active()` returns a tuple of three axis activity indicators: a 0 (disabled) or a 1 (active) for each axis
- `set_axis_active([x=None, y=None, z=None])` sets one or more axis as an active axis
- `get_properties()` returns a tuple of values indicating the `TapThresholdValue`, `TapDurationValue`, `TapLatencyValue`, and `TapIntervalValue` variables.
- `set_properties([DblTapThresholdValue = None, DblTapDurationValue = None, DblTapLatencyValue = None, DblTapIntervalValue = None])` sets the properties of variables given.

The 'active axis' determines how the double tap is determined. For example, if the X axis is turned off, but the Y and Z axes are turned on, then only changes in the Y and Z values will be used to determine double tapping.

These calls will be used and more deeply explained later in the section on gestures.

- The `AccelerometerXYZAxisData` and `RotationData` class constructors take an optional parameter that gives the name of a function used to implement a noise filtering algorithm. The possible choices are `MedianFilter()` or `LowPassFilter()`.
- A median filter will select the middle value from a collection of data, and for data that is relatively close together it is a good general-purpose noise reducer.
- A low pass filter will focus on values at the lower end of the data range and ignore high values. For noisy data that can produce wilder, out-of-range values, a low-pass filter smoothes out the signal and removes short spikes in the retrieved data.
- Not specifying a filter in the constructor call will allow raw data to be retrieved from the sensor.

11.5 Monitoring sensor data

Sensor channels cannot be polled: you can't simply create a sensor channel object and query the current value of the data. Instead, the sensor framework is designed to be monitored and the data returned to the application in callbacks as it arrives.

The sequence of setting up and retrieving data is as follows:

- Initialize the sensor by creating an instance of the channel class
- Register a callback function by calling the channel object's `set_callback()` function
- Start monitoring the channel by calling the channel object's `start_listening()` function
- Collect data for some time period
- Stop retrieving data (i.e., stop using the callback function) by calling the `stop_listening()` function of the sensor object.

The following code shows how to use the ambient-light sensor channel class to monitor the light level and print its logical name:

```
light = sensor.AmbientLightData()
def reportTheLight():
   global light
   level = light.ambient_light
   print "Light level is", level, "or", sensor.get_
logicalname(sensor.SensrvAmbientLightData, level)
light.set_callback(reportTheLight)
light.start_listening()
```

The output of the code is something like:

```
Light level is 60 or AmbientLightLight
```

A call to `light.stop_listening()` will stop the monitoring.

The following example shows how to monitor the orientation of the device (omitting the call to "`side.stop_listening()`" to stop monitoring):

```
side = sensor.OrientationData()
def reportOrientation():
    global side
    print sensor.get_logicalname(sensor.SensrvDeviceOrientation,
side.device_orientation)
side.set_callback(reportOrientation)
side.start_listening()
```

Now, if I start with the phone facing me in portrait orientation, then rotate it counter-clockwise, here is the output:

```
OrientationDisplayUp
OrientationDisplayRightUp
OrientationDisplayDown
OrientationDisplayLeftUp
OrientationDisplayUp
```

For the final example, we monitor the accelerometer coordinates as the phone is rotated (counter-clockwise):

```
meter = sensor.AccelerometerXYZAxisData(data_filter=sensor.LowPass-
Filter())
```

```
def reportXYZ():
    global meter
    print "(",meter.x,",",meter.y,",",meter.z,")"
meter.set_callback(reportXYZ)
meter.start_listening()
```

The result is a stream of (x, y, z) coordinate data:

```
( -1 , 6 , 0 )
( -1 , 11 , 1 )
( -1 , 16 , 2 )
( -2 , 23 , 3 )
( -3 , 29 , 4 )
( -4 , 34 , 6 )
( -5 , 40 , 9 )
( -5 , 46 , 11 )
( -6 , 51 , 12 )
( -6 , 57 , 13 )
( -7 , 57 , 14 )
( -8 , 58 , 14 )
( -10 , 59 , 13 )
( -11 , 59 , 11 )
( -10 , 59 , 10 )
( -9 , 58 , 10 )
( -7 , 57 , 9 )
( -7 , 57 , 9 )
( -6 , 57 , 9 )
( -6 , 56 , 7 )
```

```
( -5 , 56 , 7 )
( -5 , 57 , 8 )
( -3 , 55 , 9 )
( 0 , 54 , 10 )
( 1 , 54 , 12 )
( 1 , 56 , 11 )
( 1 , 57 , 11 )
( 1 , 58 , 10 )
( 1 , 58 , 10 )
( 2 , 58 , 11 )
( 3 , 58 , 11 )
```

Obviously, my hand did not remain perfectly still along the Z axis, but let's ignore that for now. You can see that the movement of the phone started slowly along the X axis but was faster along the Y axis. If we plot all 211 points on a X-Y graph, we get the graph shown in Figure 11.2.

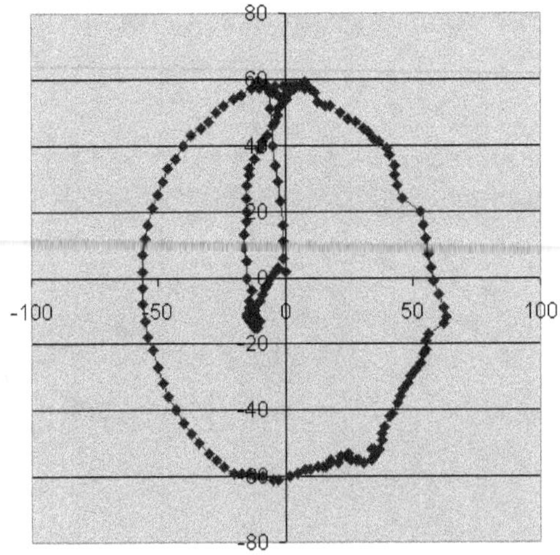

Figure 11.2 Plot of phone coordinates moving in space

You can see the phone roughly moved in a circle, except when I had to change hands, which slowed movement along one axis.

11.6 Sensor controlled bouncing ball

This section gives a more complex example. The `ball.py` example distributed with the PyS60 installation implements a ball dropping and bouncing on the screen in response to arrow keys. We modify this to control the bouncing ball using sensors.

The first question to ask is, "which sensors to use?". We want the ball to respond to movement of the phone, so we could use the rotation sensor or the accelerometer (other sensors like the ambient light sensor do not make sense for this use case). The rotation sensor responds to rotation in degrees around a single axis, and it will not render data that corresponds to movement along a single axis or give data that measures distances. So, the accelerometer appears to be the sensor of choice.

The following code provides chunks afterwards.the full solution. We examine this code in:

```
import appuifw, e32
from sensor import *
from graphics import *

# Some initial initializations
X = 0
```

```
Y = 1
img = None

# Here, we define some callbacks.
# First, we define the callback for the accelerometer.  We record
the direction of the movement along
# X and Y axes.
def deviceMoved():
    global accelerometer, prevX, prevY, dirx, diry

    dirx = prevX - accelerometer.x
    diry = prevY - accelerometer.y
    prevX = accelerometer.x
    prevY = accelerometer.y

# This is a callback for redrawing canvas graphics
def handleRedraw(rect):
    if img:
        canvas.blit(img)

# We ignore canvas events
def handleCanvasEvent(event):
    pass

# Application QUIT callback
def quit():
    global running
    running=0
```

```
if ! SENSOR_AVAILABLE:
   exit();

# Now we set up the accelerometer object and start listening to
the accelerometer
accelerometer = AccelerometerXYZAxisData(data_
filter=LowPassFilter())
accelerometer.set_callback(data_callback=deviceMoved)
accelerometer.start_listening()

# Here we set up the application screen to be the canvas and full
screen
appuifw.app.screen = 'full'
appuifw.app.body = \
    canvas = \
    appuifw.Canvas(event_callback=handleCanvasEvent, redraw_
callback=handleRedraw)
appuifw.app.exit_key_handler = quit

# New (empty) image
img = Image.new(canvas.size)

# Some final initializations before we begin.  Ball is in the mid-
dle of the screen.
prevX = prevY = 0
location = [img.size[X]/2,img.size[Y]/2]
speed = [0.,0.]
```

```
blobsize = 16
width,height = img.size[X]-blobsize,img.size[Y]-blobsize
gravity = 0.03
acceleration = 0.1
frames = 0
dirx = 0
diry = 0

# Start things going.  Stop the simulation when "running" = 0
running = 1
while running:
    # Clear the screen, draw the ball.
    img.clear(0)
    img.point((location[X]+blobsize/2,location[Y]+blobsize/2),
              0x00ff00,width=blobsize)
    handleRedraw(())

    # Yield active object (thread) execution for a moment
    e32.ao_yield()

    # Adjust the speed to slow a bit and to obey gravity.  Then
adjust the location.
    speed[X] *= 0.999
    speed[X] *= 0.999
    speed[X] += gravity if dirx > 0 else -gravity
    speed[Y] += gravity if diry > 0 else -gravity
    location[X] += speed[X]
    location[Y] += speed[Y]
```

```
    # If we hit a wall, bounce back!
    if location[X]>width:
        location[X]=width-(location[X]-width)
        speed[X]=-0.80*speed[X]
        speed[Y]=0.90*speed[Y]
    if location[X]<0:
        location[X]=-location[X]
        speed[X]=-0.80*speed[X]
        speed[Y]=0.90*speed[Y]
    if location[Y]>height:
        location[Y]=height-(location[Y]-height)
        speed[X]=0.90*speed[X]
        speed[Y]=-0.80*speed[Y]
    if location[Y]<0:
        location[Y]=-location[Y]
        speed[X]=0.90*speed[X]
        speed[Y]=-0.80*speed[Y]

    # Adjust the speed to reflect the movement of the accelerom-
eter.  Note we assume
    # that the accelerometer callback has adjusted the direction
variables
    speed[X] += dirx*acceleration
    speed[Y] -= diry*acceleration

    # Only go for a finite number of iterations.  Then stop.
    frames += 1
```

```
    if frames>400:
        running = 0
        accelerometer.stop_listening()
```

The code starts by initializing some data, then it sets up callbacks for the accelerometer and the canvas. First let's look at the accelerometer callback:

```
def deviceMoved():
    global accelerometer, prevX, prevY, dirx, diry

    dirx = prevX - accelerometer.x
    diry = prevY - accelerometer.y
    prevX = accelerometer.x
    prevY = accelerometer.y
```

The function records values to indicate direction of movement and saves values for the next call. It takes no arguments, instead using global variables to set and retain accelerometer values. As the callback will be called while the main code is executing, sharing access to these variables could potentially be a problem. As it is, this function is the only code that changes these values, so no concurrency issues need to be considered.

We set up the accelerometer with the following code, using a low pass filter to eliminate as much noise as possible and to smooth the data. We start listening to the sensor right away.

```
accelerometer = AccelerometerXYZAxisData(data_
```

```
filter=LowPassFilter())
accelerometer.set_callback(data_callback=deviceMoved)
accelerometer.start_listening()
```

Once the sensor has data, the variables `dirx` and `diry` will change according to the movement of the phone. We use this change to control the speed along both axes:

```
speed[X] += dirx*acceleration
speed[Y] -= diry*acceleration
```

Previously, I noted that the `deviceMoved()` function executes concurrently with the main code in the program. It executes as an active object (in Symbian platform parlance) and interrupts the main code when it needs to execute. This interruption can cause the main code to slow down. It is wise to explicitly share the CPU with the active object. We do that in the code as follows:

```
e32.ao_yield()
```

This call yields execution back to the system and asks the system to wake up the thread when necessary, such as for a sensor event. The system treats the thread as a Symbian C++ active object, which is an efficient asynchronous method of handling system events. Without the yield, the thread will loop repeatedly, even when there is no event to process. If there is no event, the code will redraw the ball in the same location as the previous iteration, which will cause the code to slow down due to wasted graphics manipulation. This performance degradation can be dramatic: in one trial, code to execute 400 frames or iterations ran in 36 seconds using the yield statement and 65 seconds without it.

11.7 Detecting gestures

An interesting use of sensor data is to detect gestures: movements of a phone that can be used to control applications. For this example, we will focus on two gestures: a shake up and down and a shake by moving your wrist to the left and back.

To detect a shake, we start by observing gesture data to determine exactly what a shake gesture looks like in three dimensional space. The following code records accelerometer data into a file:

```
import time, sensor, e32

datafile = open("E:\Python\sensordata", "w")
meter = sensor.AccelerometerXYZAxisData(data_filter=sensor.LowPass-
Filter())
def reportXYZ():
    global meter,datafile
    line = "(%d,%d,%d):%s\n" % (meter.x,meter.y,meter.z,time.
strftime("%H:%M:%S"))
    datafile.write(line)
meter.set_callback(reportXYZ)
meter.start_listening()
e32.ao_sleep(5)
meter.stop_listening()
datafile.close()
```

This code will write three coordinates and a time-stamp to a file. The output is a series of lines that look like this:

```
(1,5,2):14:56:51
(3,10,4):14:56:51
(4,15,6):14:56:51
(6,21,8):14:56:51
(7,26,10):14:56:51
(9,31,12):14:56:51
(10,37,14):14:56:51
(11,42,16):14:56:51
(13,47,19):14:56:51
(15,53,21):14:56:51
(15,53,21):14:56:51
(15,53,21):14:56:51
(15,53,21):14:56:52
(15,53,20):14:56:52
(15,52,20):14:56:52
(15,52,21):14:56:52
(15,52,21):14:56:52
(15,53,21):14:56:52
...
```

By analysing the data, we discover that a downward shake takes between 1.5 and 2 seconds and varies across the Y axis by between 40 and 70 points. So we need code that records the Y coordinates with a time stamp. If, over that last 1.8 seconds, the maximum Y point minus the minimum Y point is greater than

40 AND we are within 5 points of 1.8 seconds ago, we have a shake along the Y axis.

Consider the following (note that this also looks for a shake along the X axis).

```
import time,sensor,e32

meter = sensor.AccelerometerXYZAxisData(data_filter=sensor.LowPass-
Filter())

start = time.time()
timeWindow = [start]
xaxisWindow = [0]
yaxisWindow = [0]

def recordEvents():
    global meter,timeWindow,xaxisWindow,yaxisWindow

    now = time.time()
    timeWindow.append(now)
    xaxisWindow.append(meter.x)
    yaxisWindow.append(meter.y)

    while now - timeWindow[0] > 2:
        timeWindow = timeWindow[1:]
        xaxisWindow = xaxisWindow[1:]
        yaxisWindow = yaxisWindow[1:]
```

```
    if now - timeWindow[0] < 1.8: return

    if xaxisWindow[0]-meter.x < 5 and max(xaxisWindow)-
min(xaxisWindow)>40:
        print "XSHAKE"
        timeWindow = [now]
        xaxisWindow = [meter.x]
        return
    if yaxisWindow[0]-meter.y < 5 and max(yaxisWindow)-
min(yaxisWindow)>40:
        print "YSHAKE"
        timeWindow = [now]
        yaxisWindow = [meter.y]
        return

meter.set_callback(recordEvents)
meter.start_listening()
e32.ao_sleep(20)
meter.stop_listening()
```

The code starts by initializing several lists:

- `timeWindow` is a list of timestamps, initialized with the current time
- `xaxisWindow` and `yaxisWindow` are lists of X coordinates and Y coordinates, respectively.

We do not keep them in (X,Y) pairs so we can use the `min()` and `max()` functions on each axis separately. The idea here is that each window should contain recorded data for 1.8 seconds. This is a moving window, so as time shifts, data shifts in and out of each list.

The `recordEvents()` function maintains these moving lists and evaluates if a shake has occurred. The function starts by simply recording the current time and (X,Y) coordinates:

```
now = time.time()
timeWindow.append(now)
xaxisWindow.append(meter.x)
yaxisWindow.append(meter.y)
```

The function then shifts each list until we have approximately 2 seconds of data:

```
while now - timeWindow[0] > 2:
    timeWindow = timeWindow[1:]
    xaxisWindow = xaxisWindow[1:]
    yaxisWindow = yaxisWindow[1:]
```

At this point, the data at the start of each list is less than 2 seconds from the data at the end of the list. If the time difference is less than 1.8 seconds we need to get more data. We simply return in this case and do not consider the data further.

If we have a valid collection of data, we simply need to apply our criteria to it:

```
if xaxisWindow[0]-meter.x < 5 and max(xaxisWindow)-
min(xaxisWindow)>40:
    print "XSHAKE"
    timeWindow = [now]
    xaxisWindow = [meter.x]
    return
if yaxisWindow[0]-meter.y < 5 and max(yaxisWindow)-
min(yaxisWindow)>40:
    print "YSHAKE"
    timeWindow = [now]
    yaxisWindow = [meter.y]
    return
```

When we determine that a shake has occurred, we print a message and reset the data collections.

The code will detect a shake of a phone in a downward direction and the preceding code works because down is positive. For the code to react the same way for an upward shake, absolute values of Y axis data must be appended to the `yaxisWindow` list. For this, the math module will need to be imported and the `math.fabs()` should be used. The same change could be applied for an X axis shake to the right.

While it is perhaps natural for a downward or upward shake to be used as a gesture, a sideways shake is not as natural. It seems more natural to move one's wrist left, which involves both X and Y axis movements. In fact, the movements combine left X axis movements with downward Y axis movements. The distance travelled is less than a single axis movement. We could detect a wrist shake with a small code addition:

```
if xaxisWindow[0]-meter.x < 5 and max(xaxisWindow)-
min(xaxisWindow)>25
   and yaxisWindow[0]-meter.y < 5 and max(yaxisWindow)-
min(yaxisWindow)>25:
    print "WRIST SHAKE"
    timeWindow = [now]
    xaxisWindow = [meter.x]
    yaxisWindow = [meter.y]
    return
if xaxisWindow[0]-meter.x < 5 and max(xaxisWindow)-
min(xaxisWindow)>40:
    print "XSHAKE"
    timeWindow = [now]
    xaxisWindow = [meter.x]
    return
if yaxisWindow[0]-meter.y < 5 and max(yaxisWindow)-
min(yaxisWindow)>40:
    print "YSHAKE"
    timeWindow = [now]
    yaxisWindow = [meter.y]
    return
```

Finally, to act on shaking, we should replace the print statements with some other kind of functionality. We would normally use a callback function but the `reportEvent()` function is itself a callback and we cannot send it our own parameters (as would be needed to specify our own callback). The alternative is to hardcode a call into the code and specify the function later in the program.

Another common gesture might be to move a phone backwards or forwards along the Z axis. Extending the preceding code to look for these types of gestures is left as an exercise for you the reader.

11.8 Legacy sensor API

The sensor framework is available on devices based on the Symbian platform, and on older S60 devices (S60 3rd Edition, FP2 and later). Earlier platforms (S60 3rd Edition, S60 3rd Edition Feature Pack 1 and some S60 3rd Edition Feature Pack 2 devices) use a legacy "sensor API" instead.

The legacy sensor API is limited compared to sensor framework we've already discussed. It provides:

- Access to a much smaller set of sensors than the sensor framework: accelerometer, tapping sensor and rotation sensor.
- Limited ability to register for specific sensor information. Unlike the sensor framework, the sensor API provides a single callback for data from all sensors. Applications can use in-built filters to capture orientation changes and rotation changes, but have to create their own filters for other events.

The interfaces are not readily extensible.

11.9 Summary

This chapter showed how to use the framework and gave examples of using the accelerometer to control an application, and to interpret gestures.

The sensor framework allows applications to query for specific sensors and to register for notification of data from sensors of interest. The API is readily extensible so applications will not be adversely affected by the addition of new sensors in future.

12

Platform Services

This chapter explains how to access platform services through the generic *script-ext* API. The services provided include:

- Application manager
- Calendar
- Contacts
- Landmarks
- Location
- Logging
- Messaging
- Media management
- Sensors
- System information.

12.1 Introduction

Python on Symbian provides access to many platform services through platform specific modules. In earlier chapters we showed how to use modules including *calendar*, *messaging*, *logs*, *location*, *positioning*, *sensor* and others.

Python on Symbian also provides access to platform services through a simple generic API defined in the **scriptext** module. These services include the application manager, calendar, contacts, landmarks, location, logging, messaging, media management, sensors and system information.

The functionality provided by each of these mechanisms has considerable overlap, and in many cases it is possible for developers to choose which API better suits their programming style. In other cases the APIs are complementary - for example, the logs module can only read log entries while the scriptext API can also be used to create and delete log entries. Therefore, both the platform services (scriptext) and individual platform service modules are required to gain full access to all of the platform service functionality offered by Symbian devices.

Figure 12.1 shows the range of services offered.

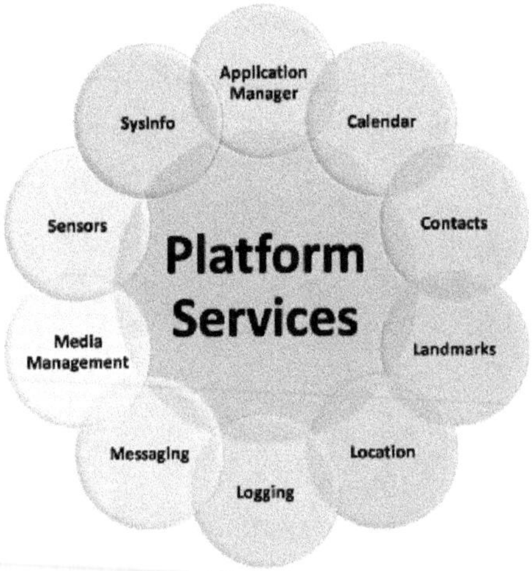

Figure 12.1: Platform services

12.2 Loading and calling platform services

Platform services can be accessed in PyS60 using the scriptext module. Scriptext uses two simple methods, `load()` and `call()`, to initiate and using the services respectively.

12.2.1 Load

A service object can be instantiated using the load() method. The syntax for using the API is as follows:

```
import scriptext
scriptext_handle = scriptext.load(<provider>, <interface>)
```

Here, <provider> is a string specifying the name of the service provider (for example 'Service.AppManager') and <interface> is a string specifying one of the names of supported interfaces of the <provider> (e.g. 'IAppManager'). For example, to load the messaging service with its supported interface IMessaging we do the following:

```
import scriptext
messaging_handle = scriptext.load("Service.Messaging", "IMessag-
ing")
```

12.2.2 Call

The call() method is used to request a service or operation from a service provider. The request may be synchronous or asynchronous. The syntax for requesting synchronous services is:

```
result = service_instance_object.call(<operation>, param-
eters)
```

where <operation> specifies the requested service and parameters is a dictionary specifying input parameters for the requested service. In the following code, GetList is the <operation> and {'Type': u'Inbox'} represents the parameters.

```
sms_iter = messaging_handle.call('GetList', {'Type':
u'Inbox'})
```

GetList is the name of the request and Inbox is the argument for the services. The code returns all of the SMS in the inbox in a map, which may be iterated and can be used for retrieving more details.

The syntax of the call() method for requesting asynchronous services is:

```
result = service_instance_object.call(<operation>, param-
eters, callback=callback_function)
```

In addition to operation and parameter arguments, an asynchronous service also needs a callback function that is called when the service completes the asynchronous request. The callback function can be any user-defined function, for example:

```
import scriptext

def media_callback(trans_id, event_id, output_params):
    print trans_id
    print event_id
    print output_params
```

```
media_handle = scriptext.call('Service.MediaManagement', 'IData-
Source')

media_trans_id = media_handle.call('GetList', {'Type':
u'FileInfo', u'FileExtension', 'StartRange': u'.mp3'},'Sort':
{'Key': u'FileName', 'Order': u'Ascending'}}, callback=media_call-
back)
```

The preceding code requests the list of mp3 files from the media player in an ascending order and then prints them. The callback function `media_callback` is called for every mp3 file that is found.

The callback function that is called after an asynchronous service request has three arguments (you must define your callback to take three parameters!):

- **`transactionID`** - the unique transaction ID associated with the particular asynchronous request. It is returned as part of the result of the initial asynchronous call.
- **`eventID`** - the status of the asynchronous operation. The values of an event id can include
  - `EventCompleted`
  - `EventCanceled`
  - `EventError`
  - `EventStopped`

  and so on. A complete list of event ids is available at ***pys60.garage.maemo.org/doc/s60/node177.html#subsec:appenevent*** with a brief description of what they indicate.
- **`outParam`** - contains the output of the asynchronous call in a dictionary

object.

- `outParam['ReturnValue']` - information requested by the asynchronous call that initiated the callback. Not all asynchronous calls return this property. The existence of `'ReturnValue'` depends on the platform service API and the method that was called. If `ReturnValue` is not present, the `outParam` would only contain `ErrorCode` and `ErrorMessage`.
- `outParam['ErrorCode']` - Specifies an error code. A complete list of pre-defined error codes is available at ***pys60.garage.maemo.org/doc/s60/node176.html#subsec:appenerrors***.
- `outParam['ErrorMessage']` - describes the error message.
- To cancel an outstanding asynchronous request, `Cancel` is passed as an argument to the call function as illustrated in the following code fragment:

```
serviceInstance.call('Cancel', {'TransactionID': serviceTransac-
tionID})
```

For example, the following line shows how we cancel the asynchronous request made in the preceding code snippet.

```
media_handle.call('Cancel', {'TransactionID': media_trans_id })
```

12.3 Application manager

The application manager service allows us to retrieve information about the installed applications and to launch applications and specific documents. The basic services `GetList`, `LaunchApp` and `LaunchDoc` are illustrated in Figure 12.2.

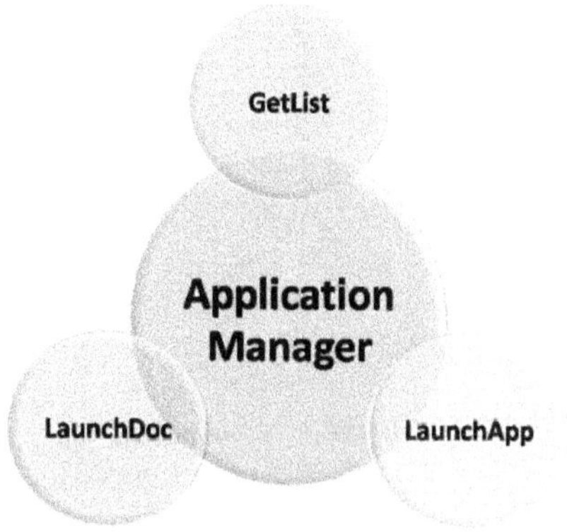

Figure 12.2: Application manager services

The application manager API has to be loaded before using any of the services it provides:

```
import scriptext
appmanager_handle = scriptext.load('Service.AppManager', 'IAppMan-
ager')
```

12.3.1 GetList

`GetList` can be used in synchronous mode to retrieve information about the all applications, user installed packages and handler applications. The following code example shows how `GetList` is used.

```
import scriptext

#initialize empty list for application info
application_info= []
#Load the Application Manager API
```

```
appmanager_handle = scriptext.load('Service.AppManager', 'IAppMan-
ager')
# Call the GetList function
appmanager_info = appmanager_handle.call('GetList', {'Type':
u'Application'})
# Populate the empty list with information of installed applica-
tions
for item in appmanager_info:
      application_info= .append(item['UID'])
      application_info= .append(item['Path'])
      application_info= .append(item['Caption'])
      application_info= .append(item['ShortCaption'])
print application_info
```

12.3. 2 LaunchApp

`LaunchApp` can be used both synchronously and asynchronously to launch an application. It takes the UID of the application as an argument.

The code fragment shows how to use `LaunchApp` to synchronously launch the application with UID `0xE674C90B`:

```
appmanager_id = appmanager_handle.call('LaunchApp', {'Applicatio-
nID': u's60uid:// 0xE674C90B'})
```

The same application can be launched asynchronously by doing this:

```
appmanager_id = appmanager_handle.call('LaunchApp', {'Applicatio-
nID': u's60uid:// 0xE674C90B'},  callback= callback_function)
```

In this case, `callback_function` is called once the application has launched.

12.3.4 LaunchDoc

Like `LaunchApp`, `LaunchDoc` can also be used either synchronously or asynchronously to launch a document in embedded mode. It takes the document path, `MimeType` (optional) and options (optional) as an argument.

The next code fragment shows how to call `LaunchDoc` synchronously, specifying a JPG image to be displayed.

```
appmanager_id = appmanager_handle.call('LaunchDoc', {'Document':
{'DocumentPath': u'C:\\data\\Image.jpg'}})
```

The following line of code would launches the jpg image viewer asynchronously to display `Image.jpg`. When the image has launched the `callback_function` is called.

```
appmanager_id = appmanager_handle.call('LaunchDoc', {'Document':
{'DocumentPath': u'C:\\data\\Image.jpg'}}, callback= callback_
function)
```

12.4 Calendar

The calendar service API enables Python developers to access, create, and manage calendars and their entries stored on a device. As shown in Figure 12.3, calendar services API provides 6 services: `GetList`, `Add`, `Delete`, `Import`, `Export` and `RequestNotification`.

Figure 12.3: Calendar services

The Calendar API has to be loaded before using any of the services it provides. Use `Service.Calendar` to identify the service provider and `IDataSource` to identify the supported interface, as illustrated in the following code.

```
import scriptext
calendar_handle = scriptext.load('Service.Calendar', 'IData-
Source')
```

12.4.1 `GetList`

The `GetList` service can be used synchronously to retrieve a list of available calendars or a list of calendar entries. The information to be retrieved can filtered by the arguments passed when using the service. Entries in the calendar can be of type Meeting, ToDo, Anniversary, DayEvent and Reminder.

For example, the following code can be used to list all the ToDo entries in the calendar.

```
ToDo_list = calendar_handle.call('GetList', {'Type':
u'CalendarEntry', 'Filter': {'CalendarName': u'C:Calendar',
'Type': u'ToDo'}})
```

Once a list of events is retrieved using `GetList`, various attributes of the events can be queried.

For example, the following code snippet retrieves a list of ToDo events and prints some of its attributes. Please refer to the ***pys60.garage.maemo.org/doc/s60/node128.html*** for more information on attributes of event types.

```
import scriptext

# Load Calendar service
calendar_handle = scriptext.load('Service.Calendar', 'IData-
Source')
ToDo_list = calendar_handle.call('GetList', {'Type':
u'CalendarEntry', 'Filter':  {'CalendarName': u'C:Calendar',
'Type': u'ToDo'}})
for ToDo in ToDo_list:
      print 'Id = ' + ToDo['id']
      print 'Summary = ' + ToDo['Summary']

      value = ToDo['EndTime']
      print "ToDo End time is ", value.day, value.month, value.
year, value.hour, ":", value.minute, ":", value.second

        value = meeting['AlarmTime']
```

```
        print "ToDo Alarm time is ", value.day, value.month, val-
ue.year, value.hour, ":", value.minute, ":", value.second

       print 'Status =' + ToDo['Status']
```

12.4.2 **Add**

Add is used synchronously to add a new calendar, new calendar entries, or to modify an existing calendar entry on the device.

For example, the following code adds a To Do entry to the calendar:

```
alarm_time = datetime.datetime(2009,12,12,13,0,0)
end_time = datetime.datetime(2009,12,12,14,0,0)

calendar_handle.call('Add', {'Type': u'CalendarEntry', 'Item':
{'Type': u'ToDo', 'Summary': u'This is the ToDo Summary', 'End-
Time': end_time, 'AlarmTime': end_time}})
```

Other event entries, such as Meeting, Anniversary, DayEvent and Reminder can be added to the calendar in a similar manner. The attributes specified may vary for different event type entries. Please refer to ***pys60.garage.maemo.org/doc/s60/node121.html*** for more information on the attributes of event types. An existing entry may be modified by specifying the id as an argument.

12.4.4 **Delete**

Delete can be used either synchronously or asynchronously to remove/delete a calendar or a calendar entry from the device. The default calendar of the device cannot be deleted.

Using `Delete` synchronously:

```
event_id = calendar_handle.call('Delete', {'Type':
u'CalendarEntry', 'id': del_id_list})
```

Using `Delete` asynchronously:

```
event_id = calendar_handle.call('Delete', {'Type':
u'CalendarEntry', 'id': del_id_list}, callback= callback_function)
```

where `del_id_list` is the list of the entries to be deleted and `callback_function` is the user defined callback function.

For example, the following code asynchronously deletes all ToDo entries from the calendar:

```
import scriptext

# Load Calendar service
calendar_handle = scriptext.load('Service.Calendar', 'IData-
Source')

# Populate ToDo_list with all the ToDo entries in the calendar
ToDo_list = calendar_handle.call('GetList', {'Type':
u'CalendarEntry', 'Filter':  {'CalendarName': u'C:Calendar',
'Type': u'ToDo'}})

# Callback function will be called when the requested service is
complete
```

```
def callback_function(trans_id, event_id, input_params):
    print "Entry Deleted"

# Delete the entries in ToDo_list
event_id = calendar_handle.call('Delete', {'Type':
u'CalendarEntry', 'IdList': ToDo_list}, callback= callback_func-
tion)

print "Waiting for the request to be completed"
lock.wait()
print "Request Complete"
```

Import

The Import service can be used synchronously or asynchronously to import entries into the calendar from a file. Currently, the file formats supported by import service are `ICal` or `VCal`.

The following code fragment shows how to use `Import` synchronously:

```
calendar_handle.call('Import', {'Type': u'CalendarEntry', 'File-
Name': u'C:\\data\\Imported.txt', 'Format': u'ICal'})
```

The code imports calendar entries in `ICal` format from `Imported.txt`. The same format must be used while exporting the entries to the calendar using the `Export` service.

To use `Import` asynchronously:

```
calendar_handle.call('Import', {'Type': u'CalendarEntry', 'File-
Name': u'C:\\data\\ Imported.txt', 'Format': u'VCal'}, callback=
callback_function))
```

This code will import the calendar entries from `Imported.txt` to the calendar and call `callback_function` when the operation completes.

12.4.5 `Export`

`Export` service can be used synchronously or asynchronously to export entries from the calendar to a file. Like the Import service, `ICal` and `VCal` are the supported file formats for `Export` service.

The code below shows how to use `Import` synchronously to export all the calendar entries to the `Exported.txt` file using `VCal` file format.

```
calendar_handle.call('Export', {'Type': u'CalendarEntry', 'File-
Name': u'C:\\Data\\Exported.txt', 'Format': u'VCal'})
```

Similarly, we can call `Import` asynchronously to perform the same task; again, `callback_function` is called when the export is finished:

```
calendar_handle.call('Export', {'Type': u'CalendarEntry', 'File-
Name': u'C:\\data\\Exported.txt', 'Format': u'VCal'}, callback=
callback_function))
```

12.4.6 `RequestNotification`

Applications can use the `RequestNotification` service to be notified (asynchronously) when the calendar entries are added, modified or deleted.

For example, the following code requests calendar entry notifications. Whenever a calendar entry is modified, edited or deleted, the callback function is called with arguments `trans_id`, `event_id` and `input_params`.

```
import scriptext
import e32

lock = e32.Ao_lock()
calendar_handle = scriptext.load('Service.Calendar', 'IData-
Source')

def calendar_callback(trans_id, event_id, input_params):
    if event_id != scriptext.EventCompleted:
# Check the event statusSound
        print "Error in retrieving required info"
        print "Error code is: " + str(input_params["ReturnValue"]
["ErrorCode"])
        if "ErrorMessage" in input_params["ReturnValue"]:
            print "Error message is: " + input_
params["ReturnValue"]["ErrorMessage"]
    else:
        print "Modification is: " + str(input_params["ReturnValue"]
["ChangeType"])
    lock.signal()
```

```
# Make a request to get notification
event_id = calendar_handle.call("RequestNotification", {'Type':
u'CalendarEntry'}, callback=calendar_callback)

lock.wait()
```

12.5 Contacts

The contacts service allows you to manage the contacts list on the device. Using the API you can retrieve contact or group information, add a contact or group, edit a particular contact or group, import and export a contact and delete a contact or a group item. These services are illustrated in figure 12.4.

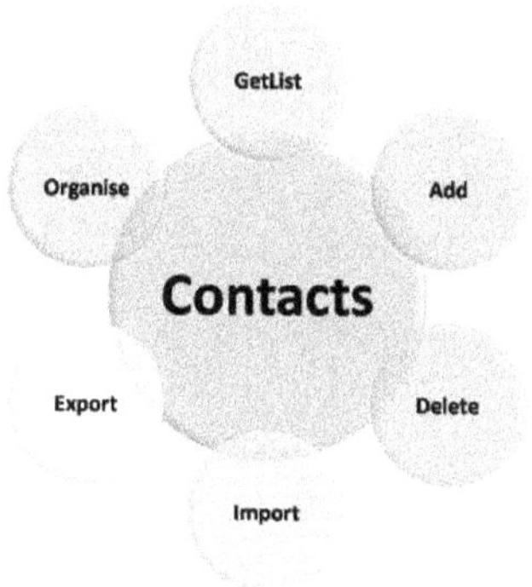

Figure 12.4: Contacts services

The Contacts API has to be loaded before using any of the services it provides. Use `Service.Contact` to identify the service provider and `IDataSource` to identify the supported interface, as illustrated by the following code.

```
import scriptext
contact_handle = scriptext.load('Service.Contact', 'IDataSource')
```

12.5.1 GetList

The `GetList` service is very similar to the one offered by the calendar service. The only difference is `GetList` for contacts can be used synchronously as well as asynchronously. `GetList` service can be used to retrieve list of contacts, contact groups, or contacts databases.

The list of contacts and contact groups can be retrieved from the specified contact database. If no database is specified, the default database is used.

The following code uses `GetList` synchronously. It populates the list `list_contacts` with the list of contacts with '`Pankaj`' in their First Name and Last Name fields:

```
list_contacts = contacts_handle.call('GetList', {'Type':
u'Contact', 'Filter': {'SearchVal': u'Pankaj'}})
```

The following code performs the same `GetList` operation asynchronously, the main difference being that the `callback_function` is called after the contacts are retrieved.

```
event_id = contacts_handle.call('GetList', {'Type': u'Contact',
'Filter':{'SearchVal': u'Pankaj'}}, callback=callback_function)
```

Note: In S60 3rd Edition and S60 3rd Edition FP1, `SearchVal` searches in all the contact fields. However in S60 3rd edition FP2 onwards, `SearchVal` searches only in First Name and Last Name field.

12.5.2 Add

`Add` can be used synchronously or asynchronously to add or edit a contact or contact group to a contacts database. If the contact or contact group already exists in the database, it is replaced with the new entry.

For example, the following code adds the contact details for Jeremy Burton to the contacts database.

```
contacts_handle.call('Add', {'Type': u'Contact', 'Data':
            {'FirstName': {'Label': u'first name', 'Value':
u'Burton'},
             'LastName': {'Label': u'last name', 'Value':
u'Jeremy'},
             'MobilePhoneGen': {'Label': u'mobile', 'Value':
u'9009132813'},
             'EmailHome': {'Label': u'email', 'Value': u'Burton@
Jeremy.com'}}})
```

Delete

The `Delete` service can be used synchronously or asynchronously to delete one or more contacts or contact groups from a given contact database. If no database is given, the default database is used.

The following example shows how to delete the contact with the `req_id` and calls the `callback_function` when this is done.

```
event_id = contacts_handle.call('Delete', {'Type': u'Contact',
'Data': {'IdList': [req_id]}}, callback=callback_function)
```

12.5.3 Import

`Import` can be used synchronously or asynchronously to import contacts from a vCard file.

Using `Import` synchronously:

```
event_id = contacts_handle.call('Import', {'Type': u'Contact','Dat
a':{'SourceFile':u'c:\\Data\\contacts.txt'}})
```

Using `Import` asynchronously:

```
event_id = contacts_handle.call('Import', {'Type': u'Contact','Da
ta':{'SourceFile':u'c:\\Data\\ contacts.txt'}},callback=callback_
function)
```

12.5.4 Export

`Export` can be used synchronously or asynchronously to export contacts to a vCard file.

Using `Export` synchronously:

```
event_id = contacts_handle.call('Export', {'Type': u'Contact','Dat
a':{'SourceFile':u'c:\\Data\\contacts.txt'}})
```

Using `Export` asynchronously:

```
event_id = contacts_handle.call('Export', {'Type': u'Contact','Da
ta':{'SourceFile':u'c:\\Data\\contacts.txt'}},callback=callback_
function)
```

`Organize`

`Organize` can be used synchronously or asynchronously, to add contacts to a contact group or remove contacts from a contact group.

Using `Organize` asynchronously:

```
event_id = contacts_handle.call('Organise', {'Type':
u'Group','Data': {'id': unicode(req_groupid[0]),'IdList': [req_
id]}, 'OperationType': u'Associate'},callback=export_contact)
```

12.6 Landmarks

Landmarks are used to record positions of interest as GPS coordinates. It is possible to sort the saved locations into different categories, such as businesses, and add other information to them, such as addresses. Landmarks can be used in other compatible applications like GPS Data and Nokia Maps. GPS coordinates are expressed in the degrees and decimal degrees format using the international WGS-84 coordinate system.

Scriptext provides the Landmarks service API for handling landmark information. Using this API, developers can read, add, delete, import, export and organize the landmarks on a local database, as shown in figure 12.5. Note that Python only supports operations associated with local databases - remote server-based databases are not supported.

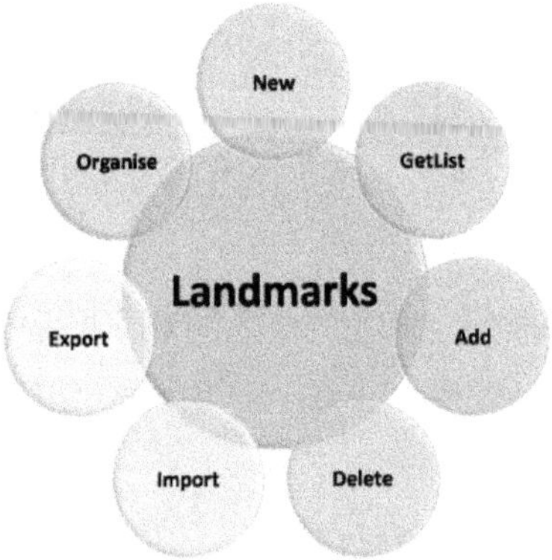

Figure 12.5: Landmarks services

A category is a characteristic of a landmark. Categories are used to classify the landmarks on the basis of geographical or architectural interest, attraction or activity-related types of objects.

The Landmarks API can be loaded by the following code:

```
import scriptext
landmark_handle = scriptext.load('Service.Landmarks', 'IData-
Source')
```

12.6.1 New

New can be used synchronously to add a landmark or a landmark category. It should be noted that the landmark created by the `New` service is supposed to be an empty landmark.

For example, to create a new empty landmark:

```
new_landmark = landmark_handle.call('New', {'Type': u'Landmark'})
```

To create a new landmark category:

```
new_category = landmark_handle.call('New', {'Type': u'Category'})
```

12.6.2 GetList

`GetList` can be used synchronously or asynchronously to retrieve information about existing landmarks, landmark categories, or landmark databases. The target landmark database may be specified. If no database is specified, the default database is used.

Using `GetList` synchronously:

```
Landmarks_info = landmark_handle.call('GetList', {'Type':
u'Landmark', 'Filter':{'uDatabaseURI':  u'dataBaseUri', 'Landmark-
Name': landmark_name}, 'Sort' :{'Key': u'LandmarkName', 'Order':
order_of_list}})
```

where `landmark_name` (Unicode) is the name of the landmark and `order_of_list` is `u'Ascending'` or `u'Decending'`.

Using `GetList` asynchronously:

```
event_id = landmark_handle.call('GetList', {'Type': u'Landmark','
Filter':{'uDatabaseURI':u'dataBaseUri','LandmarkName': },'Sort':{
'Key':u'LandmarkName','Order': order_of_list}}, callback=callback_
function)
```

where `order_of_list` is `u'Ascending'` or `u'Decending'` and `callback_function` is the user defined callback function.

12.6.3 Add

`Add` can be used synchronously to add or modify a landmark. The following example adds the landmark `landmark_name` (Unicode) to the database.

```
add_output = landmark_handle.call('Add', {'Type': u'Landmark',
'Data': {'LandmarkName':  landmark_name}})
```

12.6.4 Delete

`Delete` can be used synchronously to delete the specified landmark from the specified database. If no database is specified, the active/default database is used.

For example, the following code opens the default or active database for reading landmarks and categories. A default database is created (if it does not exist) and is set as active. The landmark `land1` is deleted from the active or specified database.

```
delete_output = landmark_handle.call('Delete', {'Type':
u'Landmark','Filter': {'LandmarkName': u'land1'}})
```

12.6.5 `Import`

`Import` can be used synchronously to import a set of landmarks from a file. For example, the following code will import landmarks from the landmarks_import.txt file to the database. Since the database is not specified, landmarks are imported to the default database. The only supported `MimeType` is `application/vnd.nokia.landmarkcollection+xml`.

```
import_output = landmark_handle.call('Import', {'Type':
u'Landmark', 'Data': {'SourceFile': u'c:\data\land-
marks_import.txt', 'MimeType': u'application/vnd.nokia.
landmarkcollection+xml'}})
```

12.6.6 `Export`

`Export` can be used synchronously to export a set of specified landmarks to a file. For example, the following code exports the landmark "land1" to export_landmarks.txt.

```
getlist_output = landmark_handle.call('GetList', {'Type':
u'Landmark', 'Filter': {'LandmarkName': u'land1'}})

retval = getlist_output['ReturnValue']
id_val = retval['id']

export_output = landmark_handle.call('Export', {'Type':
u'Landmark', 'Data': {'DestinationFile': u'c:\data\export_land-
marks.txt', 'idList': [id_val], 'MimeType': u'application/vnd.
nokia.landmarkcollection+xml'}})
```

12.6.7 `Organise`

`Organise` can be used synchronously to associate or disassociate a list of landmarks from a category.

For example, the following code will associate the landmarks `land1` and `land2` with all the available categories in the active/default database. The `Operation Type` can be 'Associate' or 'Disassociate'.

```
getlist_category_output = landmark_handle.call('GetList', {'Type':
u'Category'})
retval_category = getlist_category_output['ReturnValue']
cat_id = retval_category['id']

getlist_output1 = landmark_handle.call('GetList', {'Type':
u'Landmark', 'Filter': {'LandmarkName': u'land1'}})
retval1 = getlist_output1['ReturnValue']
id_val1 = retval1['id']

getlist_output2 = landmark_handle.call('GetList', {'Type':
u'Landmark', 'Filter': {'LandmarkName': u'land2'}})
retval2 = getlist_output2['ReturnValue']
id_val2 = retval2['id']

organise_output = landmark_handle.call('Organise', {'Type':
u'Landmark','Data': {'id': unicode(cat_id), 'idList': [id_val1,id_
val2]}, 'Operation Type': 'Associate'})
```

12.7 Location

Through the Location service API, scriptext not only gives you access to the physical location of the device but also allows you to track the movements of the device and perform calculations based on location information. Refer to Chapter 10 for information on how the physical location of the device can be interpreted.

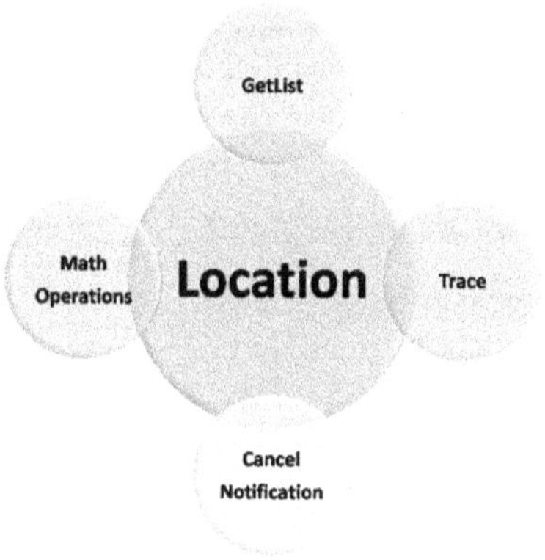

Figure 12.6: Location services

The Location API can be loaded using the following code:

```
import scriptext
location_handle = scriptext.load('Service.Location', 'IData-
Source')
```

Note that use of the Location API requires the `Location` platform security capability.

12.7.1 `GetList`

`GetList` can be used synchronously or asynchronously to retrieve the current location of the device.

The fragment below shows how to call `GetList` synchronously:

```
Location_List = location_handle.call(‘GetList’, {‘LocationIn-
formationClass’: u’BasicLocationInformation’, ‘Updateoptions’:
{‘UpdateInterval’:u’1’, ‘UpdateTimeOut’: u’15’, ‘UpdateMax-
Age’ :u’0’, ‘PartialUpdates’: u’False’}})
```

The asynchronous operation is similar `GetList`, except that `callback_function` is called after the location is retrieved:

```
event_id = location_handle.call(‘GetList’, {‘LocationInformation-
Class’:  u’BasicLocationInformation’, ‘Updateoptions’: {‘UpdateIn-
terval’: u’1’, ‘UpdateTimeOut’: u’15’, ‘UpdateMaxAge’: u’0’, ‘Par-
tialUpdates’: u’False’}}, callback= callback_function)
```

12.7.2 `Trace`

`Trace` can be used to track the movement of the device - it gives updates on the location of the device based on a predefined update interval, and it can only be used asynchronously.

```
event_id = location_handle.call(‘Trace’, {‘LocationInformation-
Class’: u’GenericLocationInfo’, ‘Updateoptions’: {‘UpdateInter-
val’: u’10’, ‘UpdateTimeOut’: u’50’, ‘UpdateMaxAge’: u’5’, ‘Par-
tialUpdates’: u’True’}})
```

12.7.3 `CancelNotification`

`CancelNotification` can be used synchronously to cancel asynchronous calls – for example – `Add` and `Trace`, as shown by the following code.

```
cancel_output = location_handle.call('CancelNotification', {'Can-
celRequestType': u'GetLocCancel'})
```

12.7.4 `MathOperations`

`MathOperations` is used to perform calculations on retrieved or user-provided location information.

The mathematical operations provided by `MathOperations` include finding distance between two given locations, finding the bearing between two given locations and calculating a new location based on movement from a source location.

For example, the following code is used to find the distance (in metres) between two provided locations:

```
distance = location_handle.call('MathOperations', {'MathRequest':
u'FindDistance', 'DistanceParamSource': {'Longitude': u'10', 'Lat-
itude': u'15', 'Altitude': u'20'}, 'DistanceParamDestination':
{'Longitude': u'40', 'Latitude': u'55', 'Altitude': u'20'}})
```

12.8 Logging

Logs are a useful way of monitoring communication on Symbian devices. Calls, messages and data are recorded in the device's Logs engine.

The logging service API offers greater control over the information in the device's logs than the logs module because it also gives you the ability to add and delete events, not just read them.

As shown in figure 12.7, logging provides 4 services: `Add`, `GetList`, `Delete`, and `RequestNotification`.

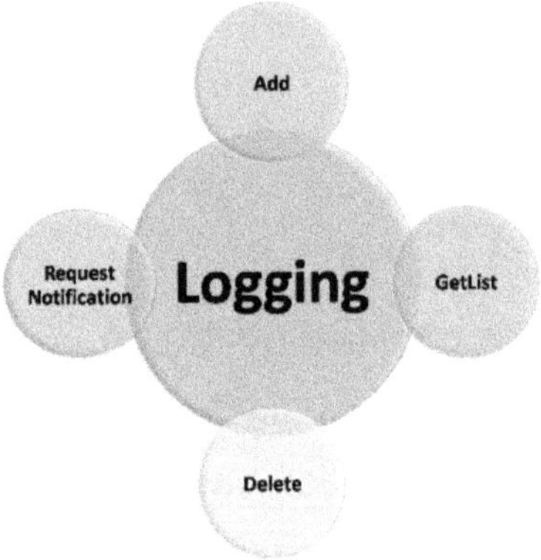

Figure 12.7: Logging services

The Logging API is loaded as follows:

```
import scriptext
logging_handle = scriptext.load('Service.Logging', 'IDataSource')
```

12.8.1 `Add`

This service is used to create events to the phone's Logs application. The general form of the handle's `call()` method is `call('Add', {'Type': , 'Item': {'EventType': , 'Direction': , 'EventDuration': , 'DeliveryStatus': , 'PhoneNumber': }})`, where appropriate values are to be associated with each parameter. A table containing possible values and descriptions for the parameters is available ***at pys60.garage.maemo.org/doc/s60/node150.html***. The method returns a unique identifier for the event in the logs database.

Here is an example of how to add a dialed call and a received SMS to the device's logs:

```
import scriptext

logging_handle = scriptext.load('Service.Logging', 'IDataSource')

#The call
log_id = logging_handle.call('Add', {'Type': u'Log', 'Item':
{'EventType': 0, 'Direction': 1, 'EventDuration': 20, 'PhoneNum-
ber': u'1234567890'}})
#The line above reads: add a log item consisting of an outgoing
(Direction 1) call (EventType 0) that lasted 20 seconds (EventDu-
ration 20) towards the number 1234567890 (PhoneNumber 1234567890)

#The SMS
log_id = logging_handle.call('Add', {'Type': u'Log', 'Item':
{'EventType': 3, 'Direction': 0, 'DeliveryStatus': 1, 'PhoneNum-
ber': u'1234567890'}})
#This line reads: add a log item consisting of an incoming (Direc-
tion 0) SMS (EventType 3) that was successfully sent (DeliverySta-
tus 1) to the number 1234567890 (PhoneNumber 1234567890)
```

12.8.2 GetList

The `GetList` service retrieves all the events from the phone's logs as a list of dictionaries. The information in each dictionary can then be accessed by using the name of its field as a key, as follows:

```
import scriptext

logging_handle = scriptext.load('Service.Logging', 'IDataSource')

#Get all the entries of type Log
logging_info = logging_handle.call('GetList', {'Type': u'Log',})
#Display their information
for entry in logging_info:
    print entry['EventType']
    print entry['RemoteParty']
    print entry['Direction']
    print entry['EventTime']
    print entry['Subject']
    print entry['PhoneNumber']
    print entry['Description']
    print entry['EventData']
```

`GetList` can be used synchronously as well as asynchronously (in this case by adding a callback function as the last paramater of the `call` method).

12.8.3 `Delete`

`Delete` can be used to remove events from the log:

```
 logging_handle.call('Delete', {'Type': u'Log', 'Data': {'id':
log_id,}})
#log_id is the ID of the entry we wish to delete
```

`RequestNotification`

The `RequestNotification` service can be used to provide asynchronous notification when log entries are added or deleted. This is useful to ensure your application information remains up to date when it is not the only application that is manipulating log data.

```
import scriptext, e32

app_lock = e32.Ao_lock()

def logging_callback(trans_id, event_id, input_params):
    #We anticipate the situation in which the request cannot be
serviced
    if trans_id != logging_id and event_id != scriptext.EventCom-
pleted:
        print "Error in servicing the request"
        print "Error code is: " + str(input_params["ReturnValue"]
["ErrorCode"])
        if "ErrorMessage" in input_params["ReturnValue"]:
            print "Error message is: " + input_
```

```
params["ReturnValue"]["ErrorMessage"]
    else:
        print "Changes notified accordingly"

    #Continue executing the rest of the script after the request
is processed
    app_lock.signal()

logging_handle = scriptext.load('Service.Logging', 'IDataSource')
logging_id = logging_handle.call('RequestNotification', {'Type':
u'Log', 'Filter': {'DelayTime': 600000}}, callback=logging_call-
back)

print "Waiting for the request to be processed"
app_lock.wait()

print "Request complete!"
```

12.9 Messaging

The messaging service offers functionality that combines much of what is offered in the messaging and inbox modules. It allows you to access and delete messages, change their status and register for new message notifications.

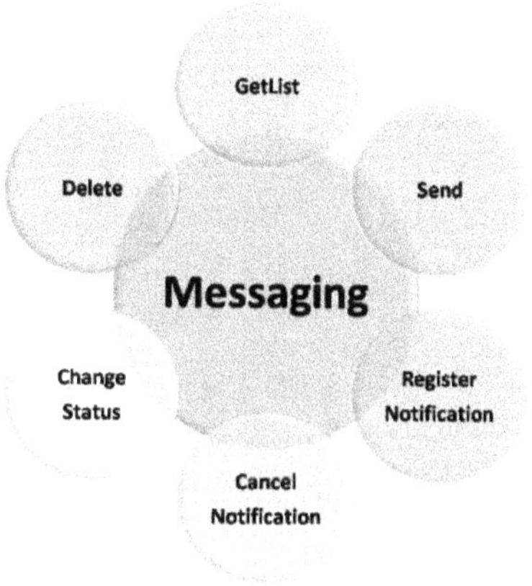

Figure 12.8: Messaging services

12.9.1 `Send`

The `Send` service allows you to send SMS and MMS messages. It can be used both synchronously and asynchronously.

Here is an example of Send being used synchronously to send an SMS and an MMS with an attachment:

```
import scriptext

#Load the provider
messaging_handle = scriptext.load('Service.Messaging', 'IMessag-
ing')

#Send the SMS
```

```
messaging_handle.call('Send', {'MessageType': u'SMS', 'To':
u'1234567890', 'BodyText': u'This is the message'})
 #Send the MMS
messaging_handle.call('Send', {'MessageType': u'MMS', 'To':
u'1234567890', 'BodyText': u'This is the message', 'Attachment':
u'C:\\Data\\photo.jpg'})
```

As with all the other services, a complete list of parameters for the call method, possible error codes, and their interpretations is available at ***pys60.garage.maemo.org/doc/s60/node156.html***.

12.9.2 `GetList`

`GetList` is used to get a list of messaging objects from the messaging center, where an object contains information about one message. This service can only be used synchronously. The following code shows how to display the SMS 'Sender' IDs from all the messages in the inbox:

```
import scriptext

messaging_handle = scriptext.load('Service.Messaging', 'IMessag-
ing')

# This 'GetList' request returns all the SMS in the inbox as an
iterable map
sms_iter = messaging_handle.call('GetList', {'Type': u'Inbox'})

#Create an empty list which will be populated with the sender IDs
sender_list = []
```

```
#For every SMS in the inbox, add the sender ID to the list
for sms_dict in sms_iter:
    if sms_dict['MessageType'] == 'SMS':
        sender_list.append(sms_dict['Sender'])

#Display the result
print "ID list :", sender_list
```

`RegisterNotification` and `CancelNotification`

`RegisterNotification` is used to receive notifications for new messages. It can only be use asynchronously, as shown below.

```
import scriptext, e32

app_lock = e32.Ao_lock()
messaging_handle = scriptext.load('Service.Messaging', 'IMessag-
ing')

def new_sms_callback(trans_id, event_id, output_params):
    if trans_id == sms_id and event_id == scriptext.EventComplet-
ed:
        print "SMS received from" + output_params['ReturnValue']
['Sender'])
    else:
        print "Error in callback"
    #Cancel notification request
```

```
    messaging_handle.call('CancelNotification', {'Type':
u'NewMessage'})
    app_lock.signal()

#The callback 'new_sms_callback' will be called when an SMS is re-
ceived
sms_id = messaging_handle.call('RegisterNotification', {'Type':
u'NewMessage'}, callback=new_sms_callback)

app_lock.wait()
```

The `CancelNotification` service is used when we wish to stop receiving notifications about new messages.

ChangeStatus

It is sometimes useful to manipulate the status of the messages in the inbox (read/unread). In order to do this, the messaging service offers `ChangeStatus`, which can only be used synchronously.

The following code displays a list of all the messages in the inbox (their text) and, once the user selects one, changes its status to unread, if possible.

```
import scriptext, appuifw

messaging_handle = scriptext.load('Service.Messaging', 'IMessag-
ing')

sms_iter = messaging_handle.call('GetList', {'Type': u'Inbox'})
```

```
id_list = []
body_list = []
#Populate the lists with the IDs and bodies of all the SMS mes-
sages
for sms_dict in sms_iter:
    if sms_dict['MessageType'] == 'SMS':
        id_list.append(sms_dict['MessageId'])
        body_list.append(sms_dict['BodyText'])

message_index = appuifw.selection_list(body_list)

try:
    messaging_handle.call('ChangeStatus', {'MessageId': id_
list[message_index], 'Status': u'Unread'})
except scriptext.ScriptextError, err:
    print "Error setting message status to unread"
else:
    print "Message status changed to unread"
```

12.9.3 Delete

`Delete` can be used synchronously to remove a certain message from the inbox:

```
import scriptext, appuifw, e32

app_lock = e32.Ao_lock()
```

```
messaging_handle = scriptext.load('Service.Messaging', 'IMessag-
ing')

sms_iter = messaging_handle.call('GetList', {'Type': u'Inbox'})

id_list = []
body_list = []
for sms_dict in sms_iter:
    if sms_dict['MessageType'] == 'SMS':
        id_list.append(sms_dict['MessageId'])
        body_list.append(sms_dict['BodyText'])

#Select the message to be deleted
message_index = appuifw.selection_list(body_list)

try:
    messaging_handle.call('Delete', {'MessageId': id_list[message_
index]})
except scriptext.ScriptextError, err:
    print "Error deleting SMS :", err
else:
    print "Message deleted successfully"
```

12.10 Media management

The media management service provides an application with information about the media files in the device's media management applications (including gallery and music player).

12.10.1 GetList

The `GetList` service returns the metadata of the media files based on the input parameters. It is only available in asynchronous mode.

The following code snippet shows how to get a list of all MP3 files:

```
import scriptext, e32

def media_callback(trans_id, event_id, output_params):
    if trans_id == media_trans_id:
        if event_id == scriptext.EventCompleted:
            song_list = []
            for item in output_params['ReturnValue']:
                song_list.append(item['FileName'])
            print "List of files retrieved:", song_list
        else:
            print "Event ID was not EventCompleted"
    else:
        print "Invalid Transaction ID"
    app_lock.signal()

app_lock = e32.Ao_lock()
media_handle = scriptext.load('Service.MediaManagement', 'IData-
Source')
```

```
#Request for the list of MP3s in ascending order
media_trans_id = media_handle.call('GetList', {'Type':
u'FileInfo',
                                   'Filter': {'FileType': u'Music',
                                              'Key': u'FileExtension',
                                              'StartRange': u'.mp3'},
                                   'Sort': {'Key': u'FileName',
                                            'Order': u'Ascending'}},
                          callback=media_callback)
```

A complete list of key values that can be used to filter information is available in at ***pys60.garage.maemo.org/doc/s60/node163.html***.

12.11 Sensors

The data provided by sensors on the device allow you to capture user actions and gestures and handle them in your applications.

Let's familiarize ourselves with the following terminologies to start with:
Sensor is a physical sensor on a device (a piece of hardware combined with a software plug-in). A single sensor can provide multiple sensor channels, such as a raw data channel and event channels, or incorporate multiple sensor readings into a single sensor channel.

Channel is an abstraction of a physical sensor. Data from one physical sensor can be mapped to multiple sensor channels.

Channel property is a configuration value of a sensor channel. The property affects all clients listening to the channel.

The Sensor service provides access to data provided by various physical sensors that exist in the device. The data from a given sensor is mapped to one or more sensor channels, which the API can listen to. With the sensor service you can:

- `FindSensorChannel:` Search for sensor channels available on a device
- `RegisterForNotification:` Listen for data provided by one or more sensor channels
  - `GetChannelProperty`: Retrieve information about sensor channel properties

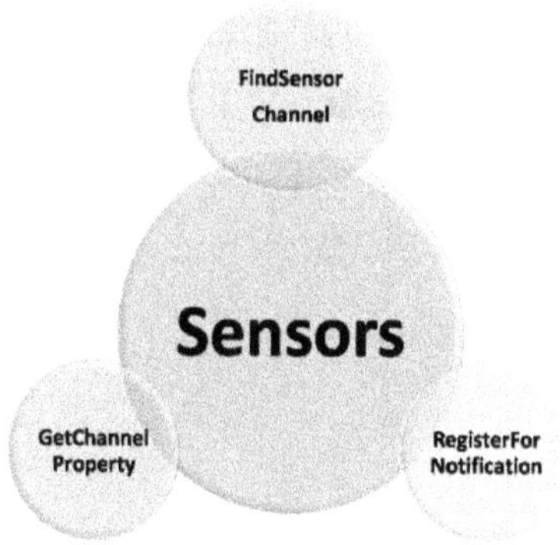

Figure 12.9: Sensor services

The API can be loaded by the following code:

```
import scriptext
sensor_handle = scriptext.load('Service.Sensor', 'ISensor')
```

12.11.1 FindSensorChannel

`FindSensorChannel` can be used synchronously to search for sensor channels available in the device. The following code performs a search operation for sensor channels available in the device, based on the specified criteria `Rotation`. The other search criteria which can be used are `All`, `AccelerometerAxis`, `AccelerometerDoubleTapping`, `Orientation` and `Rotation`.

```
sensor_handle.call('FindSensorChannel', {'SearchCriterion':
u'Rotation '})
```

RegisterForNotification

`RegisterForNotification` can be used asynchronously to register for notification with a sensor channel to receive channel data or channel property changes. This is associated with the transaction ID of an asynchronous request.

The notifications are continuous in nature and are stopped by invoking the Cancel command on the retrieved transaction ID.

For example:

```
sensor_handle.call('RegisterForNotification',
                  {'ListeningType': u'ChannelData',
                   'ChannelInfoMap': {'ChannelId': result['ChannelId'],
                                     'ContextType': result['ContextType'],
                                     'Quantity': result['Quantity'],
                                     'ChannelType': result['ChannelType'],
                                     'Location': result['Location'],
```

```
                                'VendorId': result['VendorId'],
                                'DataItemSize': result['DataItemSize'],
                                'ChannelDataTypeId':
result['ChannelDataTypeId']}},
                callback=callback_function)
```

where `callback_function` is the user defined callback function.

GetChannelProperty

`GetChannelProperty` can be used synchronously to get the channel property of the specified sensor channel.

For example, the following code is used to receive the requested property details in result.

```
result = sensor_handle.call('GetChannelProperty',
               {'ChannelInfoMap':{'ChannelId': result['ChannelId'],
                               'ContextType': result['ContextType'],
                                   'Quantity': result['Quantity'],
                               'ChannelType': result['ChannelType'],
                                  'Location': result['Location'],
                                  'VendorId': result['VendorId'],
                          'DataItemSize': result['DataItemSize'],
               'ChannelDataTypeId': result['ChannelDataTypeId']},
               'propertyId': u'DataRate'})
```

12.12 Sys Info

This service allows you to read and, in some cases, modify system parameters on the device. It is also possible to register to system events in order to receive notifications when changes occur.

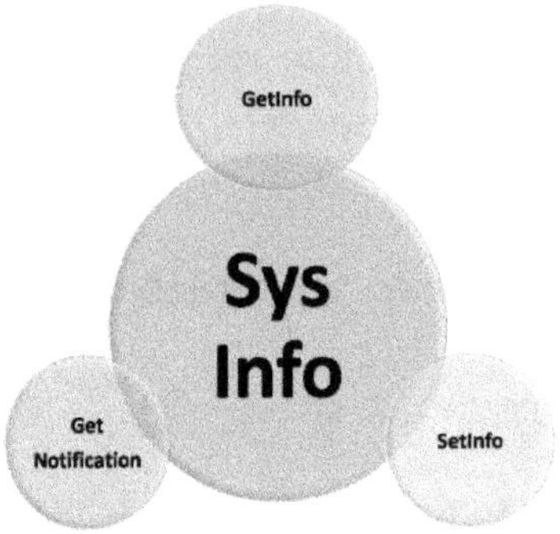

Figure 12.10: Sys Info services

12.12.1 `GetInfo`

The `GetInfo` service retrieves the value of a system attribute. For example, we define a function that will be called after the system query is made and that is passed the returned values as arguments. If all goes well (meaning there is no error), the battery strength is displayed.

```
import scriptext, e32
 #Using e32.Ao_lock() so that the main function can wait until the
callback is hit.
lock = e32.Ao_lock()

#Callback function will be called when the requested service is
complete
```

```
def print_battery_strength(trans_id, event_id, input_params):
      #Check the event status
      if event_id != scriptext.EventCompleted:
            print "Error in retrieving required info"
            print "Error code is: " + str(input_
params["ReturnValue"]["ErrorCode"])
            if "ErrorMessage" in input_params["ReturnValue"]:
                  print "Error message is: " + input_
params["ReturnValue"]["ErrorMessage"]
      else:
            print "Battery strength is: ", input_
params["ReturnValue"]["Status"]

      lock.signal()

#Load sysinfo service
sysinfo_handle = scriptext.load("Service.SysInfo", "ISysInfo")

#Make a request to query the required information
event_id = sysinfo_handle.call("GetInfo", {"Entity": u"Battery",
"Key": u"BatteryStrength"}, callback=print_battery_strength)

print "Waiting for the request to be processed!"
lock.wait()
print "Request complete!"
```

12.12.2 SetInfo

Some system attributes can be changed. As an example, the following snippet sets vibration as active:

```
import scriptext

#Load sysinfo service
sysinfo_handle = scriptext.load('Service.SysInfo', 'ISysInfo')

#Make a request to set vibra mode
try:
    sysinfo_handle.call("SetInfo", {"Entity": u"General", "Key":
u"VibraActive", "SystemData": {"Status": 1}})
    print "Request complete!"
except scriptext.ScriptextError:
    print 'Error in servicing the request'
```

12.12.3 `GetNotification`

The `GetNotification` service provides notification when changes occur in certain system parameters.

The following code registers to receive a message when the battery's charging status changes.

```
import scriptext, e32

lock = e32.Ao_lock()
sysinfo_handle = scriptext.load('Service.SysInfo', 'ISysInfo')
```

```
def battery_status_callback(trans_id, event_id, input_params):
      #Check the event status
      if event_id != scriptext.EventCompleted:
            print "Error in retrieving required info"
            print "Error code is: " + str(input_
params["ReturnValue"]["ErrorCode"])
            if "ErrorMessage" in input_params["ReturnValue"]:
                  print "Error message is: " + input_
params["ReturnValue"]["ErrorMessage"]
      else:
            print "Current battery charging status: " + str(input_
params["ReturnValue"]["Status"])
      lock.signal()

#Make a request to get notification
event_id = sysinfo_handle.call("GetNotification", {"Entity":
u"Battery", "Key": u"ChargingStatus"}, callback=battery_status_
callback)
lock.wait()
```

12.13 Summary

This chapter introduced the platform services APIs. These provide a consistent interface for deep access to a wide range of different services.

We hope that you are inspired by the plethora of features that are offered to Python on Symbian applications. Feel free to dip into this chapter and come back whenever you need to use/apply the information in practice.

In the next chapter, we provide an overview of how to extend the functionality of Python on Symbian using native Symbian C++, and also how to call Python scripts from C++ code.

13

Extending Python on Symbian

This chapter provides a brief overview of how Python on Symbian can be extended using C++. It also touches on the mechanisms to call Python from within Symbian C++ code.

13.1 Introduction

Python is a rich and flexible programming language. Its core modules provide access to most of the functionality expected in a modern programming language, including support for adding and extending Python using Python itself (using classes and modules, as we discussed in Chapter 2).

Python for Symbian extends the core Python offering by giving access to many useful Symbian platform C++ APIs, which are encapsulated in developer-friendly Python APIs. To access new or different platform functionality, you are free to write your own extensions, or you can simply add code to optimize functionality that runs faster if written in C++.

This chapter provides a *taste* of what is needed to write C++ extensions, and provides references to where you can find more information. A full explanation is beyond the scope of this book because it requires a fairly deep understanding of Symbian C++, which is a variant of C++ that uses its own idioms and introduces new data types and objects.

In this chapter, we also provide a very shallow introduction to the converse approach of accessing Python functionality from a Symbian C++ application. This approach is useful if Python code accesses a C++ API that uses callbacks (since the C++ code must call back into Python).

13.2 Using C++ from Python

This section describes how Python functionality can be enhanced by incorporating C++ code into a Python program. This is referred to as **extending Python.**

13.2.1 Why Use Python Extensions?

There are a number of reasons why C++ code should be used by Python. One is performance. The Python interpreter on a Symbian device runs very quickly but, when performance is important, C++ code is typically faster than comparable Python code (because Python is interpreted by a software layer while C++ code runs directly on the phone processor).

As an example, consider an implementation of a C++ module called "`mymath`" that implements a cosine computation. The following Python code uses this computation and tests it against the Python cosine implementation:

```
import time, math
import mymath

start = time.time()
for x in range(360):
      r = mymath.docos(x)
```

```
print time.time()-start

start = time.time()
for x in range(360):
    r = math.cos(x)
print time.time()-start
```

This code compares the two cosine computations, and the C++ implementation runs 23% faster than the Python implementation.

Another reason to use C++ code from Python is to access hardware features of the phone that are not built into a Python module. This applies to new hardware features or to hardware features you want to use in a different way than is available through standard Python interfaces. For example, you may need to access new buttons on a device before access to them is provided in a Python module.

Since C++ is the system programming language for the Symbian platform, it is the first language to have access to all phone features and functionality. While the Python interface to the operating system is quite extensive, there are likely to be system calls that you need to be accessed in a new or different way. Extending Python is an easy way to make this happen.

13.2.2 Writing and Using a C++ Extension

Let's continue the cosine example from the previous subsection. Here is the C++ code to implement the `docos()` cosine computation:

```
#include "Python.h"
#include <math.h>
```

```
static PyObject *
docos(PyObject *self, PyObject *args)
{
      double value, result;

      if (!PyArg_ParseTuple(args, "d", &value)) return NULL;

      result = cos(value);
      return Py_BuildValue("d", result);
}

static PyMethodDef mymath_methods[] = {
    {"docos",   docos,   METH_VARARGS},
    {0, 0}
};

/* module entry-point (module-initialization) function */
PyMODINIT_FUNC
initmymath(void)
{
    /* Create the module and add the functions */
    PyObject *m = Py_InitModule("mymath", mymath_methods);
}
```

Note that we are not very clever in the `docos()` implementation: we simply call the cosine function built into the C/C++ math library.

Let's point out some elements of the definition of the `docos()` function:

- The definition requires a reference to the object defining it and to function parameters. These are required for Python functions and are also present in the previous code, where all the parameters are contained in the `args` C++ parameter.
- Note that the return is a tuple, built by a C++ function call.
- Note that multiple use of `PyObject` objects. These objects are Python tuples formatted so that Python can work with them. C++ works with these objects and tuples through special functions that can interpret and build them.

This last element is at the core of Python extensions. `PyObject` objects represent data and class objects in Python. Any communication between C++ and Python happens using `PyObject` objects.

The code that implements a C++ extension must pay attention to several constraints:

- It must start with:

```
#include "Python.h"
```

- The `#include` directive includes redefinition of some C++ structures and must be used before all others.
- The C++ code should take care to convert Python objects. This includes

the data objects we discussed previously as well as Python exceptions (not discussed here). Python exceptions should be used to represent all error conditions, including those generated by the operating system, as well as the implementation code.

- The C++ code must include a method table. This table is a C++ array that holds `PyMethodDef` structs. These structs inform the Python runtime system which methods are implemented by the C++ code. For example, in the previous cosine implementation, we would declare the following table:

```
static PyMethodDef mymath_methods[] = {
    {"docos",    docos,    METH_VARARGS},
    {0, 0}
};
```

The `PyMethodDef` struct declares the name of the function, the implementation that name refers to, and the type of parameters used with the function. The typical method is `METH_VARARGS`, which indicates the Python style used in the example, but other methods exist, such as `METH_NOARGS`, where no parameters are used, and `METH_KEYWORDS`, where keywords are used for positional parameter assignment.

Finally, the function implementation needs an entry point, a kind of constructor used to initialize the implementation. The initialization is performed through a call to `Py_InitModule`, which creates a `PyObject` representation of the class to which the function belongs.

> **Note**
> Names are important in the code that implements the C++ extension. The method table must be named "`module_methods`", where module is replaced by the name of the module you are implementing. Likewise, the entry point function must be named "`initmodule`", where module is replaced by the name of the module you are implementing.

The DLL must be given the platform security capabilities of all the applications that might attempt to use it - in practice this means that you need to give it as many capabilities as possible. This is done in the C++ project's MMP file, as shown in the following section. You should also take care to document any capabilities that are needed by users of your module. If you're unfamiliar with the topic, platform security is discussed further in Chapter 15.

When the extension code is complete, it is compiled into a dynamically loaded library (DLL). Compilation can be performed either from the command line of an operating system shell or through the Carbide.c++ Integrated Development Environment (IDE). Details on using Carbide.c++ are provided later in this chapter.

The extension DLL must be bundled with the Python programs that use it. Python extension users do not need to think about this process, they simply package their application as described in Chapter 16 and the application packager automatically includes any DLLs that have been referenced in the module and that are included in the application packager module repository. As an extension developer however, you need to ensure that the DLL is copied to the right place in the application packager - this is discussed in the reference documentation, ***pys60.garage.maemo.org/doc/s60/modulerepo.html***.

It is important to note that extension modules bundled with a Python program are not available to other Python applications on the device. A unique copy of the extension module is made available for every application that bundles it (named using the application UID).

13.2.3 Using Carbide.c++

Developing the C++ code necessary for Python extension is a fairly straightforward process. Deploying this code, however, can be complicated and involves several configuration files. While the compilation and deployment of this library can be done from the command line, it is much more easily done through the Carbide.c++ IDE. This subsection will briefly walk through the steps necessary.

To use Symbian C++ for Python extension, you must install kits for Symbian C++ development. You can find the tools here: ***croozeus.com/tools_and_kits***. You must install both the Application Development Toolkit and the Symbian C++ SDK. Then you must find the Python overlay for the C++ SDK and overlay that code on the SDK installation.

Once you have the proper installation environment, follow these steps using Carbide.c++:

1. Begin by creating a new project. This should be a "Symbian OS C++ Project" found under the "File > New" menu. Selecting that menu option will bring up the new project dialog window shown in Figure 13.1:

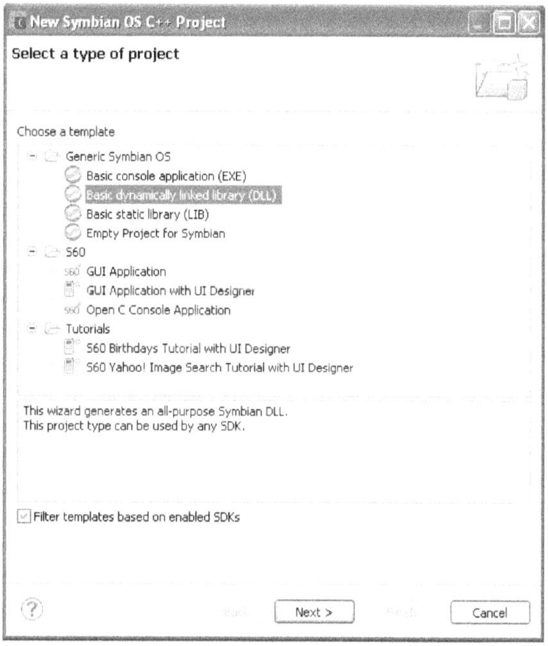

Figure 13.1 New project dialog window

In this window, select "Basic dynamically linked library (DLL)". Give the project a name in the next dialog window and select the SDK in the next window. Then click the "Finish" button. Carbide.c++ will create a project for you containing template code.

2. Using the descriptions in this chapter, design and implement the code you need for your Python extension.

3. When your code is to the point where you need to make the DLL, start with the MMP file. This is found under the "group" folder in the Project Explorer (see Figure 13.2):

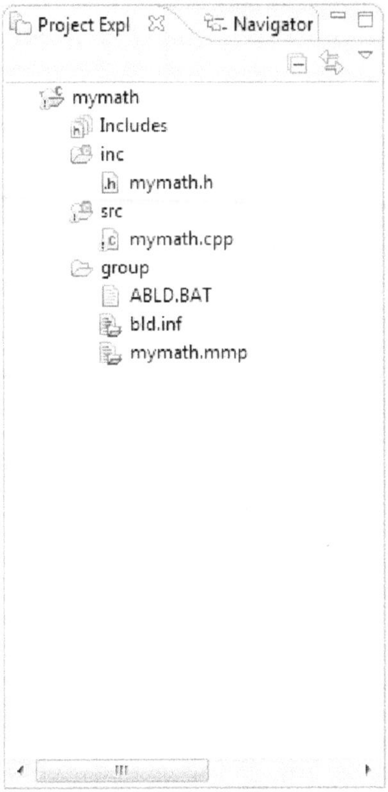

Figure 13.2 Starting the MMP file

You must add specifiers to the basic MMP file generated for you. You may select the provided links in Carbide.c++ or you can simply find the source (select the name of the MMP file on the bottom of the editor) and type in a few statements yourself. The MMP file for the "mymath" example is shown as follows.

```
/*
=============================================================
================
 Name        : mymath.mmp
 Author      :
 Copyright   : Your copyright notice
 Description : This is the project specification file for my-
math.
=============================================================
================
*/

TARGET            kf_mymath.pyd
TARGETTYPE   DLL

USERINCLUDE       ..\inc
SYSTEMINCLUDE   \epoc32\include
SYSTEMINCLUDE   \epoc32\include\stdapis
SYSTEMINCLUDE   \epoc32\include\python25

SOURCEPATH   ..\src
SOURCE            mymath.cpp

CAPABILITY LocalServices NetworkServices ReadUserData
UserEnvironment WriteUserData
LIBRARY python25.lib
LIBRARY estlib.lib
```

```
EPOCALLOWDLLDATA

NOSTRICTDEF
DEFFILE mymath.def
```

- Note the inclusion of more system include files as well as the `EPOCALLOWDLLDATA` specifier, the definition file additions, and the new library specifications (the "mymath" example needs the "estlib.lib" library for the "`cos()`" function). The `TARGETTYPE` should be `DLL`. Also note the name: "kf_module.pyd", where module is replaced by the name of the module you are implementing.
- Note also that this DLL has been given all the user capabilities (using the `CAPABILITY` keyword). As discussed in the preceding section, in practice you'd seek to give it as many capabilities as possible.
- Once the MMP file is in place, you can build the C++ library file. When you are ready, you can build for the release target on the phone for which you are building. You will be able to find this in the SDK installation directory under "epoc32\release\gcce\urel".
- Now you need to place the library where the bundling software can find it. This place is located in the installation directory under the "module-repo\dev modules" directory. In this directory, you need to create a folder with the name of your module. For the "mymath" example, this is the directory "C:\Program Files\PythonForS60-2.0\module-repo\dev-modules\mymath". In this new directory, place two files. The first is the library file ("kf_mymath.pyd" for our example). The second is a configuration file called "module_config.cfg", which needs to contain a single line, as follows:

```
{'type': 'repo', 'deps': []}
```

The final step is use the application packager to bundle the Python code with the library file you created.

13.3 Using Python from C++

While the typical way for Python and C++ to interact is to extend Python functionality, another way to mix the two languages is to use Python as part a larger application. This technique is referred to as embedding Python in an application. The difference between extending and embedding is that when you extend Python, the main components of the application is the Python interpreter and runtime environment, while if you embed Python, the main component may occasionally call the Python interpreter to run some Python code. The process of embedding Python is less straightforward than implementing an extension. However, many ideas and skills developed extending Python with C++ are useful when embedding Python.

At a very high level, embedding Python in C++ uses a very high level interface. This high level embedding is intended to execute a Python script that does not interact with the application directly. Consider the following simple code:

```
#include <Python.h>

int main(int argc, char *argv[])
{
  Py_Initialize();
  PyRun_SimpleString("from time import time,ctime\n"
                     "print 'Today is',ctime(time())\n");
```

```
  Py_Finalize();
  return 0;
}
```

This code starts by initializing the Python interpreter with `Py_Initialize()`. It then executes a Python script that is contained in a single string by calling `PyRun_SimpleString()`. The call to `Py_Finalize()` terminates the Python interpreter.

Obviously, this is a simple and contrived introduction to interacting with Python from C++. There are many other ways to interact at this high level, such as getting the Python code from a file with `PyRun_SimpleFile()` or compiling Python code with `Py_CompileString()`. The most effective interactions, however, come from deeper, more intimate collaborations with the Python runtime; there are many ways to work with a Python interpreter.

There are several reasons to embed Python in a C++ application. Providing scripting layers that allow the user write Python scripts to automate common tasks or extend a feature set is a common use. Allowing users to tailor an application to their needs by writing some scripts in Python is useful if some of the functionality can be written in Python more easily than in some other configuration language. Another use of embedding is as a configuration medium for an application. Sometimes complication configurations are better handled by languages that already exist and might be more familiar to a user.

Documentation on C++ interfaces to Python can be found from links outlined in the next section.

13.4 Further Reading

For further reading into combining Python with C++, here are some places to start:

- PyS60 project documentation on extending and embedding for the Symbian platform: ***pys60.garage.maemo.org/doc/s60/extendandembed.html***.
- Documentation for extending and embedding in Python "in general": ***pys60.garage.maemo.org/doc/ext/ext.html***.
- A general look at multi-language programming in general can be found on the Symbian developer website. The article, entitled "Multi-Language Programming - An Overview" describes several languages that can work together, including Python.
- A more detailed look at extending Python with C++ can be found in this article: ***croozeus.com/Combining_Python_with_FlashLite_C++***. As the name suggests, the article has more detail about Python with C++ as well as using other languages with C++ (e.g., Flash Lite).

13.6 Summary

This chapter provides a look at what is needed to write C++ extensions, the use of C++ code from Python. It also briefly introduces the idea of embedding Python into C++ code.

We provide a small example of how to create a C++ extension, including how to use the Carbide.c++ integrated development environment to accomplish this:

croozeus.com/PythonOnSymbianBookExampleCode_ExtendingPython.zip

14

Advanced Network Programming

This chapter extends the concepts discussed in Chapter 9, employing high level libraries to create advanced, connected applications.

14.1 Introduction

While Chapter 9 is useful to acquire a basic understanding of TCP/IP, and discusses how client-server applications can be constructed using the socket library, it does not explore the Python libraries available for developing networked programs.

In this chapter, some important libraries like urllib, xmlrpclib, JSON and Beautiful Soup are discussed and illustrated using fully functional examples written in Python for Symbian. We also present some techniques for inter-process communication and explain how to create multi-threaded programs.

14.2 HTTP Principles and urllib module

14.2.1 urllib

urllib is a versatile Python module for fetching data across the Internet. It has several interesting features:

- Opening URLs with an interface similar to that one found in file operations
- Functions for processing URLs, like escaping HTML and parameter

processing
- Proxy and HTTP basic authentication support.

Powerful programs can be created with urllib. For instance, suppose you want to fetch the content of a page from ***wiki.forum.nokia.com*** and save it into local file wikiforumnokia.html. This can be performed by urllib using a few lines of code:

```
import urllib
# returns a file like interface
furl = urllib.urlopen("http://wiki.forum.nokia.com/")
# reading the "file"
contents = furl.read()
# saving the page contents
flocal = open("wikiforumnokia.html","wt")
flocal.write(contents)
```

Or, if you prefer, the `urlretrieve()` method can achieve this with just two lines of code:

```
import urllib
urllib.urlretrieve("http://wiki.forum.nokia.com/","wikiforumnokia.
html")
```

`urlopen()` performs an HTTP GET request and fetches the contents of the desired page, stripping the HTTP header. If additional parameters are necessary in your request, they may be added to the URL like a typical URL GET request.

```
import urllib
params = urllib.urlencode({'name': 'My name is Bond',
'phone':'007007'})
url = "www.exemplo.com/yourname?" + params
print url
```

The output is an URL with all parameters encoded, as you can see in the address bar when searching at Yahoo! or Google.

```
htp://www.exemplo.com/yourname?phone=007007&name=My+name+is+Bond
```

It is possible to simulate an HTTP POST request as well. POST requests do not use the URL to encode the parameters. Instead, parameters are included in the body of the request. Forms are a good example of POST requests where all form parameters are hidden inside the html body.

We can access ***www.exemplo.com*** with the same arguments as previously, but now using POST, as demonstrated in the following code snippet:

```
import urllib
params = urllib.urlencode({'name': 'My name is Bond',
'phone':'007007'})
result = urllib.urlopen("www.exemplo.com/yourname", params).read()
```

In this case, an additional parameter must be supplied to `urlopen()`, indicating the POST request parameters.

14.2.2 Accessing Wordpress statistics

As an example, urllib may be used to retrieve information about blog views and post views from wordpress statistics (***stats.wordpress.com/csv.php***). It is necessary to use an api_key (***faq.wordpress.com/2005/10/19/api-key***) and to create an appropriate HTTP GET request (see ***en.wikipedia.org/wiki/Hypertext_Transfer_Protocol#Request_methods*** for more details about HTTP requests). Blog views may be fetched with the following URL:

```
http://stats.wordpress.com/csv.php?api_key=your_api_key&
blog_uri=http://yourblogname.wordpress.com&blog_id=0&table=views
```

All post views may be fetched with the following URL:

```
http://stats.wordpress.com/csv.php?api_key=your_api_key&
blog_uri=http://yourblogname.wordpress.com&blog_
id=0&table=postviews
```

Wordpress can send the response in CSV (comma separated values) or XML. I will use CSV, parsing just a few fields. It is necessary to use a smarter strategy to avoid problems with commas in post titles, for example (or switch to XML). Moreover, you may have a lot of headaches when transforming HTML in Unicode (avoided here as well).

The code is as follows and it is not difficult to understand after this urllib lesson.

```
# Wordpress Stats demo
import urllib
```

```
from appuifw import *
import e32

class WPStats(object):
    """ This classe uses urllib for accessing wordpress blog sta-
tistics.
        Only blogs hosted at wordpress.com may be used.
    """

    STAT_URL = "http://stats.wordpress.com/csv.php?"

    def __init__(self,api_key,blog_uri,blog_id=0,max_days=30):
        """ Init WPStats parmeters.

            Please use:
                api_key: copy it from http://yourblogname.word-
press.com/wp-admin/profile.php
                blog_uri: your blog uri (http://yourblogname.word-
press.com)
                max_days: all accesses will provided statistics
for the last max_days
        """
        self.api_key = api_key
        self.blog_uri = blog_uri
        self.blog_id = blog_id
        self.max_days = max_days

    def __request_stats(self,custom_params):
```

```
        """ Common request function. Additional parameters may be
            encoded for GET using custom_params dictionary
        """
        params = {"api_key":self.api_key,
                  "blog_id":self.blog_id,
                  "blog_uri":self.blog_uri,
                  "format":"cvs",
                  "days":self.max_days}
        params.update(custom_params) # add custom_params values to
params

        try:
            f = urllib.urlopen(self.STAT_URL + urllib.
urlencode(params))
        except Exception, e:
            raise e

        data = []
        rsp = f.read()
        if rsp:
            # this split may fail for post title with "\n" on it -
improve it
            data = rsp.split("\n")[1:-1] # discard column names
and last empty element

        return data

    def get_post_views(self,post_id = 0):
```

```
    """ Get the number of views for a given post id or
        number of views for all posts (post id = 0)

        Response is an array of tuples like below:
        [(date,post_id,views),date,post_id,views),...]
    """
    params = {"table":"postviews"}
    if post_id:
        params['post_id'] = post_id
    data = self.__request_stats(params)
    res = []
    for d in data:
        # this split may fail for post title with "," on it
        row = d.split(",")
        res.append((row[0],row[1],row[-1]))
    return res

def get_blog_views(self):
    """ Get the number of views

        Response format is an array of tuples like below:
        [(date,views),(date,views),...]
    """
    params = {"table":"view"}
    data = self.__request_stats(params)
    res = []
    for d in data:
        res.append(tuple(d.split(",")))
```

```
        return res


class WPStatClient(object):
    """ Get statistics from wordpress
    """
    def __init__(self):
        self.lock = e32.Ao_lock()
        app.title = u"WP Stats demo"
        app.menu = [(u"Get blog views", self.blog_views),
                    (u"Get post views", self.post_views),
                    (u"Exit", self.close_app)]
        self.body = Listbox([(u"Please, update statistics",u"")])
        app.body = self.body
        app.screen = "normal"
        self.wpstats = WPStats("put_api_key_here","http://your_
blog_name_here.wordpress.com")
        self.lock.wait()

    def blog_views(self):
        try:
            bv = self.wpstats.get_blog_views()
        except:
            note(u"Impossible to get stats","error")
        else:
            if bv:
                items = []
                for stat in bv:
                    items.append((unicode(stat[0]),
```

```
                                u"Views:" + unicode(stat[1])))
                self.body.set_list(items)
            else:
                self.body.set_list([(u"",u"")])

    def post_views(self):
        try:
            pv = self.wpstats.get_post_views()
        except:
            note(u"Impossible to get stats","error")
        else:
            if pv:
                items = []
                for stat in pv:
                    items.append((unicode(stat[0]),
                                u"PostID:"+unicode(stat[1]) + u"
Views:"+unicode(stat[2])))
                self.body.set_list(items)
            else:
                self.body.set_list([(u"",u"")])

    def close_app(self):
        self.lock.signal()
        app.set_exit()

if __name__ == "__main__":
    WPStatClient()
```

Figure 14.1 shows some screenshots:

Figure 14.1: Wordpress Stats demo screenshots

14.2.3 Accessing public Qik streams from Symbian devices

Qik is a new and innovative service that allows you stream video live from your cell phone to the web. The videos can be shared with your friends and are available for viewing and downloading. In this section, we'll describe how to use urllib and JSON-RPC to create an API for browsing public streams, given a Qik account.

14.2.4 Object serialization using JSON

JSON is a lightweight data-interchange format, easily readable for humans and equally easily parsed and generated by machines. Several languages, including Python, have one or more JSON implementations. In this section, the Python library known as simplejson will be used. This library was also ported for Symbian devices and it is available for download from ***pys60gps.googlecode.com/svn/trunk/lib/simplejson.py***.

Using simplejson, almost all basic types may be encoded as strings and sent over an Internet connection. Two simplejson methods (`dumps()` and `loads()`) are responsible for encoding data as a JSON representation and decoding it afterwards.

For instance, consider the following dictionary and its posterior serialization/de-serialization:

```
import simplejson

d = { "name":"John Symbian", "age": 36, "weight":1.77,
"devices":["N95", "E72", "N900"] }
ser = simplejson.dumps(d)

print len(ser)
print type(ser)
print ser

rd = simplejson.loads(ser)

print len(rd)
print type(rd)
print rd
```

The serialization output is a string, ready to be transmitted over TCP/IP connections:

```
>>> 81
>>> <type 'str'>
>>>   '{"age": 36, "devices": ["N95", "E72", "N900"], "name": "John
Symbian", "weight": 1.77}'
```

This string can be converted to a Python object again using the `loads()` method, as showed in the following output:

```
>>> 4
>>> <type 'dict'>
>>> {u'age': 36, u'weight': 1.77, u'name': u'John Symbian',
u'devices': [u'N95', u'E72', u'N900']}
```

14.2.5 Qik API foundations

The current Qik API is based on JSON-RPC and REST (only available for the Qik-ly API and not used in this section). JSON-RPC Qik API uses HTTP for transfer data between client and Qik engine. For instance, the public streams of Qik user marcelobarrosalmeida can be retrieved with the following HTTP data:

```
POST /api/jsonrpc?apikey=YOUR_API_KEY HTTP/1.0
Content-Length: 80
Host: engine.qik.com
Content-Type: application/json; charset=UTF-8
```

```
{"method": "qik.stream.public_user_streams","params": ["marcelo-
barrosalmeida"]}
```

The response is as follows:


```
HTTP/1.1 200 OK
Server: nginx/0.7.59
Date: Fri, 07 Aug 2009 14:31:06 GMT
Content-Type: text/json
Connection: close
Content-Length: 1706
X-Qik-Origin: 229

[[{"url": "http://qik.com/video/2363785", "live": false, "user_
id": 365150, "small_thumbnail_url": "http://media.qik.com/media.th
umbnails.128/2a7c74d9862b4f2caa9ea6d7296b9225.jpg", "title": "Un-
titled",
"duration": 54, "created_at": "2009-07-31 13:23:30", "views": 7,
"id": 2363785}, {"url": "http://qik.com/video/2366002",
 "live": false, "user_id": 365150, "small_thumbnail_url": "http://
media.qik.com/media.thumbnails.128/93befe9eb93c464aadbd92d8ea16
ac77.jpg",
 "title": "Pint da Guinness", "duration": 30, "created_at": "2009-
07-31 18:15:29", "views": 18, "id": 2366002},
{"url": "http://qik.com/video/2363998", "live": false, "user_id":
365150, "small_thumbnail_url": "http://media.qik.com/media.thumbna
ils.128/566d3f87915b46479ad72eff0c0a21ca.jpg", "title": "Trafalgar
square",
```

```
"duration": 41, "created_at": "2009-07-31 14:01:39", "views": 11,
"id": 2363998}, {"url": "http://qik.com/video/2357498",
 "live": false, "user_id": 365150, "small_thumbnail_url": "http://
media.qik.com/media.thumbnails.128/cd4e173774884249968e757d-
364fe34d.jpg",
 "title": "Untitled", "duration": 55, "created_at": "2009-07-30
21:06:58", "views": 5, "id": 2357498}, {"url": "http://qik.com/
video/2356796",
 "live": false, "user_id": 365150, "small_thumbnail_url": "http://
media.qik.com/media.thumbnails.128/2053be143c2c4e708b9bcd51d6
2a7359.jpg",
 "title": "Untitled", "duration": 97, "created_at": "2009-07-30
19:54:10", "views": 7, "id": 2356796}, {"url": "http://qik.com/
video/2363619",
 "live": false, "user_id": 365150, "small_thumbnail_url": "http://
media.qik.com/media.thumbnails.128/d230dcf8cf3e4f9fb6980f-
512b66265c.jpg",
 "title": "Untitled", "duration": 61, "created_at": "2009-07-31
12:54:22", "views": 5, "id": 2363619}]]
```

The responses use JSON as well, and will vary depending on the required command (check qikapi.pbworks.com for details).

14.2.6 Implementing Qik API in Python for Symbian

Using simplejson and urllib, it is possible to create an API for accessing Qik services from a mobile device. Since we need to include special HTTP headers, instead of using `urllib.urlopen()` we create an URL opener (using `urllib.URLopener()`), and add required headers to it:

```
urlopener = urllib.URLopener()
urlopener.addheaders = [('Host','engine.qik.com'), ('Content-
Type','application/json; charset=UTF-8')]
```

The desired remote procedure call can be reached using the `open()` method and a serialized version of your data. The simplejson method `dumps()` is used to accomplish this task.

```
import simplejson as json

data = json.dumps(data)
url = 'http://engine.qik.com/api/jsonrpc?apikey=YOUR_API_KEY'
f = urlopener.open(url,data)
```

Finally, using the file descriptor returned by `open()` and `loads()` to deserialize the data, it is possible to get the response and decode it:

```
data = json.loads(f.read())[0]
```

The code can be run in Python for Symbian devices or PC, but you will need an API key to use it, which you can request from ***qikapi.pbworks.com***.

```
# -*- coding: utf-8 -*-
# License: GPL3

import simplejson as json
import urllib
```

```
class QikApi(object):
    """ Simple class for Qik videos proxy support
    """
    def __init__(self, api_key, qik_usr):
        """ Create a new Qik API instance with given API key and
user name
        """
        self.qik_url = 'http://engine.qik.com/api/jsonrpc?apikey='
+ api_key
        self.qik_usr = qik_usr
        self.qik_id = -1

    def __urlopener(self):
        """ Return an urlopener with Qik required headers already
set
        """
        urlopener = urllib.URLopener()
        urlopener.addheaders = [('Host','engine.qik.com'),
                                ('Content-Type','application/json;
charset=UTF-8')]
        return urlopener

    def __open(self,url,params=""):
        """ Open a given URL using GET or POST and Qik headers
        """
        if params:
            f = self.__urlopener().open(url,params) #post
```

```
        else:
            f = self.__urlopener().open(url) #get

        return f

    def __qik_request(self,data):
        """ Qik request. Encode data in json format, do the re-
quest and
            decode json response
        """
        data = json.dumps(data)
        f = self.__open(self.qik_url,data)
        res = json.loads(f.read())[0]
        return res

    def __check_id(self,qik_id):
        """ Check if user ID was retrieved or not. If not, down-
load it
        """
        if qik_id == -1:
            if self.qik_id == -1:
                self.qik_id = self.get_user_public_profile()[u'id']
            qik_id = self.qik_id
        return qik_id

    def get_public_user_streams(self,usr=''):
        """ Return all public stream for a given user
            (or for the current user, if it not provided)
```

```
        """
        if not usr:
            usr = self.qik_usr
        data = {'method': 'qik.stream.public_user_
streams','params': [usr]}
        return self.__qik_request(data)

    def get_user_public_profile(self,usr=''):
        """ Return public profile for a given user
            (or for the current user, if it not provided)
        """
        if not usr:
            usr = self.qik_usr
        data = {'method': 'qik.user.public_profile','params':
[usr]}
        return self.__qik_request(data)

    def get_user_public_detailed_profile(self,usr=''):
        """ Return detailed public profile for a given user
            (or for the current user, if it not provided)
        """
        if not usr:
            usr = self.qik_usr
        data = {'method': 'qik.user.public_detailed_
profile','params': [usr]}
        return self.__qik_request(data)

    def get_user_followers(self,qik_id=-1):
```

```
        """ Return the list of followers for a given user
            (or for the current user, if it not provided)
        """
        qik_id = self.__check_id(qik_id)
        data = {'method': 'qik.user.followers','params': [qik_id]}
        return self.__qik_request(data)

    def get_user_following(self,qik_id=-1):
        """ Return the list of following for a given user
            (or for the current user, if it not provided)
        """
        qik_id = self.__check_id(qik_id)
        data = {'method': 'qik.user.following','params': [qik_id]}
        return self.__qik_request(data)

    def get_public_stream_info(self,vid_id):
        """ Get detailed information about some public video
        """
        data = {'method': 'qik.stream.public_info','params': [vid_
id]}
        return self.__qik_request(data)
```

14.2.7 Demo application and source code

It is simple to create a demo application to show user streams and their Qik following/followers lists, each one in a different tab. To play the videos on a Flash-lite capable device, a local HTML file with links to the embedded video is created (see QIK_TEMPLATE variable) and the native web browser is called to show it. The user interface was created using the handy article found at ***wiki.forum.nokia.com/index.php/Basic_framework_for_creating_user_interface***.

You can see this application in action here: ***www.youtube.com/watch?v=AjPZKXrQq4k&feature=player_embedded.***

Check ***code.google.com/p/wordmobi/source/browse/trunk/qikapi*** for newer versions and updates. To run it, just copy all files (window.py, qikapi.py, qikview.py, simplejson.py) to your memory card (into e:\Python) and use the Python interpreter to execute qikview.py.

```
# Qik view demo
import sys
sys.path.append('e:\\Python')

import window
from appuifw import *
from qikapi import QikApi
import time

API_KEY = 'YOUR_API_KEY'

QIK_TEMPLATE = u"""
<html><head><meta http-equiv="Content-Type" content="application/
vnd.wap.xhtml+xml; charset=utf-8" /><title>__TITLE__</title></
head><body>
<object classid="clsid:d27cdb6e-ae6d-11cf-96b8-444553540000"
```

```
codebase="http://fpdownload.macromedia.com/pub/shockwave/cabs/
flash/swflash.cab#version=7,0,0,0" width="220" height="185"
id="player" align="middle">
<param name="movie" value="http://qik.com/swfs/qik_player_lite.
swf?file=http://qik.com/flv/__FILENAME__.flv&amp;thumbnail=http://
qik.com/redir/__FILENAME__.jpg&amp;size=false&amp;aplay=true&amp;a
utorew=false&amp;layout=small&amp;title=__TITLE__"/>
<param name="menu" value="false" />
<param name="quality" value="high" />
<param name="bgcolor" value="#999999" />
<embed src="http://qik.com/swfs/qik_player_lite.swf?file=http://
qik.com/flv/__FILENAME__.flv&amp;thumbnail=http://qik.com/redir/__
FILENAME__.jpg&amp;size=false&amp;aplay=true&amp;autorew=false&a
mp;layout=small&amp;title=__TITLE__" menu="false" quality="high"
bgcolor="#999999" width="220" height="185" name="player"
align="middle" allowScriptAccess="sameDomain" type="application/x-
shockwave-flash" pluginspage="http://www.macromedia.com/go/getflash-
player"/>
</object></body></html>
""".encode('utf-8')

class QikView(window.Application):
    def __init__(self):
        self.qik_usr = u""
        self.qik_api = None
        self.data = {'profile':[], 'streams':[], 'followers':[],
'following':[]}
        # menus
```

```
        streams_menu = [(u"Show stream",self.show_video)]
        common_menu = [(u"Update",self.update),
                       (u"Setup",self.setup)]
        # bodies
        self.streams = Listbox([(u"Please, setup and 
update",u"")],self.show_video)
        self.following = Listbox([(u"Please, setup and 
update",u"")])
        self.followers = Listbox([(u"Please, setup and 
update",u"")])

        window.Application.__init__(self,
                                     u"Qik View",
                                     [(u"Streams",self.streams,streams_
menu),
                                      (u"Following",self.following,[]),
                                      (u"Followers",self.followers,[])],
                                     common_menu)

    def update(self):
        if not self.qik_usr or not self.qik_api:
            note(u"Please, setup the Qik user",u"error")
        else:
            self.lock_ui()
            try:
                self.set_title(u"Updating profile...")
                self.data['profile'] = self.qik_api.get_user_pub-
lic_profile()
```

```
                self.set_title(u"Updating streams...")
                self.data['streams'] = self.qik_api.get_public_
user_streams()
                self.set_title(u"Updating followers...")
                self.data['followers'] = self.qik_api.get_user_
followers()
                self.set_title(u"Updating following...")
                self.data['following'] = self.qik_api.get_user_
following()
            except:
                note(u"Network error. Please, try again","error")
            else:
                self.update_bodies()
            self.set_title(u"Qik View")
            self.unlock_ui()
            self.refresh()

    def update_bodies(self):
        streams = []
        followers = []
        following = []

        for s in self.data['streams']:
            h1 = s['title'] + (u" (%ds)" % s['duration'])
            h2 = s['created_at']
            streams.append((h1,h2))

        for f in self.data['followers']:
```

```
            followers.append((f[u'username'],f[u'full_name']))

        for f in self.data['following']:
            following.append((f[u'username'],f[u'full_name']))

        if streams:
            self.streams.set_list(streams)
        else:
            self.streams.set_list([(u"No streams available",u"")])

        if followers:
            self.followers.set_list(followers)
        else:
            self.followers.set_list([(u"No followers
available",u"")])

        if following:
            self.following.set_list(following)
        else:
            self.following.set_list([(u"No following
available",u"")])

    def setup(self):
        usr = query(u"Qik user:","text",self.qik_usr)
        if usr is not None:
            self.qik_usr = usr
            self.qik_api = QikApi(API_KEY,self.qik_usr)
```

```
    def show_video(self):
        if self.data['streams']:
            # retrieve information about video
            idx = self.streams.current()
            if 'stream_info' not in self.data['streams'][idx]:
                vid = self.data['streams'][idx][u'id']
                self.lock_ui(u"Downloading stream info...")
                try:
                    self.data['streams'][idx]['stream_info'] =
self.qik_api.get_public_stream_info(vid)
                except:
                    note(u"Network error. Please, try
again","error")
                    ret = True
                else:
                    ret = False
                self.set_title(u"Qik View")
                self.unlock_ui()
                self.refresh()
                if ret:
                    return
            tit = self.data['streams'][idx]['stream_info']
[u'title'].encode('utf-8')
            fn = self.data['streams'][idx]['stream_info']
[u'filename'].encode('utf-8')
            html_code = QIK_TEMPLATE.replace('__FILENAME__',fn).
replace('__TITLE__',tit)
            html_file = "html_" + time.strftime("%Y%m%d_%H%M%S",
```

```
time.localtime()) + ".html"
            try:
                fp = open(html_file,"wt")
                fp.write(html_code)
                fp.close()
            except:
                note(u"Could not create HTML file","error")
                return

            viewer = Content_handler(self.refresh)
            try:
                viewer.open(html_file)
            except:
                note(u"Can not open browser","error")

if __name__ == "__main__":
    app = QikView()
    app.run()
```

14.3 Beautiful Soup and an HTML/XML parser

Beautiful Soup (***www.crummy.com/software/BeautifulSoup***) is a Python HTML/XML parser with many useful methods to collect data from pages or for navigating, searching, and modifying a parse tree. It is very flexible and can be executed on Symbian devices, creating interesting mobile applications. Since Beautiful Soup does not come bundled with a standard Python distribution, you will need to download it and extract the file BeautifulSoup.py to your project root. At the time of writing the version 3.0.8.1 was the most recent.

14.3.1 Beautiful Soup basics

Suppose you have a large (and confusing) HTML file. It is possible to organize and indent it using the `prettify()` method. Just create a `BeautifulSoup` object and feed it the HTML as follows:

```
from BeautifulSoup import BeautifulSoup

html = u"""<html><body><h1 style="text-align:center">Heading 1</
h1>
<p>Page content goes here.
<h2>And here.</h2></p><a href="http://croozeus.com/blogs"
alt="Croozeus link">Croozeus</a><br/>
<a href="http://www.python.org">Python</a><br/>
<h1>The end.</h1></body>
</html>"""

soup = BeautifulSoup(html)
print soup.prettify()
```

The output is as follows:

```
<html>
 <body>
  <h1 style="text-align:center">
   Heading 1
  </h1>
  <p>
```

```
    Page content goes here.
    <h2>
     And here.
    </h2>
   </p>
   <a href="http://croozeus.com/blogs" alt="Croozeus link">
    Croozeus
   </a>
   <br />
   <a href="http://www.python.org">
    Python
   </a>
   <br />
   <h1>
    The end.
   </h1>
  </body>
</html>
```

The parser tree is available with nice operations like `findAll()`. For instance, how about printing all the links on the page ? Just use a dictionary with all the tags you want as argument:

```
links = soup.findAll({'a':True})
for link in links:
    print "-->", link['href'].encode('utf-8')
```

The output is as follows:

```
--> http://croozeus.com/blogs
--> http://www.python.org
```

Or, you may want to add the alt attribute to all links, modifying the parser tree, which is simple:

```
for link in links:
    link['alt'] = link['href']
print soup.prettify()
```

The output is as follows:

```
...
  <a href="http://croozeus.com/blogs" alt="http://croozeus.com/
blogs">
   Croozeus
  </a>
  <br />
  <a href="http://www.python.org" alt="http://www.python.org">
   Python
  </a>
...
```

As you can see, each link is like a dictionary and it is really straightforward to modify it.

The contents between <p> and </p> tags can be retrieved with a call to `find()`, which just looks for the first instance of tag <p> and returns an object that holds the contents between <p> and </p>. Using the contents attribute, you can iterate over an array of child elements. In this case, the first is a string and the second is a new parseable element of the tree:

```
p = soup.find('p')
print p.contents
print p.contents[0]
print p.contents[1]
print p.contents[1].contents
```

The output is as follows:

```
[u'Page content goes here.\n', <h2>And here.</h2>]
Page content goes here.
<h2>And here.</h2>
[u'And here.']
```

There is a complete set of functions to navigate through the tree. For instance, it is possible to start our search at first tag 'p' after locating its child with the following code:

```
p = soup.p
h2 = p.findChild()
print h2
```

The output is as follows:

```
<h2>And here.</h2>
```

Or start the search at first tag ‘h1’ but now looking for next siblings:

```
h1=soup.h1
while h1:
    print h1
    h1 = h1.findNextSibling('h1')
```

The output is as follows:

```
<h1 style="text-align:center">Heading 1</h1>
<h1>The end.</h1>
```

14.3.2 Link checker application

Now it’s time to use this knowledge in a new application: a basic link checker for Symbian devices. The idea is to download the contents of some URL and check all links inside it using Beautiful Soup and urllib.

There is a known problem related to fetching pages from Wikipedia using Python. Wikipedia does not accept the default urllib user agent, so you need to change it. The class `LCOpener` was created to solve this issue, defining a new user agent (Mozilla/5.0).

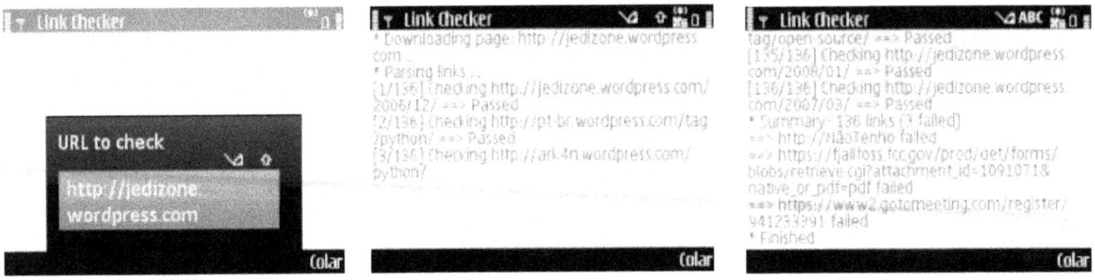

Figure 14.2: Link checker screenshots

```
# Link Checker demo
import sys
sys.path.append('e:\\Python')
try:
    # Try to import 'btsocket' as 'socket'
    sys.modules['socket'] = __import__('btsocket')
except ImportError:
    pass
import socket
from BeautifulSoup import BeautifulSoup
import os
import e32
import urllib
import hashlib
from appuifw import *

class LCOpener(urllib.FancyURLopener):
```

```
    """ For mediawiki it is necessary to change the http agent.
        See:
        http://wolfprojects.altervista.org/changeua.php
        http://stackoverflow.com/questions/120061/fetch-a-wikipe-
dia-article-with-python
    """
    version = 'Mozilla/5.0'

class LinkChecker(object):
    def __init__(self):
        self.lock = e32.Ao_lock()
        self.dir = "e:\\linkchecker"
        if not os.path.isdir(self.dir):
            os.makedirs(self.dir)
        self.apo = None
        self.url = u'http://www.'
        self.running = False
        app.title = u"Link Checker"
        app.screen = "normal"
        app.menu = [(u"Check URL",self.check_url),
                    (u"Exit", self.close_app)]
        self.body = Text()
        app.body = self.body
        self.lock.wait()

    def close_app(self):
        self.lock.signal()
```

```
    def sel_access_point(self):
        """ Select and set the default access point.
            Return the access point object if the selection was
done or None if not
        """
        aps = socket.access_points()
        if not aps:
            note(u"No access points available","error")
            return None

        ap_labels = map(lambda x: x['name'], aps)
        item = popup_menu(ap_labels,u"Access points:")
        if item is None:
            return None

        apo = socket.access_point(aps[item]['iapid'])
        socket.set_default_access_point(apo)

        return apo

    def check_url(self):
        if self.running:
            note(u"There is a checking already in
progress",u"info")
            return
        self.running = True
        url = query(u"URL to check", "text", self.url)
        if url is not None:
```

```
            self.url = url
            self.apo = self.sel_access_point()
            if self.apo:
                self.body.clear()
                self.run_checker()
        self.running = False

    def run_checker(self):
        self.body.add(u"* Downloading page: %s ...\n" % self.url)
        fn = os.path.join(self.dir,'temp.html')
        try:
            urllib.urlretrieve(self.url,fn)
        except Exception, e:
            try:
                self.body.add(repr(e))
            except:
                self.body.add(u"Could not download " + self.url)
            return
        self.body.add(u"* Parsing links ...\n")
        page = open(fn,'rb').read()
        try:
            soup = BeautifulSoup(page)
        except:
            self.body.add(u"* BeautifulSoup error when decoding
html. Aborted.")
            return
        tags = soup.findAll({'img':True,'a':True})
        links = {}
```

```
        bad_links = []
        for n,tag in enumerate(tags):
            if 'href' in tag:
                link = tag['href']
            elif 'img' in tag:
                link = tag['src']
            else:
                link=u''
            # just check external links
            if link.startswith(u'http'):
                # not handling internal links
                link = link.split(u'#')[0]
                # using a hash to avoid repeated links
                h = hashlib.md5()
                h.update(link.encode('utf-8'))
                links[h.digest()] = link
        nl = len(links)
        for n,k in enumerate(links):
            link = links[k]
            msg = u"[%d/%d] Checking %s " % (n+1,nl,link)
            self.body.add(msg)
            (valid,info) = self.check_link(link.encode('utf-8'))
            if valid:
                msg = u"==> Passed\n"
            else:
                msg = u"==> Failed: %s\n" % info
                bad_links.append(link)
            self.body.add(msg)
```

```
        msg = u"* Summary: %d links (%d failed)\n" % (nl,len(bad_
links))
        self.body.add(msg)
        for link in bad_links:
            self.body.add(u"==> %s failed\n" % link)
        self.body.add(u"* Finished")

    def check_link(self,link):
        """ Check if link (encoded in utf-8) exists.
            Return (True,'') or (False,'error message')
        """
        try:
            page = LCOpener().open(link)
        except Exception, e:
            return (False,unicode(repr(e)))
        else:
           return (True,u'')

lc = LinkChecker()
```

14.4 Multi-threaded programming

It is impossible to talk about network programming without discuss multi-threading.

Many servers are implemented using multi-threading strategies, spawning new threads for each client connection that they receive. Multi-threaded programs require specific inter process communications like semaphores, critical sections and queues. Python support for multi-threading is provided by the threading-module and queues can be created using the Queue module, both available in Python for Symbian. They will be used in this chapter for constructing multi-threaded clients and servers.

Threads

Threads can be created from functions or `Thread` objects. For instance, in the following example a new thread is created to show n messages, waiting m seconds between two consecutive messages.

```
# Multi-thread demo1
from threading import Thread
from time import sleep

def mythread(n,m):
    for i in xrange(n):
        print "-->",i
        sleep(m)

t = Thread(target=mythread,args=(5,2))
t.start()
t.join()
```

Figure 14.3: Multi-thread demo result

Since you have created the function with your thread code, it is necessary to create a `Thread` object using target to indicate the thread and args to specify the thread parameters. Thus, it is possible to start a new thread from the main thread (your script) just by calling the method `start()`. The `join()` method is used to block the main thread while the dispatched runs, avoiding any premature termination of the main thread.

If you want to use classes, it is necessary to create a new class using Thread as the base class and defining your thread code inside the `run()` method, as follows:

```
# Multi-thread demo2
from threading import Thread
from time import sleep

class MyThread(Thread):
    def __init__(self,n,m):
```

```
        self.n = n
        self.m = m
        Thread.__init__(self)
    def run(self):
        for i in xrange(self.n):
            print "-->",i
            sleep(self.m)

t = MyThread(5,2)
t.start()
t.join()
```

14.4 1 Semaphores

Multi-threaded applications need to use synchronization mechanisms to control access to shared resources. The following example shows how to use a semaphore to control access to a list that can be modified by different threads. For instance, suppose you have a list that can be modified by your threads, as in the following example:

```
# Semaphore demo
from threading import Thread, Semaphore
from time import sleep
from random import randint

class MyThread(Thread):
    resource = []
    def __init__(self,tid,s):
        self.tid = tid
```

```
        self.sema = s
        Thread.__init__(self)
    def insert(self,v):
        self.sema.acquire()
        MyThread.resource.append(v)
        self.sema.release()
    def run(self):
        for i in xrange(5):
            self.insert((self.tid,i))
            sleep(randint(1,4))

s = Semaphore(1)
tsks = [ MyThread(n,s) for n in xrange(5) ]
[ t.start() for t  in tsks ]
[ t.join() for t  in tsks ]

print MyThread.resource
```

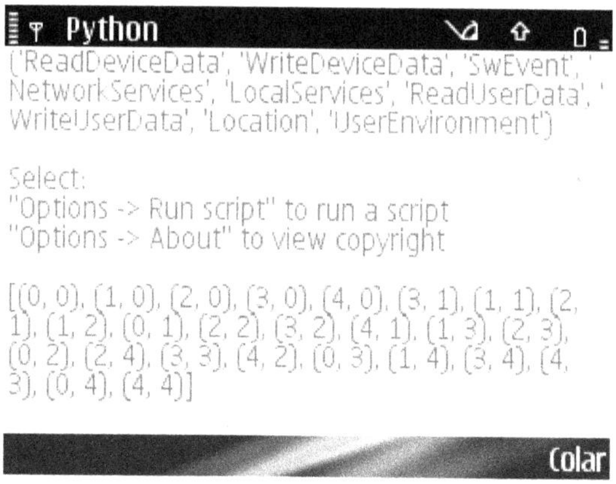

Figure 14.4: Semaphore demo result

The semaphore object is created with a resource-counting object as argument, indicating the number of resources available. In this case, only one resource is used (a global list) and we avoid any concurrent access to it by using a semaphore. The `insert()` function can be understood as a critical section, and all code between `acquire()` and `release()` methods will be protected. Successive calls to `acquire()` without previous calls to `release()` will block the calling thread until the resource becomes available.

14.4.2 Queues

Python implements multi-producer, multi-consumer queues via the Queue module, which is available for Python for Symbian. The `put()` and `get()` methods are the basic Queue methods, inserting and removing objects into/from the Queue. Both methods support timeouts and can block or not. In the next code snippet, several worker threads are created. These threads receive their jobs using a `Queue` object:

```
# Queue demo
from threading import Thread
from Queue import Queue
from random import randint
from time import sleep

def worker_thread(ti,q):
    while True:
        job = q.get()
        if job == "exit":
            print "[%d] exit" % ti
```

```
            break
        else:
            print "[%d] New job: %s" % (ti,job)
            sleep(randint(0,3))
q = Queue()
max_jobs = 12
max_threads = 3

# creating and starting all threads
threads = [ Thread(target=worker_thread,args=(x,q)) for x in
xrange(max_threads) ]
[ t.start() for t in threads ]

# dispatching jobs
[ q.put("Job%d" % x) for x in xrange(max_jobs) ]

# sending exit
[ q.put("exit") for x in xrange(max_threads) ]

# waiting all threads
[ t.join() for t in threads ]
```

A possible output could be:

```
[0] New job: Job0
[1] New job: Job1
[2] New job: Job2
[2] New job: Job3
```

```
[2] New job: Job4
[0] New job: Job5
[0] New job: Job6
[0] New job: Job7
[2] New job: Job8
[1] New job: Job9
[0] New job: Job10
[2] New job: Job11
[2] exit
[1] exit
[0] exit
```

You may also want to check the `task_done()` and `join()` `Queue` methods (available since Python 2.5) for a simpler way to create worker threads.

14.4.3 Multi -threaded page download example

In this example, we will use threads to concurrently download several web pages. You just need to create a file with all pages that you want to download, as follows:

```
http://www.google.com
http://www.yahoo.com
http://invalid.com
```

In this case, the last page was intentionally mistyped to test when the download fails. A queue is used to send progress messages from threads to the main user interface. All files will be saved into "e:\python" using the page name as a file name. The code is as follows:

```
# Multi-thread page downloader
import urllib
from threading import Thread
from Queue import Queue
from appuifw import *
import os
import e32

class get_page(Thread):
    def __init__(self,url,qlog):
        self.url = url
        self.fname = os.path.join(u"e:\\python\\",url[url.
rfind('/')+1:])
        self.qlog = qlog
        Thread.__init__(self)

    def add_msg(self,msg):
        # send a message to UI
        self.qlog.put(msg)

    def run(self):
        self.add_msg(u"Saving %s into %s" % (self.url,self.fname))
        try:
            urllib.urlretrieve(self.url,self.fname)
        except:
            self.add_msg(u"Error downloading %s" % (self.url))
        else:
```

```
            self.add_msg(u"%s finished" % (self.url))

class mt_page_download(object):
    def __init__(self):
        self.lock = e32.Ao_lock()
        self.qlog = Queue()
        app.title = u"MT Demo"
        app.screen = "normal"
        app.menu = [(u"Load URL list", self.load_list),
                    (u"Exit", self.close_app)]
        app.body = Text()
        self.lst = u"e:\\python\\urls.txt"
        self.running = True
        self.run()

    def load_list(self):
        lst = query(u"Path to URL list",'text',self.lst)
        if lst is not None:
            self.lst = lst
            self.create_threads()

    def create_threads(self):
        try:
            urls = open(self.lst,'rt').readlines()
            urls = [ url.replace('\n','') for url in urls if
len(url) ]
            urls = [ url.strip() for url in urls if len(url.
strip()) ]
```

```
        except:
            self.add_msg(u"Could not open %s" % self.lst)
        else:
            self.add_msg(u"Creating threads for %s" % self.lst)
            [ get_page(url,self.qlog).run() for url in urls ]

    def close_app(self):
        self.running = False
        self.lock.signal()

    def add_msg(self,msg):
        app.body.add(msg + u"\u2029")

    def run(self):
        while self.running:
            # create a loop and check to incoming messages
            e32.ao_yield()
            try:
                msg = self.qlog.get(True,1)
            except:
                continue
            else:
                self.add_msg(msg)
        self.lock.wait()
        app.set_exit()

mt = mt_page_download()
```

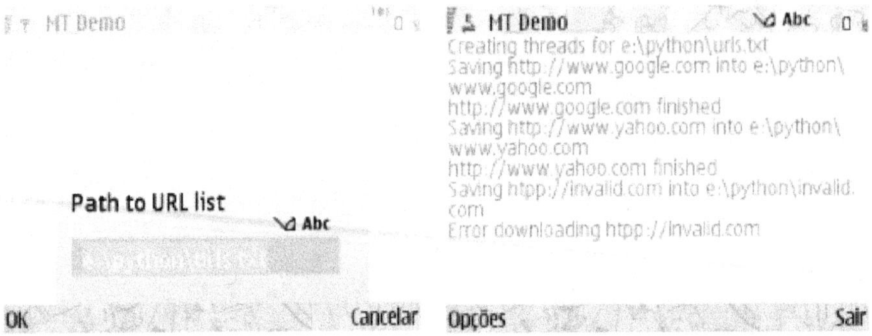

Figure 14.5: Multi-threaded example screenshots

14.4.4 Recreating a Python shell with multi-threading support

Some scripts in this section will lock if you try to run the code in Python for Symbian shells from series 1.4 or before 1.9.1. Those Python for Symbian shell were created using ensymble with `package_mode=pys60`, but for proper multi-threading and socket usage you need a shell with `package_mode=pycore` and you'll need to recreate the sis file, changing the package mode.

Note: This topic may be considered out of scope but since it is extremely important to run multi-threaded programs that use sockets, it will described briefly here. You should also check ***garage.maemo.org*** for more information.

You will need a copy of the current shell file, available in the Python for Symbian source code as the file `ext\amaretto\scriptshell\default.py`. Extract and copy it into a directory, for instance c:\temp\pyshellmt\. Do not use spaces in any directory name.

Using the application Ensymble GUI you can recreate your shell. Ensymble GUI is available from the PythonForSymbian 2.0.0 installation package. Fill all fields as shown in the next figure.

We recommend that you add some additional platform security capabilities to your shell (if you're unsure about what this means, further information about Symbian platform security is available in Chapter 15). In this example we used:

```
caps=LocalServices+NetworkServices+ReadUserData+WriteUserDat
a+UserEnvironment
```

Press Create and your new shell will be created inside c:\temp\pyshellmt\. Install and use it for running all examples in this section.

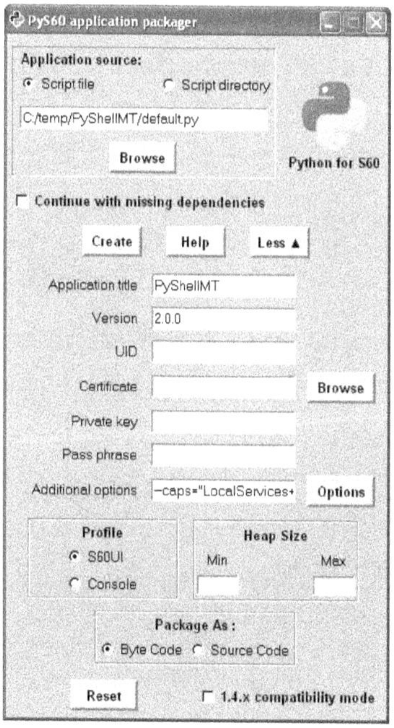

Figure 14.6: Creating a new Python shell

14.5 XML-RPC

The xmlrpclib module is also available for Python for Symbian, allowing communication between an application and several XML-RPC based services, like Wordpress, Flickr and Drupal. Using xmlrpclib it is possible to call remote methods (with parameters) and get back structured responses.

The following code snippet will show how to retrieve a list of recent posts from a Wordpress blog account. Before you run it, replace put_user_here and put_pass_here with blog credentials with administration rights, and check if your blog allows XML-RPC connections. Moreover, do not forget to use your own blog URL, in general following the format your_blog_domain/xmlrpc.php.

For further explanations about the methods and parameters available, please consult the documentation at ***www.sixapart.com/developers/xmlrpc/metaweblog_api***.

```
# XML-RPC demo
import xmlrpclib
blog = ‘http://wordmobi.wordpress.com/xmlrpc.php’
server = xmlrpclib.ServerProxy(blog)
rposts = server.metaWeblog.getRecentPosts(0,”put_user_here”,”put_
pass_here”, 5)
for post in rposts:
    print ”-> %s” % post[‘title’]
```

The output is as follows:

```
-> I think you already know but I will say ...
```

```
-> I update the latest Wordmobi version to ...
-> Nice things happens when you share :) Th...
-> Returning to Python 1.9.6 and new Wordmobi 0.9.3
-> Python 1.9.7 is crashing wordmobi due to an error in mktime()
function.
```

The list of categories can be retrieved using the method `wp.getCategories()` (see ***codex.wordpress.org/XML-RPC***_wp for documentation):

```
# XML-RPC demo
cats = server.wp.getCategories(0,"put_user_here","put_pass_here")
for c in cats:
    print c['categoryName']
```

Output:

```
Announce
Bugs
Complains
Development
New Versions
Translation
Uncategorized
```

Recent services such as Flickr will require more advanced authentication methods. Please check the documentation for individual services before using them.

14.5.1 Express post demo application

In the next application, xmlrpclib is used to add small posts to a Wordpress-based blog. It is necessary to submit blog domain and access credentials, as cited in the previous section. If want to develop a new application for Wordpress, there is a xmlrpclib wrapper called Wordpresslib (***www.blackbirdblog.it/download/software/wordpresslib.zip***) that can be useful.

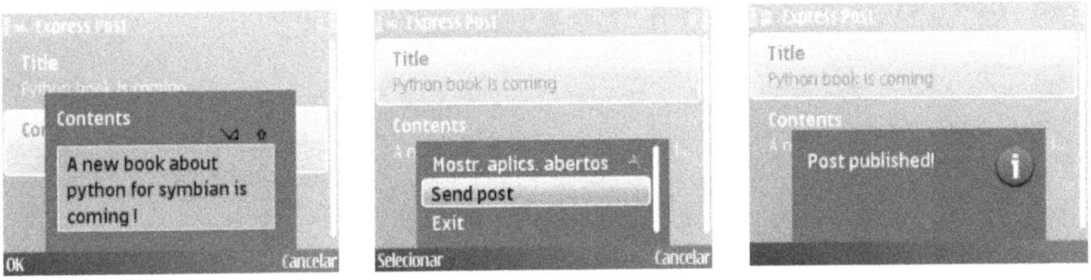

Figure 14.7: Express post application screenshots

```
# Wordpress demo
import socket
from appuifw import *
import xmlrpclib
import e32

WP_USER = “YOUR_USERNAME”
WP_PASS = “YOUR_PASSWORD”
WP_BLOG = “http://YOUR_BLOG_DOMAIN/xmlrpc.php”

class ExpressPost(object):
```

```
def __init__(self):
    self.lock = e32.Ao_lock()
    app.title = u"Express Post"
    app.screen = "normal"
    self.title = u""
    self.contents = u""
    app.menu = [(u"Send post",self.send_post),
                (u"Exit", self.close_app)]
    self.body = Listbox([(u"",u"")],self.edit)
    app.body = self.body
    self.blog = xmlrpclib.ServerProxy(WP_BLOG)
    self.update()
    self.lock.wait()

def edit(self):
    idx = self.body.current()
    if idx == 0:
        title = query(u"Title", "text", self.title)
        if title is not None:
            self.title = title
    elif idx == 1:
        contents = query(u"Contents", "text", self.contents)
        if contents is not None:
            self.contents = contents
    self.update()

def update(self):
    self.body.set_list([(u"Title",self.
```

```
title),(u"Contents",self.contents)])

    def send_post(self):
        "Adding a new post to the blog"
        post = { 'title' : self.unicode_to_utf8(self.title),
                 'description' : self.unicode_to_utf8(self.con-
tents)}
        try:
            # use 0 instead 1 at the end if you want a draft post
            self.blog.metaWeblog.newPost(0,WP_USER,WP_PASS,post,1)
        except:
            note(u"Could not send the post!","error")
        else:
            note(u"Post published!","info")

    def unicode_to_utf8(self,s):
        "Converting string to the default encoding of wordpress"
        return s.encode('utf-8')

    def close_app(self):
        self.lock.signal()

ExpressPost()
```

14.6 Source Code

All examples shown in this chapter are available for download from ***File:Python OnSymbianBookExampleCode Ch14AdvNetProg.zip***.

References

If you are reading a printed version of this book, the following links may be useful:

- Hypertext Transfer Protocol: ***en.wikipedia.org/wiki/Hypertext_Transfer_Protocol***
- JSON-RPC: ***en.wikipedia.org/wiki/JSON-RPC***
- Simplejson: ***simplejson.googlecode.com/svn/tags/simplejson-2.0.9/docs/index.html***
- Simplejson for S60: ***pys60gps.googlecode.com/svn/trunk/lib/simplejson.py***
- Qik API: ***qikapi.pbworks.com***
- Basic framework for creating user interface: ***wiki.forum.nokia.com/index.php/Basic_framework_for_creating_user_interface***
- Beautiful Soup HTML/XML parser: ***www.crummy.com/software/BeautifulSoup***
- Wordpresslib: ***www.blackbirdblog.it/download/software/wordpresslib.zip.***

14.7 Summary

In this chapter, we discussed how to create fully-functional networked programs using important libraries such as urllib, xmlrpclib, JSON and Beautiful Soup. Multi-threaded applications and interprocess communications were briefly described too, since they are frequently found in networked applications.

15

Platform Security and Application Signing

This chapter explains Symbian platform security and application signing from a Python developer's perspective.

15.1 Introduction

On Symbian, application signing and platform security make it very difficult for malicious or badly-written software to subvert the normal operation of a device, while still ensuring that the phone is easy for the user to operate and that honest developers can create powerful and compelling applications.

Application signing is used to determine which applications are trusted, while platform security allows only trusted applications to call sensitive APIs and access areas of the file system.

15.2 Platform security

The two most important platform security concepts are capabilities and data caging.

15.2.1 What are capabilities?

Capabilities are access tokens that an executable must have in order call sensitive APIs or access protected areas of the file system. For example, in order to access the Internet, an application must have the `NetworkServices` capability. If an application calls an API without having the associated capability, then it will crash (in Symbian terms it will panic with code `KERN-EXRC 46` (`KErrPermissionDenied`)).

The most common capabilities are the following 'user capabilities'. These may be granted by the user at install time:

- `NetworkServices` for any operation that results in a network connection
- `LocalServices` for operations that access to bluetooth, USB, or infra-red connections
- `Location` for positioning information
- `ReadUserData` to read the device user's data including contacts and calendar information
- `WriteUserData` to write the device user's data including contacts and calendar information
- `UserEnvironment` to record audio, use the camera, or otherwise use services that provide data from users' physical surroundings.

Other capabilities are less commonly needed by applications, and can only be granted to applications through Symbian Signed. The System, Restricted and Device manufacturer capabilities groups are discussed in detail on the Symbian developer wiki: ***croozeus.com/Fundamentals_Symbian_Platform_Security.***

15.2.2 How do I add capabilities to my app?

The application packager gives your application the user capabilities by default.

If your application needs different capabilities you can replace the default set using caps keyword in the 'Additional options' field (capability names are separated using the '+' symbol):

```
--caps=LocalServices+NetworkServices+...
```

Note that `caps` replaces the existing capabilities - if you need the user capabilities, these will need to be entered again.

15.2.3 What capabilities should I give my application?

The application packager gives your application user capabilities by default. If you're self-signing the application and you don't mind the user being presented with a prompt asking for capabilities that the application doesn't use, then there is no need to change them.

If you're signing your application through Symbian Signed, then you should give your application the minimal set of capabilities it needs to access the functionality it uses. Working out which ones you need is usually easy. Many applications won't need any capabilities at all - no capabilities are required to call standard Python functions. Of those that do, the vast majority will only need the User capabilities listed above. There are a few exceptions - for example, `SwEvent` is needed by the KeyCapture module; these should be documented in your module documentation.

Note that if your application uses more advanced capabilities you will also need to request a developer certificate from Symbian Signed in order to be able to install the application during development.

15.2.4 What capabilities should I give my Python extensions?

Advanced users can extend Python using C++, as discussed in Chapter 13.

Python extensions are DLLs and must obey the same rules as other DLLs on the Symbian platform. A DLL must have all the capabilities of the loading executable:

- If the DLL is solely for the use of a single application then give it the same capabilities as the application.
- If the DLL is shared (to be loaded into many processes) then give it all the capabilities of all the processes (System DLLs have all capabilities except TCB so that they can be loaded into any process).

Note also that some DLLs also require capabilities because they call protected APIs. In this case both the DLL and the loading process must be granted the capability.

15.2.5 What if I don't use the right capabilities?

If your application has insufficient capabilities, it will crash with `KERN-EXEC 46` (`KErrPermissionDenied`).

First, you should check that the application has the capabilities that grant the broad functionality it uses (e.g. `NetworkServices` for Internet access). There are further suggestions for debugging platform security errors in the Symbian developer wiki article: ***croozeus.com/Troubleshooting_platform_security_problems***.

15.2.6 What is data caging?

Data cages are file system directories that are protected against reading or writing (or both). Attempts to access files in these directories returns an error code. Python applications are given their own "private directory" (a private data cage) to which they have sole access (where their resources and data files can be securely stored). The location is based on the name of the Python application's UID. For example, an application with UID 0xE80B00C9 has a private directory \private\E80B00C9\.

Note that one implication of data caging is that file browser applications cannot read certain protected directories, including /sys/bin (all executable code), /resource/ (Symbian resource files) or \private (application private directories). To read these areas requires the (very hard to get) device manufacturer capability `AllFiles`; to write needs the capability TCB.

15.3 Application signing

Symbian uses an application testing and signing program called Symbian Signed to determine which applications may be trusted, and with what platform security capabilities. While you're developing an application, it can also be signed with a special developer certificate (also from Symbian Signed) or self-signed, both of which grant lesser levels of trust to the application and hence result in certain limitations.

15.3.1 What are the signing options?

The signing options are:

- Symbian Signed
- Express Signed
- Certified Signed
- Developer Certificate Signed
- Open Signed Online
- Open Signed Offline
- Self-signing.

Each of the options gives different warnings to the user on installation and provides different access to capabilities - for more information on the capability to signing option mapping see: ***croozeus.com/Capabilities_(Symbian_Signed))***. The options are discussed in the following sections.

Symbian Signed

Symbian Signed is an application testing and signing program. Most Python applications can be Symbian Signed using the Express Signed route discussed below; few Python applications will need the restricted or device manufacturer capabilities granted through Certified Signed.

Symbian Signed applications are encoded with a tamper-proof digital certificate that identifies the vendor, grants all the capabilities of the contained binaries, and allows the application to install without warnings on Symbian devices. Many distribution channels, including Handango and the Nokia Ovi Store require that applications be Symbian Signed.

The purpose of the Symbian Signed is to determine which applications can be trusted to run on Symbian platform devices. Much of the trust comes from the fact that the identity of the vendor is known - applications submitted to ***www.symbiansigned.com*** must be signed with a Publisher ID from Trustcenter.

Applications may be Symbian Signed using either Express Signed or Certified Signed routes. In both cases the application is expected to comply with the Symbian Signed Test Criteria. The difference is that every Certified Signed application is tested by a test house, while Express Signed applications are only occasionally audited (if they fail, the developer will subsequently need to use Certified Signed for several signing runs). Express Signing is consequently much cheaper, but as because it conveys less trust, can only grant user and system capabilities. Certified Signed applications may additionally have restricted capabilities if these are needed.

15.3.2 Developer certificates

Applications that use only the user capabilities can be self signed, and will not need a developer certificate.

Developer Certificates (DevCerts) are limited certificates that are are locked to a particular mobile device or set of devices and always display a warning that the application is untrusted on installation. They are issued by Symbian Signed and are primarily intended for giving access to more advanced capabilities during development.

Symbian Signed makes developer certificates available to companies through Open Signed Offline on request. The certificate returned to you is locked to the

IMEIs that you specify when you request the certificate (at most 1000 devices). Open Signed Onlinecan be used to DevCert sign an application for a single IMEI through the ***www.symbiansigned.com*** website. This mechanism grants more capabilities than self signing and can be used as a distribution mechanism for freeware that needs more than the user capabilities. It can also be used as a mechanism for signing your application during testing if you are not a 'company' and hence can't request an offline developer certificate. Note however that using the turnaround time for signing using Open Signed Online results in a much slower development cycle.

15.3.3 Self-signed

Self-signing is where an application is signed with a certificate created by the developer. As the platform has no basis for trusting the application:

- Self-signed applications that use more than the 'user capabilities' (those capabilities where the user can make an informed decision about the risk of installing the application - `NetworkServices`, `LocalServices`, `Location`, `ReadUserData`, `WriteUserData`, and `UserEnvironment`) cannot be installed.
- On installation the device user is informed that the application is untrusted. They are then told which user capabilities it requests and asked if they wish to continue the installation.
- Many distribution channels will not accept self-signed applications. For example, Ovi store requires that your application is Symbian Signed.

The application packager self-signs applications by default. Provided you don't want to distribute applications through some of the application stores and the warnings do not concern you, this may be an acceptable signing approach.

15.3.4 What signing options should I use for distribution?

Python applications that need to be distributed through application stores or which cannot have "trust warnings" are usually Symbian Signed through the Express Signed route (or Certified Signed in the rare case where restricted capabilities are required).

Applications that need only user capabilities and where warnings are not important may be self-signed.

15.3.5 What signing options should I use for testing/development?

Most Python applications only require the 'user capabilities', and can hence be self signed during development (a self signed certificate is used by the Application packager by default, so you don't need to do anything!).

Applications that need more capabilities can use Open Signed Offline or Open Signed Online.

15.3.6 What are the freeware signing options?

Self-signing can be used for applications that only request the user capabilities; if system capabilities are also required then "Open Signed Offline" can be used. Note however that in this case is case the user must sign the application through the web portal themselves, rather than you supplying them with a pre-signed signed file.

At time of writing there is no mechanism for Symbian Signing of freeware; note, however, that application stores will sometimes sponsor applications for signing.

15.3.7 How do I change the certificate used to sign my application?

The application packager automatically signs the application SIS file created for device targets with a default self-signed certificate. You can change this to specify a self-signed certificate with your own company details (which you can create using makekeys from the Symbian SDK), a developer certificate, or a publisher ID (prior to submission to Symbian Signed).

15.3.8 Special considerations for Symbian Signing PyS60 Applications

PyS60 applications can be signed using the same mechanisms and options as any native application.

The only issue is that if you want to Symbian Sign your application then you need to supply a standard Symbian .PKG file in your submission .zip file; and unfortunately the application packager doesn't use or create one. The workaround is to use the `dumpsis` command line tool from the Symbian platform C++ SDK (`\Epoc32\tools\dumpsis.exe`):

```
dumpsis filename.sis
```

The command extracts the files from the sis into a subdirectory with the same name as the original SIS file name. You can use the package file generated in your Symbian Signed submission.

15.3.9 How do I get started?

After reading this article you should have a fairly good idea which signing option you need to use based on the Capabilities (Symbian Signed) required by your application. For most applications, this will be either a Self-signed or Express Signed.

Step-by-step instructions are provided for each signing option in the articles below.

- Express Signed: ***croozeus.com/Express_Signed_(Symbian_Signed)***
- Certified Signed: ***croozeus.com/Certified_Signed_(Symbian_Signed)***
- Open Signed Offline ***croozeus.com/Open_Signed_Offline_(Symbian_Signed)***
- Open Signed Online: ***croozeus.com/Open_Signed_Online_(Symbian_Signed)***
- Self-signed: ***croozeus.com/Introduction_to_Self_Signed***

15.4 Summary

This article provided a simple introduction to platform security and application signing for Python application developers.

The Complete Guide To Symbian Signed, ***croozeus.com/Complete_Guide_To_Symbian_Signed*** and Category:Symbian Signed, ***croozeus.com/Category_Symbian_Signed,*** provide more detailed information when you're ready to start signing an application, although the articles do make the assumption that the reader has developed a native C++ application.

If you have a query, Symbian Signed requests can be raised on these forums:

- Symbian Signed Support: ***croozeus.com/Application_Packaging_Distribution***
- Application Packaging and Distribution: ***croozeus.com/Application_Packaging_Distribution***
- Python, Ruby and Other Languages: ***croozeus.com/Python_Forum***

16

Standalone Applications

This chapter tells you how to package Python scripts as standard Symbian application installation files that can then be Symbian Signed and distributed through channels like Nokia's Ovi store. We'll also look at what you can do to protect your application from being pirated and how to add multilingual support.

16.1 Introduction

In Python on Symbian, 'standalone applications' are applications that are delivered in easy-to-install SIS files that bundle everything needed to run the application. After installation, the use can launch the application by selecting its icon on the phone's user interface. This approach means improves usability accessibility for ordinary phone users.

This chapter explains how to create standalone applications from scripts using a simple and intuitive application packager tool. If you haven't already studied it, you may want to refer to Chapter 15 as you read this chapter, since it will assume an understanding of application signing and platform security.

16.2 Application packager

The application packager makes it very easy to create standalone applications from your Python scripts. It creates the SIS files for you, adding everything needed to allow the script to be launched from the phone's user interface.

The packager is delivered as part of the Python Windows installation package (i.e. `PythonForS60_2.0.0_Setup.exe`) or in the Mac/Linux archive. As the packager is itself a Python application, you will first need to install Python 2.5.x on your computer (from ***www.python.org/download/releases/2.5.4***). Once Python is installed, you can launch the packager from the Windows Start button: Start | PythonForS60 2.0.0 | PyS60 Application Packager, or by selecting it in the file system: `\PythonForS60\ensymble_gui.py`.

> ***Tip***
>
> The application packager can also be used on Linux or Mac OS, but you'll have to execute ensymble_gui.py directly as there is no start bar shortcut. The systems that the packager has been tested with are listed in the release notes (README text file in the PyS60 installation root directory.)

The application packager opens in a minimal view, as shown in Figure 16.1. Specify either a single script or a folder that you want to package as an application - if you're specifying a folder you need to ensure that it contains a script `default.py` that can be used to start your application. Do not check 'Continue with missing dependencies' unless you're a power user.

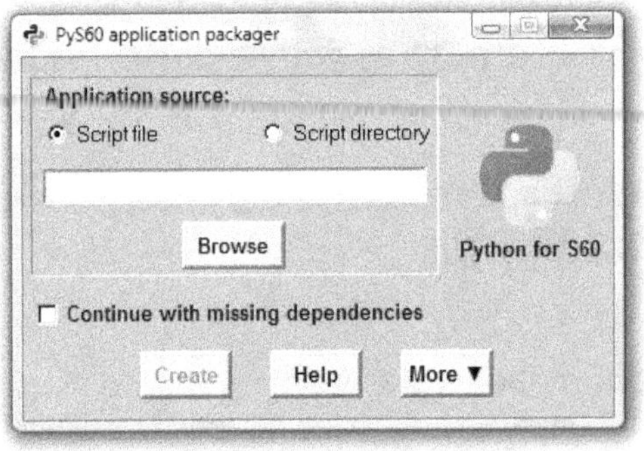

Figure 16.1: The application packager.

Press Create to create a SIS installation file that contains the specified python script and any modules it needs to run. The resulting SIS file (ScriptFileOrFolder-Name_v1_0_0.sis) can be installed and run on a device in the same way as any other Symbian application. It is self-signed using a dummy certificate and given the platform security capabilities that can be granted by the user on installation. Once installed, the application is represented in the phone's UI by the default Python logo.

If you want to distribute the application, then you will need to change some of the settings in the application packager so that you can submit it to Symbian Signed. You can edit the settings by pressing the More button as shown in Figure 16.2. Some of the settings are specified as commands entered in the field Additional Options.

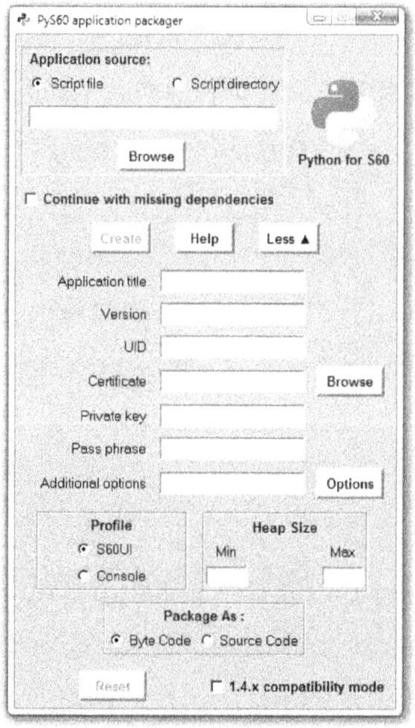

Figure 16.2: The application packager window (expanded).

We discuss the values you're likely to want to change in the next section. You can get more information on these and the other fields by pressing the Help button, and for the commands by pressing the Options button.

16.2.1 UID

Every Python standalone application has a unique identifier (UID) that defines the protected area of the file system where it can securely store its data. UIDs are free and are allocated by Symbian Signed. If you plan to Symbian Sign your application then you'll need to get a protected UID in the 0x2 range, and if you're self-signing your application, then you'll need to request an unprotected UID in the `0xA` range.

You can enter the UID into the application packager dialog in hexadecimal. Note, however, that the information isn't stored between sessions so it is often easier to instead store the value permanently in your script using the SYMBIAN_UID keyword (e.g. `SYMBIAN_UID = yourUID`).

Note that the default UID allocated by the packager is allocated in the 0xE test range (and is based on a cryptographic hash of the script file name). This is fine for development, but is not suitable for distribution because there is no guarantee in this range that there won't be UID clashes with other applications.

16.2.2 Certificates

The application packager, by default, self-signs the application SIS file with a dummy untrusted certificate containing fictional names/information. When the application is installed, the fictional information in the certificate is displayed and the user is warned that the application is untrusted. The user is also told what platform security capabilities are requested by the application and is required to acknowledge the prompt before the application is installed.

This generated certificate is fine when developing an application, but if you want to distribute the application, Symbian Sign it, or use capabilities that cannot be granted to a self-signed application, then you will need to specify a new certificate, private key and pass phrase in the fields provided.

The different certificates you can use are discussed in Chapter 15.

16.2.3 Vendor name

The vendor name is your company name (this should be changed from the default: "Ensymble"). The vendor name is specified as an entry in the "Additional options" field, shown as follows:

```
--vendor="Vendor Name"
```

In a multilingual application, the names in each language are displayed as comma separated values.

16.2.4 Version

The version number of your application should be updated with every revision. This can be done in the "Additional options" field using the version keyword. The application major version, minor version, build number should be separated by a period or comma:

```
[--version=1.0.0]
```

Note that it is usually more convenient to specify the version in your script, using the SIS_VERSION keyword (e.g. `SIS_VERSION = "1.0.0"`).

16.2.5 Icon

Adding a distinctive and attractive icon can make your application look more professional (if no icon is specified the application will be represented in the phone shell by the normal "Python" logo).

The icon is specified as a command in the 'Additional options' field:

```
--icon=\FullPathToIcon_icon.svg
```

The icon must be in SVG-Tiny format (see ***www.inkscape.org***). Note that you must include the full path, and it can't have any spaces.

16.2.6 Platform UID

It is possible to restrict your application to install only on a particular product by specifying the product ID. Alternatively, you can limit installation to a particular platform (and compatible future releases of the platform) using the platform UID. As discussed in the Targeting older devices section, one reason you may do this would do this to restrict your application to only those devices that will automatically download the Python core binaries when needed (Symbian^1/S60 5th Edition and later). To restrict installation in this way, the following text must be appended onto the 'Additional Options' field:

```
--platform-uid=0x20022E6D
```

Additional platforms/products may be specified, separating the values with commas. Lists of platform and product UIDs are available on the Symbian developer wiki - search for Device Product ID, Platform ID and HAL information.

16.2.7 Platform security capabilities

The application packager gives your application all the 'user' platform security capabilities by default. If required, the default capabilities can be replaced using the caps keyword in the "Additional options" field (capability names are separated using the "+" symbol):

```
--caps=LocalServices+NetworkServices+...
```

Capabilities are discussed further in Chapter 15, which covers platform security on Symbian.

16.2.8 Other options

The Additional Options field allows you to specify additional configuration settings (these are passed through to the underlying command line tool Ensymble). You can get a brief overview of what the options do by pressing the Options button. If you need more information, the Ensymble release notes contain very detailed explanations of what each command does, and are included in the root of your Python for Symbian installation: `PythonForS60\README`.

In addition to those already covered, a small subset of the useful commands are:

- `textfile` - A text file (or files) to be displayed during installation.
- `extrasdir` - If your application needs to make some files available in a

public area of the phone file system - for example an icon editor application might install some demonstration icons, you can specify these in a location under drive root.

- `autostart` - The application is registered to start on each device boot
- `runinstall` - The application is automatically started after installation
- `drive` - The drive where the package will be installed. There is usually no reason to change this (default is application can be installed to any drive).

The keywords `lang`, `shortcaption`, and `caption` (and a little more about vendor and `textfile`) are discussed in the section Multilingual Applications.

16.3 Targeting older devices

On newer Symbian devices, applications created using the Python 2.0.0 application packager will automatically download any missing Python core libraries when the application is started.

> ***Note***
> This feature is expected to be present on all future devices and, at the time of writing, is true for the following list: 6220 classic, N86 8 MP, N85, 6720 classic, 6730 classic, N96, 5730 XpressMusic, N78, 5630 XpressMusic, E52, E55, 6710 Navigator, E75, N79, 5800 XpressMusic, 5530 XpressMusic, 5230, X6, N97 mini, N97 and N8.

You can restrict your application to install on only these platforms using the platform UID setting in the application packager, as discussed in earlier in this chapter.

For older devices, users will need to install the Python runtime themselves (developers might add an installation note with the `textfile` option to this effect). It is also possible to bundle all the Python dependencies into your SIS file - this will increase the size of your installation files by about 3Mb (about the size of a typical song in mp3 format).

If you choose to bundle Python with your application, you will need to include the Python core libraries (installed on your PC in a SIS file by the PyS60 installer) and the Open C/C++ libraries (installed onto your Windows PC if you set up the Symbian SDK for Python development on the Emulator). Embedding the dependency SIS files can be done after creating the application SIS file using the `ensymble.py` command line tool "`mergesis`" option (see the file "README" in the Python installation root directory for instructions on how to use the command line tool).

16.4 Multilingual applications

Making your application multi-lingual can significantly increase the number of people it appeals to and boost your downloads and sales.

The application packager allows you to specify translations for all text that appears (during installation and on the phone's user interface). This includes application captions, vendor names and text files displayed during installation, so the phone can display the appropriate text and files for the current phone language at install time. It will also display the application caption in the current phone language (and change it if the phone's default language changes).

The platform is smart enough to use sensible fall-back languages; for example if you supply your files in Spanish, then these will be used even if the platform language is Latin American Spanish.

> ***Note***
>
> The application packager does not provide access to Symbian platform features like locale-specific application icons, and conditional installation of files based on the current locale. You don't need them!

Python on Symbian does not provide explicit support for localizing your scripts, and there is (at time of writing) no extension to get the current locale from the phone. It is good practice to separate your translations from the rest of your code; we outline a simple method in the following section to show you how to keep translation files as separate Python modules, and load them based on a filename convention.

16.4.1 Packaging applications

The packager allows you to define the languages your installation will support, including the translated strings for the application's caption, short caption and the vendor name. You don't have to specify those translations, but if you do, then you need to specify them as comma separated values in the same order as your initial language list.

> ***Note***
>
> The application packager does not provide access to Symbian platform features like locale-specific application icons, and conditional installation of files based on the current locale. You don't need the values!

The translations are specified as additional options using the following commands:

Table 16.2: Optional commands.

Command	Description
`lang`	Comma separated list of two-character language codes. A few common codes are: English UK (EN), French (FR), Italian (IT), German (GE), Spanish (SP), Japanese (JA), Chinese PRC (ZH). The full list can be found in the Symbian reference (or search for "Language Codes" on ***developer.symbian.org***). As an example, to specify that the package support English, French and German, you would add the following additional option to your installation package: `--lang=EN,FR,GE`
`caption`	Caption, or a comma separated list of (long) captions in all the supported languages. Note that the order is the same specified in the `lang` command: `--caption="English Caption","French Caption","German Caption"`

short-caption	Short caption, or a comma separated list of short captions in all the supported languages. Short captions are used in views where there isn't sufficient space to use the normal caption. Note the declaration order is the same as specified in the `lang` command: `--shortcaption="EngCapt","FncCapt","GmCpt"`
vendor	Vendor name or a comma separated list of all supported vendor names. Note the declaration order is the same as specified in the `lang` command: `--vendor="BigCorp","French Big Corp","German Big Corp"`

The application packager also allows you to specify a text file (in UTF8 Encoding) that is to be displayed during installation. You can create a file containing different translation for each supported language and the application will bundle these in the SIS file.

The format is something like:

```
--textfile=mytext_%C.txt
```

In the preceding example, the packager bundles files with names mytext_EN.txt, mytext_FR.txt and mytext_GE.txt. You can also specify different patterns, for example:

```
%%            - literal %
%n            - language number (01 - 99)
%c            - two-character language code in lowercase letters
%C            - two-character language code in capital letters
%l            - language name in English, using only lowercase let-
ters
%l            - language name in English, using mixed case letters
```

The language number is a number assigned to each language, that can be used instead of the code. The numbers are also documented in the Symbian Reference (or just search for "Language abbreviations in lang-code alphabetical order" on ***developer.symbian.org***).

16.4.2 Localizing Python scripts

Since Python on Symbian itself does not provide explicit support for localizing your scripts, we will present a strategy for supporting multiple languages in a PyS6. Using this strategy it is possible to define the default language and additional translations may be added whenever needed. Moreover, missing translations are replaced by the default translation, allowing incremental translations without breaking the code.

The strategy is composed of a main script file (wm_locale.py) used for dynamic loading of the desired language, and localization files that contain the actual translated text. The localization files are also Python files and they are imported as modules. Using Python introspection, the translation may be loaded and missing translations are replaced by the default language. The main script is as follows:

wm_locale.py

```
# -*- coding: utf-8 -*-

__all__ = [ "Locale" ]

class Loc_Data(object):
    "Translation data holder"
    pass

class Default(object):
    "Default language support"
    def __init__(self):
        self.loc = Loc_Data()
        self.loc.zero = u'Zero'
        self.loc.one = u'One'
        self.loc.two = u'Two'
        self.loc.three = u'Three'
        self.loc.four = u'Four'
        self.loc.five = u'Five'
        self.loc.six = u'Six'
        self.loc.seven = u'Seven'
        self.loc.eight = u'Eight'
        self.loc.nine = u'Nine'
        self.loc.change_language = u'Change Language'
        self.loc.english_us = u'English (USA)'
        self.loc.finnish = u'Finnish'
```

```
        self.loc.hungarian = u'Hungarian'
        self.loc.portuguese_br = u'Portuguese (Brazil)'
        self.loc.about = u'About'
        self.loc.exit = u'Exit'

class Locale(Default):
    "Multiple language support class"

    LOC_MODULE = "wm_locale_%s"

    def __init__(self,lang = ""):
        "Load all locale strings for one specific language or de-
fault if empty"
        self.set_locale(lang)

    def set_locale(self,lang = ""):
        "Load all locale strings for one specific language or de-
fault if empty"
        Default.__init__(self)

        try:
            lang_mod = __import__( self.LOC_MODULE % ( lang ) )
        except ImportError:
            pass
        else:
            self.merge_locale(lang_mod)

    def merge_locale(self, lang_mod):
```

```
        "Merge new location string into default locale"

        # replace existing strings and keep old ones
        # if it is missing in the locale module
        for k,v in self.loc.__dict__.iteritems():
            if hasattr(lang_mod,k):
                nv = lang_mod.__getattribute__(k)
                self.loc.__setattr__(k,nv)
```

All default translations are defined in class Default using the attribute `self.loc`. Each string in your program should be represented by a different attribute in `self.loc`. Localization modules are loaded dynamically and the files are named according to certain conventions. This is represented by the following expression:

```
LOC_MODULE = "wm_locale_%s"
```

So, if you have a pt_BR translation, create a file called wm_locale_pt_BR.py. Inside this module, translate all strings in class `Default`, removing any class or `self.loc` references. For instance, the `pt_BR` translation would be:

wm_locale_pt_BR.py

```
# -*- coding: utf-8 -*-
zero = u'Zero'
one = u'Um'
two = u'Dois'
three = u'Três'
```

```
four = u'Quatro'
five = u'Cinco'
six = u'Seis'
seven = u'Sete'
eight = u'Oito'
nine = u'Nove'
change_language = u'Mudar idioma'
english_us = u'Inglês (EUA)'
finnish = u'Finlandês'
hungarian = u'Húngaro'
portuguese_br = u'Português (Brasil)'
about = u'Sobre'
exit = u'Sair'
```

The next code snippet demonstrates how the locale class can be used.

wm_locale_demo.py

```
# -*- coding: utf-8 -*-
import sys
sys.path.append(r'e:\python')

import appuifw
import e32
import wm_locale

class Locale_Demo(object):
```

```
    def __init__(self):
        appuifw.app.exit_key_handler = self.close
        appuifw.app.title = u"Locale Demo"
        appuifw.app.screen = 'normal'
        self.update_locale()
        self.app_lock = e32.Ao_lock()

    def close(self):
        self.app_lock.signal()

    def about(self):
        appuifw.note( u"Locale Demo", "info" )

    def update_locale(self,lang=""):
        self.labels = wm_locale.Locale(lang)
        self.refresh()

    def refresh(self):
        entries = [
            self.labels.loc.zero,
            self.labels.loc.one,
            self.labels.loc.two,
            self.labels.loc.three,
            self.labels.loc.four,
            self.labels.loc.five,
            self.labels.loc.six,
            self.labels.loc.seven,
            self.labels.loc.eight,
```

```
            self.labels.loc.nine
            ]

        self.body = appuifw.Listbox(entries)

        self.menu = [
            (self.labels.loc.change_language, (
                (self.labels.loc.english_us, lambda: self.update_
locale("en_US")),
                (self.labels.loc.finnish, lambda: self.update_
locale("fi")),
                (self.labels.loc.hungarian, lambda: self.update_
locale("hu")),
                (self.labels.loc.portuguese_br, lambda: self.up-
date_locale("pt_BR"))
                )
            ),
            (self.labels.loc.about, self.about),
            (self.labels.loc.exit, self.close)
            ]

        appuifw.app.menu = self.menu
        appuifw.app.body = self.body

    def run(self):
        self.app_lock.wait()
        appuifw.app.menu = []
        appuifw.app.body = None
```

```
        appuifw.app.set_exit()


if __name__ == "__main__":

    ld = Locale_Demo()
    ld.run()
```

If you have more translation files, just add them to your project. The following translations were copied from ***wiki.forum.nokia.com/index.php/Localization_Example_for_PyS60***- you can see that there are missing translations.

wm_locale_en_US.py

```
# -*- coding: utf-8 -*-
zero = u'Zero'
one = u'One'
two = u'Two'
three = u'Three'
four = u'Four'
five = u'Five'
six = u'Six'
seven = u'Seven'
eight = u'Eight'
nine = u'Nine'
change_language = u'Change Language'
english_us = u'English (USA)'
finnish = u'Finnish'
```

```
hungarian = u'Hungarian'
portuguese_br = u'Portuguese (Brazil)'
about = u'About'
exit = u'Exit'
```

wm_locale_fi.py

```
# -*- coding: utf-8 -*-
zero = u'nolla'
one = u'yksi'
two = u'kaksi'
three = u'kolme'
four = u'neljä'
five = u'viisi'
six = u'kuusi'
seven = u'seitsemän'
eight = u'kahdeksan'
nine = u'yhdeksän'
change_language = u'Vaihda kieli'
english_us = u'englanti'
finnish = u'suomi'
hungarian = u'unkari'
about = u'Tietoja'
exit = u'Poistu'
```

wm_locale_hu.py

```
# -*- coding: utf-8 -*-
```

```
zero = u'nulla'
one = u'egy'
two = u'kett\u0151'
three = u'három'
four = u'négy'
five = u'öt'
six = u'hat'
seven = u'hét'
eight = u'nyolc'
nine = u'kilenc'
change_language = u'Nyelv változtatás'
english_us = u'angol'
finnish = u'finn'
hungarian = u'magyar'
about = u'Információ'
exit = u'Kijárat'
```

Figures 16.3 and 16.4 show some screenshots.

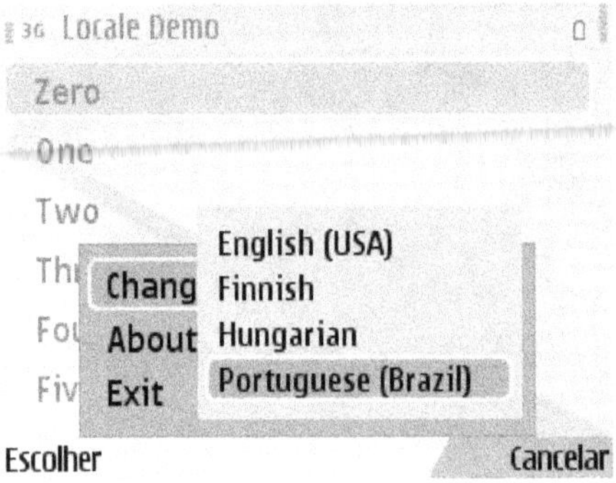

Figure 16.3: Screenshot: Localizing Python Applications

Figure 16.4: Screenshot: Localizing Python Applications

16.5 Commercial applications

Python can be used to create commercial applications for the Symbian platform. From PyS60 2.0, applications can now be Symbian Signed and distributed through channels such as Nokia's Ovi store - in the same way as applications developed in native C++. In addition, even though the Python core libraries are still not automatically included in all devices, newer devices will automatically download Python when it is needed.

A common requirement of commercial applications is the need to fully enable applications only for licensed users. This section explains how to create an application that can only be unlocked with a valid registration code. The registration code can be verified at runtime on the device, or on the server side using SMS or a GPRS/Data connection.

16.5.1 Registration code

This section illustrates a simple and minimalistic approach for implementing a registration code algorithm. The code creates a registration code from the IMEI and compares it to a value entered by the user. If the values match, the fact that the application is registered is stored on the device and used to determine which options the user interface presents to the user.

The complete code is as follows:

```
import appuifw
import e32
import os
import sysinfo

pathtoapp=os.path.dirname(appuifw.app.full_name())

is_registered=0

timer = e32.Ao_timer()
app_lock = e32.Ao_lock()

phone_imei=sysinfo.imei()
reg_code = phone_imei[2]+phone_imei[0]+phone_imei[0]+phone_imei[8]


def write_settings():
# Write registration flag
    global is_registered
    REG_DIR='C:\\system\\data\\registration'
    CONFIG_FILE=os.path.join(REG_DIR,'confg.set')
```

```
    if not os.path.isdir(REG_DIR):
        os.makedirs(REG_DIR)
        REG_FILE=os.path.join(REG_DIR,'confg.set')
    config={}
    config['is_registered']= is_registered
    f=open(REG_FILE,'wt')
    f.write(repr(config))
    f.close()

def read_settings():
# Read registration flag
    global is_registered
    REG_FILE='C:\\system\\data\\registration\\confg.set'
    print "read settings 2"
    try:
      print "read settings 3"
        f=open(REG_FILE,'rt')
        try:
            content = f.read()
            config=eval(content)
            f.close()
            is_registered=config.get('is_registered','')
        except:
            appuifw.note(u"Cannot read settings file", "error")
    except:
      print "read settings 4"
        appuifw.note(u"Creating settings file", "info")
```

```
def exit_key_handler():
    write_settings()
    appuifw.app.set_exit()


def quit():
    write_settings()
    appuifw.app.set_exit()

L_Unregistered = [u"Register",u"About", u"Exit"]

L_Registered = [u"About", u"Exit"]

def start_application():
# On start check if the application is registered or not and ac-
cordingly give menu pop-up
options
    global is_registered
    if is_registered == 0:
      appuifw.app.title = u"Not Registered"
        index = appuifw.popup_menu(L_Unregistered)
        if index == 0:
            register_application()
        elif index == 1:
                about()
        elif index == 2:
            quit()
        else:
```

```
            pass
    elif is_registered == 1:
      appuifw.app.title = u"Registered"
        index = appuifw.popup_menu(L_Registered)
        if index == 0:
            about()
        elif index == 1:
            quit()
        else:
            pass
    else:
        pass

def about():
# About the application
    appuifw.note(u"Registration Example\nPython on Symbian",
"info")
    start_application()

def promt_user():
# Prompt user for registration code
    global is_registered
    if is_registered == 0:
        appuifw.note(u"Application not registered!", "info")

def register_application():
# Ask and check for registration
    global is_registered
```

```
    if is_registered == 0:
        appuifw.note(u"Please enter the registration code",
"info")
        regtry = appuifw.query(u"Enter Registration code", "text")
        if regtry == reg_code:
            is_registered = 1 # Successfully registered!
            appuifw.note(u"Thanks for registering!","info")
        else:
            appuifw.note(u"Invalid Registration Code!","error") #
Registration failed!
    else:
        appuifw.note(u"Registered Application!","info")

    start_application()

appuifw.app.exit_key_handler = exit_key_handler
appuifw.app.screen='normal'

read_settings() # Check if registered or not
promt_user() # Prompt user if not registered
start_application() # Show application to user, accordingly
```

Lets go through the code in sections. The machine registration code is generated from the device IMEI at the start of the application using a very simple algorithm:

```
phone_imei=sysinfo.imei()
reg_code = phone_imei[2]+phone_imei[0]+phone_imei[0]+phone_imei[8]
```

We call the three functions - `read_settings()`, `prompt_user()` and `start_application()` in order. `read_settings()` checks whether the application is registered or not by checking the registration flag from a configuration file. The registration flag is stored in the `is_registered` variable and used in the other functions.

```
def read_settings():
# Read registration flag
    global is_registered
    REG_FILE='C:\\system\\data\\registration\\confg.set'
    try:
        f=open(REG_FILE,'rt')
        try:
            content = f.read()
            config=eval(content)
            f.close()
            is_registered=config.get('is_registered','')
        except:
            appuifw.note(u"Cannot read settings file", "error")
    except:
        appuifw.note(u"Creating settings file", "info")
```

The `prompt_user()` function displays a note to the user if the application is not registered.

```
def promt_user():
# Prompt user for registration code
```

```
    global is_registered
    if is_registered == 0:
        appuifw.note(u"Application not registered!", "info")
```

`start_application()` checks the registration flag (`is_registered`) read from the file in `read_settings()` function. If the application is found to be registered, the application is fully activated. On the other hand, if the application is not registered, the softkey menu shows only the registration option - the other options are not shown.

```
def start_application():
# On start check if the application is registered or not and ac-
cordingly give menu pop-up
options
    global is_registered
    if is_registered == 0:
      appuifw.app.title = u"Not Registered"
        index = appuifw.popup_menu(L_Unregistered)
        if index == 0:
            register_application()
        elif index == 1:
                 about()
        elif index == 2:
            quit()
        else:
            pass
    elif is_registered == 1:
      appuifw.app.title = u"Registered"
```

```
        index = appuifw.popup_menu(L_Registered)
        if index == 0:
            about()
        elif index == 1:
            quit()
        else:
            pass
    else:
        pass
```

If the user selects the ‘Register’ option they are asked to enter the registration code. If the registration code is successful, the ‘Thanks for registration’ note is displayed, the registration flag (`is_registered`) flag is stored in the configuration file and the application is activated. If a wrong registration code is provided, the application is not activated and the user is not able to use the application unless he/she registers.

```
def register_application():
# Ask and check for registration
    global is_registered
    if is_registered == 0:
        appuifw.note(u"Please enter the registration code",
"info")
        regtry = appuifw.query(u"Enter Registration code", "text")
        if regtry == reg_code:
            is_registered = 1 # Successfully registered!
            appuifw.note(u"Thanks for registering!","info")
         else:
```

```
            appuifw.note(u"Invalid Registration
Code!","error") # Registration failed!
    else:
        appuifw.note(u"Registered Application!","info")

    start_application()
```

The application registration is very simplistic because it does not solve real-world issues like how the user gets the registration code in the first place. There are many ways this could be done - for example the application could directly supply the phone IMEI to a registration server via SMS or the Internet, which checks payment details and returns the registration key back to the application.

There are many other limitations of this particular implementation, including the fact that the registration key algorithm is very simple, it is stored in a public area of the file system, and the mechanism used can be reverse engineered from the script. While the mechanism is not perfect, it is probably sufficient to deter "casual" piracy. A more complicated mechanism such as DRM can be used to provide further protection.

16.6 Summary

Python applications can be nearly indistinguishable from those developed in native code, both in terms of appearance and installation behavior. We showed how to package and install applications using the application packager and how to write multilingual applications. It concluded with an explanation of what you can do to protect your application from software piracy, including example code demonstrating how to implement a registration code in your application.

17

Debugging Techniques

This chapter demonstrates the main debugging techniques for Python on the Symbian platform and gives a brief overview of tools and programming practices that can help you write robust Python code.

17.1 Introduction

Defects can be introduced into software at any point in the software development lifecycle, and may be detected in any of these stages or later during unit testing and system testing or, in the worst case, by the end-user. There is plenty of evidence to show that defects are orders of magnitude easier and cheaper to fix early in the design cycle. There is also a lot of evidence to show that good programming and testing practices can eliminate and detect defects.

The first section of this chapter provides useful links to some of the techniques and tools that can help you write better code to avoid defects. The rest of the chapter demonstrates the techniques you use for debugging Python code on the Symbian platform. Unfortunately, Python on Symbian does not provide an interactive source code debugger; while you can use an IDE for your development if you choose (including the Python IDLE IDE) you can't step through your running code or debug on a target Symbian device. Instead, most of the techniques described use logging to report the state of the application as the code runs. The techniques are flexible and can be used to debug simple scripts or more complex applications.

17.2 Writing better code

The following development methodologies and tools can help improve the quality of your code.

- Release early and often. A frequent release cycle keeps your early-adopters and testers interested, and having more eyes on the code improves the chances of defects being detected. The idea of Release Early, Release Often comes from the book The Cathedral and the Bazaar by Eric S. Raymond.
- Perform code inspection by another programmer, which is an important tool for detecting defects and ensuring that code is maintainable.
- Pair programming is an agile methodology that takes the idea of code review further, and combines code generation with review. Free tools, such as Google Code, support code inspection and, even if your project does not have budget for an independent code review or pair programming, you still gain value by inspecting your own code with a critical eye.
- Test your code thoroughly. In particular, it is good programming practice to divide your code into modules andunit test each individually. Test-driven development is a methodology that deserves some attention.
- Document your code. It is important to document your code as you write it, and maintain the documentation along with any code changes. Good documentation makes it easier for others to work on your code, and to understand it when fixing defects. Python makes it very easy to write code and documentation together.
- Use version control tools. Source Code Management (SCM) allows you to keep a record of specific changes and to undo mistakes if necessary.

  - Bzr (***bazaar.canonical.com***) and Mercurial (***mercurial.selenic.com***) are excellent options for small projects.
  - CVS, Subversion and Git are more difficult to learn, but are helpful if you want to host your project on open source repositories like Sourceforge, Savanna, Maemo or Google Code.
- Use a bug tracker. For a very small project you can track defects using a spreadsheet. However, if you have a larger project, or you need to communicate your defects outside your immediate project team, a bug tracking tool is essential.
  - Sourceforge, Savanna, Maemo or Google Code have their own bug tracker system.

Mantis (***www.mantisbt.org***), Trac (***trac.edgewall.org***) and Bugzilla (***www.bugzilla.org***) are good options for a standalone bug tracker.

17.3 Debugging tools and techniques

17.3.1 Python shell

During the development phase it is common to execute all PyS60 applications from the Python shell. The most basic debug technique is to run the code within the Python shell application and use the print command to log application state to the console, as follows:

```
# instructions here
print "I am here"
# more instructions
```

```
print "now I am here"
# ...
```

You may also want to have an additional DEBUG flag to switch between the debug mode and normal execution mode. For example:

```
# script starts
import modules

# Debug
DEBUG = True

# instructions here
def myfunction():
    if DEBUG:
        print u"In myfunction()" # debug
    # more instructions

# more instructions
```

To execute your script from the Python shell, select the menu option Run script (note that you will need to copy it to `e:\Python` or `c:\data\Python` first). This technique is not particularly useful for debugging programs with a user interface because the console (and log messages) is usually hidden by the running application. Provided that the script does not call `app.set_exit()` to close the script shell, the messages will be available when the script finishes.

17.3.2 Python shell over Bluetooth

The Python shell can be run over a Bluetooth connection. This approach allows you to drive execution of your application from your computer, and ensure that log messages are visible at the point of execution. More information can be found at ***wiki.opensource.nokia.com/projects/PyS60_Bluetooth_console*** but, in summary, you need to:

1. Configure a COM port on your PC.
2. Use an application like Hyperterminal or Putty to connect to this port.
3. In your phone, open the Python shell and select Bluetooth console fro the menu. Then select the Bluetooth name of your computer.

17.3.3 Python shell over WiFi

The Python shell can also be run over WiFi connections using the Netcat utility (***netcat.sourceforge.net***). If you are running Unix, Linux or Mac OS X, type the following lines in a console:

```
# Running a TCP server on port 1025
stty raw -echo ; nc -l -p 1025 ; stty sane
```

There is a Netcat version for Windows but you can have some problems with control characters since stty is not available. In this case, use only:

```
nc -l -p 1025
```

Launch the following script on your phone. Do not forget to set the proper IP of your computer (we are using 10.0.0.10). You can improve it with calls to `appuifw.query()`, allowing users to select IP and port.

```
import btconsole
from socket import *

sock = socket(AF_INET,SOCK_STREAM)
# put the proper IP and port here
sock.connect((“10.0.0.10”,1025))
btconsole.run_with_redirected_io(sock,btconsole.interact,
None, None, locals())
```

Audio logging

An alternative method to logging with printed messages, is to use ‘speak’ the messages using the audio module’s text to speech converter:

```
import audio
# instructions here
audio.say(u”I am here”)
# more instructions
audio.say(u”now I am here”)
# ...
```

The text to speech functionality is discussed in Chapter 7.

17.3.4 Logging view

An alternative to logging to the shell console is to log to a `Text` object. Having a dedicated logging view allows us to see the logs for a running UI application, which means that we don't need to run the script in a shell environment in order to debug it.

```
from appuifw import *

logview = Text()
app.body = logview

def add_msg(msg):
    global logview
    # u"\u2029" is the new line code for Text()
    logview.add(unicode(msg) + u"\u2029")
    # put the cursor at the end
    logview.set_pos(logview.len())

add_msg(u"Starting...")
# some code here

add_msg(u"Now running at this point ...")
# more code ...
```

The previous fragment logs to a Text object that is the current `app.body`. In a user interface application we would probably have the logview as a separate view and switch to it when necessary. We could even include this code in the production version of the application, hidden from the user until it is needed to diagnose a problem.

17.3.5 Log files

Some code is harder to debug, either by its very nature (e.g. multi-threaded programs) or because they close unexpectedly with no chance for exception handling. In such cases, log files can provide essential 'post-mortem' debugging information.

A log class is suggested in the next code snippet (just save it to a file called logfile.py):

```
# logfile.py
#
import sys
import time
import thread
import os

__all__ = [ "FLOG" ]

log_path = "C:\\Logs\\"

class FileLog(object):
    def __init__(self,filename):
        if (os.path.exists(log_path)):
            # Log enabled
```

```
            self.log = True
            self.filename = log_path+filename
            print filename
            self.file = open(self.filename,'at')
            self.lock = thread.allocate_lock()
        else:
            appuifw.note(u' Log diabled')
            # Log diabled
            self.log = False

    def add(self,msg):
        if (self.log):
            # collect caller information from stack call us-
ing _getframe
            caller = sys._getframe(1).f_code.co_name
            line = str(sys._getframe(1).f_code.co_firstline-
no)
            # create log message
            timestamp = time.strftime("[%Y%m%d %H:%M:%S]
",time.localtime())
            logmsg = timestamp + caller + ":" + line + " - "
+ msg + " \n"
            # write log message, using a semaphore for con-
trolling the file access
            self.lock.acquire()
            self.file.write(logmsg)
            self.file.flush()
            self.lock.release()
```

```
        else:
            pass

    def close(self):
        if (self.log):
            self.file.close()
        else:
            pass

FLOG = FileLog("filelog.txt")
```

The `logfile` module is written in such a manner that existence of the path C:\Logs serves as a flag for enabling or disabling the logging. You may, of course, change this path according to your needs.

To use the logfile module, simply import the object FLOG and log messages with `FLOG.add(msg)`:

```
import sys
# Append the path where you placed 'logfile.py'
sys.path.append(u"C:\\data\\python")

# import FLOG from the logfile module
from logfile import FLOG

# You can log to the file by using the 'add' function
FLOG.add("Log initialized")
```

```
# Instructions and your code go here
FLOG.add("Debug 1")

# More instructions and code
FLOG.add("Debug 2")

# Closing the log file
FLOG.close()
```

Caller information is automatically added to the log using the object `sys._getframe`, and a semaphore (created using `thread.allocate_lock`) is provided to avoid re-entrancy problems when writing to the file. After writing, the file is flushed and any pending bytes are written, so you can trust that a message is written to the file after the call to `FLOG.add()`.

You may close the file by calling `FLOG.close()` when you have finished logging to the file.

17.3.6 Runtime error detection

Using the script shell is practical for debugging during development, but is not suitable for detecting runtime errors in standalone applications (which can be created as described in Chapter 16). It is not uncommon when first deploying a program as a standalone application to have errors related to missing modules, or use of the wrong paths in `sys.path`, and so on. In these situations, we use exception handling to detect and log runtime errors; we can then provide a comprehensive debug message to the user, and even notify ourselves of the problem automatically.

Tracebacks can be used extensively to extract, format and print stack traces of Python scripts. For example, the following code would print the traceback.

```
import traceback, appuifw, sys

def dangerous_function():
    appuifw.non_existing_function()

try:
    # something that would throw an exception
    dangerous_function()
except:
    # catch exception
    print "Exception in user code:"
    print '-'*30
    traceback.print_exc()
    print '-'*30
```

Different ways to print and format the stack traces can be found in the Python documentation library (***docs.python.org/library/traceback.html***).

Using a traceback module, the following code example shows how we can collect mobile device and exception data after a failure, and then create a new user interface to inform the user of how to report the problem as follows.

```
try:
    # Put you startup code here.
    # For instance, import your module and run it.
    # import my_module
    # my_module.startup()
    pass
except Exception, e:
    # Oops, something wrong. Report problems to user
    # and ask him/her to send them to you.
    import appuifw
    import traceback
    import sys
    import e32

    # Collecting call stack info
    e1,e2,e3 = sys.exc_info()
    call_stack = unicode(traceback.format_
exception(e1,e2,e3))

    # Creating a friendly user message with exception de-
tails
    new_line = u"\u2029"
    err_msg = u"This programs was unexpectedly closed due to
the following error: "
    err_msg += unicode(repr(e)) + new_line
    err_msg += u"Please, copy and past the text presented
here and "
    err_msg += u"send it to email@server.com. "
```

```
    err_msg += u"Thanks in advance and sorry for this incon-
venience." + new_line*2
    err_msg += u"Call stack:" + new_line + call_stack

    # Small PyS60 application
    lock = e32.Ao_lock()
    appuifw.app.body = appuifw.Text(err_msg)
    appuifw.app.body.set_pos(0)
    appuifw.app.menu = [(u"Exit", lambda: lock.signal())]
    appuifw.app.title = u"Error log"
    lock.wait()
```

For instance, suppose your main program is just the following (invalid) code snippet:

```
#...
try:
    import camera
    camera.take_photo(camera.RGB32) # error: invalid mode
except Exception, e:
    #...
```

A screenshot of the error message that would be presented is shown in Figure 17.1.

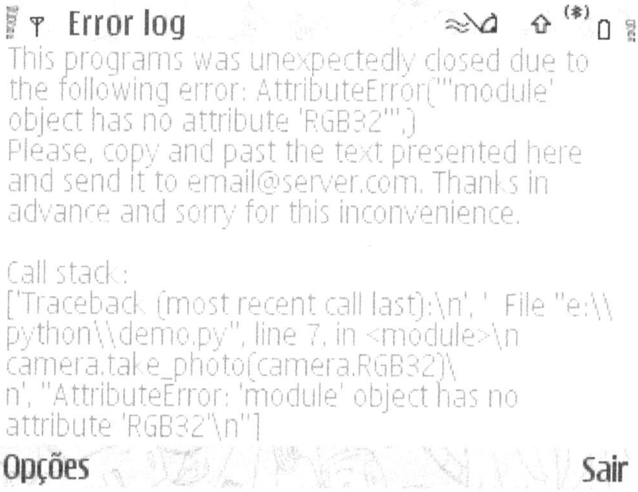

Figure 17.1:Message displayed to user in the event of an error.

17.3.7 Debugging defects on end-user phones

However careful you are in your software development process, it is still possible (even likely) that defects will escape into production code. Furthermore, with so many Symbian devices running in so many different locales, it is possible that issues will occur on devices you can't get access to. Getting your application's runtime debug information from a customer's mobile device is likely to be more useful for debugging than any amount of description they can provide, and can save a lot of time because they've already reproduced the problem for you!

The previous section showed how we might catch an exception and display a message asking the user to email it to us. The following goes one step further, modifying the previous code fragment to demonstrate how you might SMS a debug message to yourself.

```
try:
    # Put you startup code here.
    # For instance, import your module and run it.
    # import my_module
    # my_module.startup()
    import camera
    camera.take_photo(camera.RGB32) # error: invalid mode
except Exception, e:
    # Oops, something wrong. Report problems to user
    # and ask him/her to send them to you.
    import appuifw
    import traceback
    import sys
    import e32

    # Collecting call stack info
    e1,e2,e3 = sys.exc_info()
    call_stack = unicode(traceback.format_
exception(e1,e2,e3))

    # Creating a friendly user message with exception de-
tails
    new_line = u"\u2029"
    #Replace MyProgram with your app's name
    err_msg = u"MyProgram was unexpectedly closed due to the
following error: "
    err_msg += unicode(repr(e)) + new_line
    err_msg += u"Please, copy and past the text presented
```

```
here and "
    err_msg += u"send it to email@server.com. "
    err_msg += u"Thanks in advance and sorry for this incon-
venience." + new_line*2
    err_msg += u"Call stack:" + new_line + call_stack

    def send_sms():
        import messaging
        msg = appuifw.app.body.get()
        messaging.sms_send("+5516xxxxxxxx",msg) # put your
phone here
        appuifw.note(u"A message was created and sent.
Thanks a lot.","info")

    def save_screenshot():
        import graphics
        ss = graphics.screenshot()
        ss.save(u"e:\\screenshot.png")
        appuifw.note(u"Screenshot saved in e:\\ ","info")

    # Small PyS60 application
    lock = e32.Ao_lock()
    appuifw.app.body = appuifw.Text(err_msg)
    appuifw.app.body.set_pos(0)
    appuifw.app.menu = [(u"Send report via SMS",send_sms),
                        (u"Save screenshot",save_screen-
shot),
                        (u"Exit", lambda: lock.signal())]
```

```
    appuifw.app.title = u"Error log"
    lock.wait()
```

Figure 17.2 shows the screenshot received:

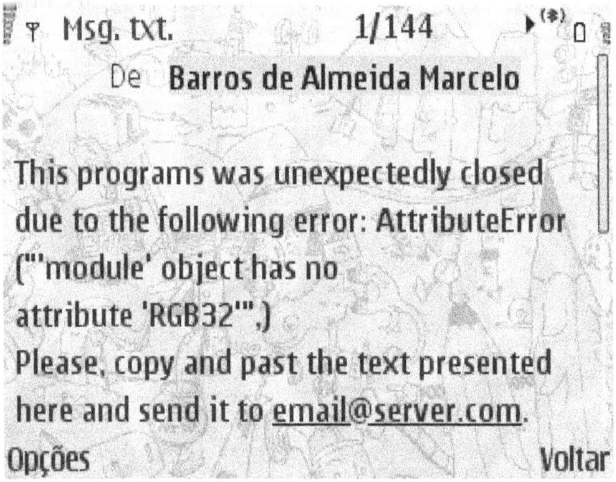

Figure 17.2: Screenshot of a debug SMS sent by an application

SMS is just one alternative to sending a debug message. Another approach might be to send the debug message using MMS, or using an Internet connection. The techniques in Chapter 14 could even be used to post defect information directly into your web-based defect management system.

17.3.8 Working on Windows using an emulator

Normally, you'll test your applications on a real Symbian device, either in the Python shell or as a stand-alone application. However, if you don't have a device, you can instead test your scripts within the Python shell console on an emulator (a simulation of the Symbian platform running on top of the Windows operating system). Instructions on how to set up the emulator for Python development are given in Chapter 1.

When the emulator is running, locate and run your Python script shell. You can debug it, as shown in Figure 17.3.

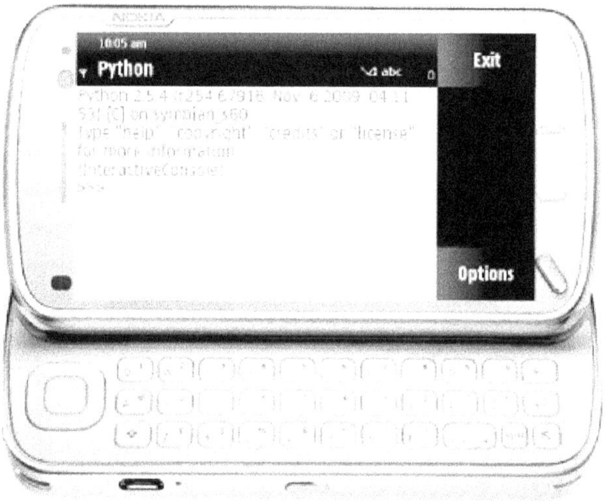

Figure 17.3: Python interactive console

If you want to debug a script, copy it into the following directory and select Run script from the Python shell menu.

```
<SDK Installation directory>\epoc32\winscw\c\Data\python
```

The other debugging techniques explained in the chapter can all be used when debugging on the emulator.

17.4 Summary

This chapter covered several techniques for debugging scripts and applications, including printing through the script shell, using a logging view, implementing robust file logging and using a crash log. The techniques described can be used for debugging both simple and complex scripts, and can help you debug and fix problems quickly and efficiently.

Example Code

Python on Symbian has the following examples. Links to individual examples are available within the chapters, and from the wiki here: ***croozeus.com/Python_on_Symbian/Example_code.***

Example	Description
PythonOnSymbianBookExample-Code AddCalendarEntry.zip	Adds an entry to the Calendar
PythonOnSymbianBookExample-Code AddContact.zip	Adds a contact to the contact database
PythonOnSymbianBookExample-Code AddToContactGroup.zip	Demonstrates how to add a contact to a group
PythonOnSymbianBookExample-Code AnniversaryEntry.zip	Adds an Anniversary entry to the Calendar
PythonOnSymbianBookExample-Code ApplicationUI.zip	Initializes the UI for a simple application
PythonOnSymbianBookExample-Code CallNotes.zip	Demonstrates the use of telephony
PythonOnSymbianBookExample-Code CanvasShapes.zip	Demonstrates drawing shapes on a Canvas
PythonOnSymbianBookExample-Code CanvasText.zip	Demonstrates writing text on a Canvas

PythonOnSymbianBookExample-Code Ch09BasicNetProg.zip	Examples from Basic Network Programming chapter
PythonOnSymbianBookExample-Code Ch14AdvNetProg.zip	Examples from Advanced Network Programming chapter
PythonOnSymbianBookExample-Code CreateContactsGroup.zip	Creates a contacts group
PythonOnSymbianBookExample-Code DeleteContact.zip	Shows how to delete a contact
PythonOnSymbianBookExample-Code DeleteContactsGroup.zip	Shows how to delete a contacts group
PythonOnSymbianBookExample-Code DisplayCalendarEntries.zip	Displays the entries from the Calendar
PythonOnSymbianBookExample-Code Double listbox.zip	Demonstrates how to use a double Listbox
PythonOnSymbianBookExample-Code ExtendingPython.zip	Simple example C++ extension
PythonOnSymbianBookExample-Code Form.zip	Demonstrates how to use the Form control
PythonOnSymbianBookExample-Code ImageEditing.zip	Shows how image editing can be done
PythonOnSymbianBookExample-Code Infopopup.zip	Creates an InfoPopup
PythonOnSymbianBookExample-Code Localization.zip	Demonstrates adding multilingual support to Python apps

PythonOnSymbianBookExample-Code Menu with submenu.zip	Creates a menu with a submenu
PythonOnSymbianBookExample-Code ModifyContact1.zip	Shows how to modify a contact without saving the changes
PythonOnSymbianBookExample-Code ModifyContact2.zip	Shows how to modify a contact and save the changes
PythonOnSymbianBookExample-Code Multi selection list.zip	Demonstrates how to use a multi selection list
PythonOnSymbianBookExample-Code Orientation.zip	Demonstrates how to change the orientation of the UI
PythonOnSymbianBookExample-Code PyMPlayer.zip	A simple music player application
PythonOnSymbianBookExample-Code PySymCamera.zip	A simple camera application
PythonOnSymbianBookExample-Code RecordVideo.zip	Demonstrates how to record video
PythonOnSymbianBookExample-Code RegistrationCode.zip	Demonstrates minimalistic approach for implementing a registration code algorithm
PythonOnSymbianBookExample-Code RepeatedAnniversaryEntry.zip	Adds a repeated Anniversary entry to the Calendar
PythonOnSymbianBookExample-Code RetrieveExistingContact-Groups.zip	Demonstrates how to fetch the existing contact groups

PythonOnSymbianBookExample-Code ScreenShot.zip	Demonstrates how to take a screenshot and save it
PythonOnSymbianBookExample-Code Screen size.zip	Demonstrates how to change the screen size for the application
PythonOnSymbianBookExample-Code SensorBall.zip	Demonstrates use of Accelerometer sensor
PythonOnSymbianBookExample-Code Simple menu.zip	Demonstrates how to create a simple menu
PythonOnSymbianBookExample-Code Single listbox.zip	Demonstrates how to use a single listbox
PythonOnSymbianBookExample-Code SmsAutoReply.zip	Demonstrates the use of messaging
PythonOnSymbianBookExample-Code SoundFiles.zip	Demonstrates how to record and play sound files
PythonOnSymbianBookExample-Code Tabs.zip	Demonstrates how to use tabs
PythonOnSymbianBookExample-Code TakeMaxresPhoto.zip	Demonstrates how to take a photo at maximum resolution
PythonOnSymbianBookExample-Code TakePhoto.zip	Demonstrates how to take a photo
PythonOnSymbianBookExample-Code Text.zip	Demonstrates how to use the Text control
PythonOnSymbianBookExample-Code TextToSpeech.zip	Demonstrates how to use text-to-speech

PythonOnSymbianBookExample-Code TicTacToe.zip	Quick and easy game –Tic-Tac-Toe
PythonOnSymbianBookExample-Code ToDoEntry.zip	Demonstrates how to create a ToDo Calendar entry
PythonOnSymbianBookExample-Code TopWindow.zip	Demonstrates how to use a TopWindow
PythonOnSymbianBookExample-Code TouchArbitaryRegions.zip	Demonstrates touch events on Arbitrary shapes like a circle
PythonOnSymbianBookExample-Code TouchOnFullscreen.zip	Demonstrates touch events on full screen
PythonOnSymbianBookExample-Code TouchWithinRectangle.zip	Demonstrates touch events within a rectangle
PythonOnSymbianBookExample-Code TouchyPaint.zip	Simple application similar to 'Paint' on Windows
PythonOnSymbianBookExample-Code UsingViewFinder.zip	Demonstrates how to use the viewfinder
PythonOnSymbianBookExample-Code WhereAmI.zip	Simple GPS Tracking and mapping application
PythonOnSymbianBookExample-Code appuifw notes.zip	Demonstrates the notes from the appuifw module
PythonOnSymbianBookExample-Code appuifw popup menu.zip	Demonstrates the popup menu from the appuifw module
PythonOnSymbianBookExample-Code appuifw queries.zip	Demonstrates the queries from the appuifw module

PythonOnSymbianBookExample-Code globalui notes.zip	Demonstrates the notes from the globalui module
PythonOnSymbianBookExample-Code globalui popup menu.zip	Demonstrates the popup menu from the globalui module
PythonOnSymbianBookExample-Code globalui queries.zip	Demonstrates the queries from the globalui module

References

Book References

- Scheible J., Tuulos V. 2007. Mobile Python - Rapid prototyping on the mobile platform, John Wiley & Sons.
- Pilgrim M. 2004. Dive into Python - Python from novice to pro, Apress.
- Magnus Lie Hetland. 2008. Beginning Python - From Novice to Professional, Apress.
- Goerzen J. 2004. Foundations of Python Netwrk Programming - The comprehensive guide to building network applications with Python, Apress.

Tutorials and Documentation

Python

- Python documentation - ***docs.python.org***
- Python for Non-Programmers - ***wiki.python.org/moin/BeginnersGuide/NonProgrammers***
- Python for Programmers - ***wiki.python.org/moin/BeginnersGuide/Programmers***

Python on Symbian

- Python on Symbian documentation - ***pys60.garage.maemo.org/doc/s60/s60.html***
- PyS60 tutorials - ***www.mobilenin.com/pys60/menu.htm*** and ***croozeus.com/tutorials.htm***

- Python on Symbian Quick Start - ***croozeus.com/Python_Quick_Star***
- Featured Applications - ***croozeus.com/blogs/?page_id=838***

Other Useful Links

- Python on Symbian Q&As - ***croozeus.com/Python_Q_n_As***
- Python on Symbian in a Nutshell - ***croozeus.com/Python_in_a_Nutshell***
- Python on Symbian Technical Overview - ***croozeus.com/Python_Technical_Overview***

Forums

- Symbian Foundation forum - ***croozeus.com/Python_Forum***
- Forum Nokia discussion boards - ***discussion.forum.nokia.com/forum/forumdisplay.php?102-Python***

Wiki

- Symbian Foundation Wiki - ***croozeus.com/Category_Python***
- Forum Nokia Wiki - ***wiki.forum.nokia.com/index.php/Category:Python***

Python on Symbian Incubation project

- Landing page - ***croozeus.com/Python_Package***
- How can one contribute? - ***croozeus.com/Python_Runtime***

Index

www.ingramcontent.com/pod-product-compliance
Lightning Source LLC
LaVergne TN
LVHW062258060326
832902LV00013B/1948
9781453747995